PROPERTY PRACTICE

The University of Law

PROPERTY PRACTICE
FIFTH EDITION

Anne Rodell

This edition published 2025 by
The University of Law
2 Bunhill Row
London EC1Y 8HQ

British Library Cataloguing in Publication Data

A catalogue record for this book is available from the British Library.

ISBN 978 1 80502 259 6

Preface

This book is part of a series of Study Manuals that have been specially designed to support the reader to achieve the SQE1 Assessment Specification in relation to Functioning Legal Knowledge. Each Study Manual aims to provide the reader with a solid knowledge and understanding of fundamental legal principles and rules, including how those principles and rules might be applied in practice.

This Study Manual covers the Solicitors Regulation Authority's syllabus for the SQE1 assessment for Property Practice in a concise and tightly focused manner. The Manual provides a clear statement of relevant legal rules and a well-defined road map through examinable law and practice. The Manual aims to bring the law and practice to life through the use of example scenarios based on realistic client-based problems and allows the reader to test their knowledge and understanding through single best answer questions that have been modelled on the SRA's sample assessment questions.

For those readers who are students at the University of Law, the Study Manual is used alongside other learning resources and the University's assessment bank to best prepare students not only for the SQE1 assessments, but also for a future life in professional legal practice.

We hope that you find the Study Manual supportive of your preparation for SQE1 and we wish you every success.

The legal principles and rules contained within this Manual are stated as at 1 May 2025.

Author acknowledgments
I should like to thank Clare Harris, Kate Lambert, Christa Sabine and Joanne Wylde for their help in the preparation of this book. I would also like to thank David Stott for his editorial support and guidance.

Contents

Preface		v
Table of Cases		xv
Table of Statutes		xvii
Chapter 1	**The Key Elements and Structure of a Freehold Property Transaction**	**1**
	SQE1 syllabus	1
	Learning outcomes	1
	1.1 Introduction	2
	1.2 Key elements and structure of freehold property transactions	2
	1.2.1 The pre-contract stage	3
	1.2.2 The pre-completion stage	4
	1.2.3 The post-completion stage	4
	1.2.4 The Law Society Conveyancing Protocol	4
	1.2.5 Summary of key elements and structure	5
	1.3 Professional conduct issues in a property transaction	6
	1.3.1 Acting for seller and buyer	6
	1.3.2 Acting for joint buyers	7
	1.3.3 Acting for borrower and lender	7
	1.3.4 Acting for joint borrowers	8
	1.3.5 Contract races	9
	1.3.6 Undertakings	9
	1.4 Sources of finance for a property transaction	10
	1.5 Types of mortgage	11
	1.5.1 Repayment mortgages	11
	1.5.2 Interest-only mortgages	12
	1.5.3 Other types of mortgage	12
	1.6 Property taxation	12
	1.6.1 Stamp Duty Land Tax ('SDLT') in England and Land Transaction Tax ('LTT') in Wales	12
	1.6.2 CGT and private residence relief	15
	1.6.3 VAT	16
	1.7 Core principles of planning law	19
	1.7.1 Statutory definition of 'Development'	19
	1.7.2 Matters that do not constitute 'Development'	19
	1.7.3 The effect of planning permission	20
	1.7.4 Matters that do not require express planning permission	21
	1.7.5 Enforcement: time limits and the range of the LPA's enforcement powers	21
	1.7.6 Building regulation control	23

	1.7.7	Listed buildings	24
	1.7.8	Conservation areas	24
	1.7.9	Planning summary	24
	1.8	Taking instructions	25
	Summary		26
	Sample questions		27
Chapter 2	**Investigation of Title**		**31**
	SQE1 syllabus		31
	Learning outcomes		31
	2.1	Introduction	32
	2.2	The distinction between registered and unregistered land	32
	2.3	How to investigate title to freehold registered land	32
	2.3.1	The way in which the seller deduces title to the buyer in registered land	32
	2.3.2	How official copies are set out in registered land	33
	2.4	How to investigate title to freehold unregistered land	36
	2.4.1	The way in which the seller deduces title to the buyer in unregistered land	37
	2.4.2	The requirements for a good root of title	38
	2.4.3	Checking each title deed listed in the epitome of title	38
	2.5	Issues that might be revealed in an investigation of title and the further action required	42
	2.5.1	Easements	42
	2.5.2	Mines and minerals exceptions and reservations	43
	2.5.3	Declaration as to rights of light and air	43
	2.5.4	Co-ownership	43
	2.5.5	Restrictive covenants	44
	2.5.6	Positive covenants	45
	2.5.7	Unknown covenants	46
	2.5.8	Mortgages	47
	2.5.9	Leases	48
	2.5.10	Notices (registered land only)	48
	2.5.11	Home rights	49
	Summary		49
	Sample questions		50
Chapter 3	**Pre-contract Searches and Enquiries**		**53**
	SQE1 syllabus		53
	Learning outcomes		53
	3.1	Introduction	54
	3.2	Who makes the searches and raises the enquiries	54
	3.3	The range and type of searches and enquiries available	54

		3.3.1 Searches and enquiries relevant to every property	54
		3.3.2 Searches and enquiries for particular properties and transactions	57
		3.3.3 Summary of the range and type of searches and enquiries available	59
		3.3.4 Online search providers	61
	3.4	Deciding which searches and enquiries are relevant for a particular property	62
	3.5	Matters commonly revealed in search results and replies to enquiries	63
		3.5.1 Planning permissions	63
		3.5.2 Road adoption	64
		3.5.3 Tree preservation orders	65
		3.5.4 Smoke control orders	65
		3.5.5 Conservation areas	65
		3.5.6 Occupiers	66
	Summary		66
	Sample questions		66
Chapter 4	**Preparation for and Exchange of Contracts**		**69**
	SQE1 syllabus		69
	Learning outcomes		70
	4.1	Introduction	70
	4.2	The purpose of a contract	70
	4.3	Standard Conditions of Sale and the Standard Commercial Property Conditions	71
	4.4	Key conditions in the SC and the SCPC	72
		4.4.1 Specified incumbrances	73
		4.4.2 Title guarantee	74
		4.4.3 Contract rate	74
		4.4.4 Deposit: stakeholder and agent	75
	4.5	The purpose of, and matters covered by, special conditions	76
	4.6	Insurance and risk	78
	4.7	Basics of VAT in a contract	79
	4.8	The requirements of a lender	80
	4.9	Acting for the lender	81
	4.10	Purpose of, and timing for issuing, a certificate of title to the lender	82
	4.11	Purpose and process of reporting to the client	83
	4.12	Preparation for and exchange of contracts	83
	4.13	The practice, method and authority to exchange	84
	4.14	The consequences of exchange	85
	Summary		86
	Sample questions		87

Chapter 5	**Completion**		**91**
	SQE1 syllabus		91
	Learning outcomes		91
	5.1	Introduction	92
	5.2	Pre-completion steps	92
	5.3	Form of transfer deed and formalities for execution	92
	5.4	Pre-completion searches	97
		5.4.1 Pre-completion search of the title	98
		5.4.2 Checking for buyer's solvency on behalf of lender	102
		5.4.3 Company search against a company seller	102
		5.4.4 Bankruptcy search against an individual seller	103
	5.5	Practical arrangements for completion	103
	5.6	Ensuring the finances are in order for completion	103
	5.7	Methods and effect of completion	104
		5.7.1 Completion in person	104
		5.7.2 Completion by post	104
		5.7.3 Effect of completion	105
	5.8	Post-completion steps	105
		5.8.1 Discharge of the seller's mortgage	105
		5.8.2 SDLT/LTT	105
		5.8.3 Registration of the new charge at Companies House	106
		5.8.4 Land Registry application(s)	106
	5.9	Remedies for delayed completion	107
		5.9.1 Contractual compensation	108
		5.9.2 Common law damages	108
		5.9.3 Notice to complete	109
		5.9.4 Rescission	109
	Summary		109
	Sample questions		111
Chapter 6	**Structure and Content of a Lease**		**113**
	SQE1 syllabus		113
	Learning outcomes		114
	6.1	Introduction	114
	6.2	Advantages and disadvantages of owning a leasehold property	114
	6.3	The structure of a typical commercial lease	115
	6.4	Options for the term of a lease	116
	6.5	Types of leasehold covenant	117
	6.6	The full repairing and insuring lease	118
	6.7	Repair	118
	6.8	Insurance	119

		6.8.1 A landlord's covenant to insure the property against defined risks (the 'insured risks')	120
		6.8.2 A covenant by the tenant to pay for the insurance policy	120
		6.8.3 A covenant by the landlord to reinstate the property	121
		6.8.4 Rent suspension	121
		6.8.5 Termination	122
		6.8.6 Interplay between the landlord's insurance covenants and the tenant's repair covenant	122
	6.9	Alterations	125
		6.9.1 Absolute covenants	125
		6.9.2 Qualified and fully qualified covenants	125
		6.9.3 Compensation for improvements	127
	6.10	User and planning	127
	6.11	Alienation	128
		6.11.1 Alienation terminology	129
		6.11.2 Assignment	130
		6.11.3 Underletting	133
	6.12	Rent and rent review	136
		6.12.1 Types of rent review	137
		6.12.2 Open market rent review: the basis of valuation	137
		6.12.3 Open market rent review: the process for determination	139
	6.13	Code for Leasing Business Premises	139
	Summary		141
	Sample questions		142
Chapter 7	**Procedural Steps for the Grant of a Lease or Underlease**		**145**
	SQE1 syllabus		145
	Learning outcomes		145
	7.1	Introduction	146
	7.2	Drafting the lease	146
	7.3	Purpose of an agreement for lease	147
	7.4	Deduction and investigation of title	148
	7.5	Pre-contract enquiries and searches	148
	7.6	Licence to underlet	149
		7.6.1 Contractual liability and how the licence deals with this	149
		7.6.2 Key provisions in the licence	149
	7.7	Pre-completion formalities	150
	7.8	Completion and post-completion steps	150
		7.8.1 Completion	150
		7.8.2 SDLT and LTT	150
		7.8.3 Registration	152

	Summary		152
	Sample questions		153
Chapter 8	**Procedural Steps for the Assignment of a Lease**		**155**
	SQE1 syllabus		155
	Learning outcomes		156
	8.1	Introduction	156
	8.2	Overview of the conveyancing procedure for the assignment of a lease	156
	8.3	Landlord's consent	158
	8.4	The licence to assign	159
		8.4.1 Purpose of a licence to assign and who prepares the draft	159
		8.4.2 Key provisions in the licence to assign	159
		8.4.3 Contractual liability and how the licence to assign deals with this	159
		8.4.4 Authorised guarantee agreement ('AGA')	160
	8.5	Deduction and investigation of title	161
	8.6	Pre-contract enquiries and searches	161
	8.7	Deed of assignment and covenants for title	162
		8.7.1 Covenants for title	162
		8.7.2 Indemnity	162
	8.8	Pre-completion formalities	163
		8.8.1 Pre-completion searches	163
		8.8.2 The licence to assign	163
		8.8.3 Apportionments	163
	8.9	Completion	163
	8.10	Post-completion steps	164
		8.10.1 SDLT/LTT	164
		8.10.2 Registered lease	164
		8.10.3 Unregistered lease	164
		8.10.4 Notice of assignment	165
	Summary		165
	Sample questions		166
Chapter 9	**Remedies for Breach of Leasehold Covenants**		**169**
	SQE1 syllabus		169
	Learning outcomes		169
	9.1	Introduction	170
	9.2	Liability on covenants in leases	170
		9.2.1 Leases granted before 1 January 1996	170
		9.2.2 Leases granted on or after 1 January 1996	170
	9.3	Remedies for breach of the covenant to pay rent	171
		9.3.1 Action in debt	172

		9.3.2 Commercial Rent Arrears Recovery ('CRAR')	172
		9.3.3 Pursue guarantors and/or rent deposit	172
		9.3.4 Forfeiture	173
		9.3.5 Choosing an appropriate remedy	174
	9.4	Remedies for breach of the covenant to repair	175
		9.4.1 Specific performance	175
		9.4.2 Damages	175
		9.4.3 Self-help/*Jervis v Harris* clause	175
		9.4.4 Forfeiture	176
		9.4.5 Choosing an appropriate remedy	176
	9.5	Remedies for breach of other covenants	178
	9.6	Surrender of the lease	178
	Summary		178
	Sample questions		179
Chapter 10	**Lease Termination and Security of Tenure under a Business Lease**		**183**
	SQE1 syllabus		183
	Learning outcomes		183
	10.1	Introduction	184
	10.2	Termination of leases at common law	184
		10.2.1 Effluxion of time	184
		10.2.2 Notice to quit	184
		10.2.3 Surrender	184
		10.2.4 Merger	185
	10.3	The 1954 Act	186
		10.3.1 Application of the 1954 Act	186
		10.3.2 Effect of the 1954 Act	186
		10.3.3 Termination by the landlord - s 25 notice	187
		10.3.4 Application to the court following service of a s 25 notice	189
		10.3.5 Renewal lease by the tenant - s 26 request	190
		10.3.6 Application to the court following service of a s 26 request	191
		10.3.7 Landlord's grounds of opposition - s 30 grounds	192
		10.3.8 Terms of the new lease	193
		10.3.9 Compensation	193
	Summary		193
	Sample questions		195
	Index		197

Table of Cases

A	Ashworth Frazer Ltd v Gloucester City Council [2002] 05 EG 133	132
H	Hadley v Baxendale [1854] EWHC J70	109
	Halsall v Brizell [1957] Ch 169	42
J	Jervis v Harris [1996] Ch 195	169, 175, 176, 179
L	Lurcott v Wakeley [1911]	119
P	Post Office v Aquarius Properties Ltd [1987] 1 All ER 1055	119
	Proudfoot v Hart [1890] 25 QBD 42	119
R	Rainbow Estates Ltd v Tokenhold Ltd [1999] Ch 64	175
	Ravenseft Properties Ltd v Davstone (Holdings) Ltd [1980] QB 12	119
	Royal Bank of Scotland v Etridge (no 2) and others [2001] UKHL 44	9
W	Welsh v Greenwich LBC [2000]	119

Table of Statutes

C	Chancel Repairs Act 1932	57
	Coal Industry Act 1994	43
	Commons Registration Act 1965	58
E	Environmental Protection Act 1990	56
	Equality Act 2010	132
F	Family Law Act 1996	49, 66
	Financial Services and Markets Act 2000	
	s 327	11
	Fraud Act 2006	
	s 1	96, 101
G	General Permitted Development Order 2015	
	art 4	21, 24, 55
L	Land Registration Act 1925	32
	Land Registration Act 2002	32, 152
	s 67	35
	s 66	96, 101
	s 86(5)	103
	Land Registration Rules 2003	162
	r 131	100
	r 136	96, 101
	r 183	94
	r 217A	99
	Landlord and Tenant Act 1927	
	s 3	125, 127, 144
	s 18	175, 177
	s 19(1)(a)	130, 131, 141, 143, 166, 134
	s 19(1A)	131, 132, 133, 143
	s 19(2)	126
	s 19(3)	128
	Pt 1	125
	Landlord and Tenant Act 1954	117, 134
	s 23	196, 186
	s 24	186
	ss 24–28	135
	s 25	187–190, 192, 194, 195, 196
	s 26	187, 190–192, 194
	s 27	187, 190, 194
	s 27(1A)	187, 190
	s 30	187, 191, 192, 194, 195
	Pt II	132, 135, 183, 187
	Landlord and Tenant Act 1988	
	s 1	131, 143, 166, 134

	Landlord and Tenant (Covenants) Act 1995	159, 167, 168, 173
	s 17	173, 174, 177, 180
	Law of Property Act 1925	
	s 44	38, 49-50
	s 45(2)	164
	s 52	39, 92, 184
	s 53(1)(b)	96
	s 54(2)	48
	s 84	45
	s 101	81
	s 146	176-179
	Law of Property (Joint Tenants) Act 1964	44
	Law of Property (Miscellaneous Provisions) Act 1989	
	s 1(2)	39
	s 2(1)	84
	Law of Property (Miscellaneous Provisions) Act 1994	
	s 4	162
	s 6	74
	Leasehold Property (Repairs) Act 1938	175, 176, 177
	Legal Services Act 2007	99
	Limitation Act 1980	172, 180
S	SRA Code of Conduct for Firms	6
	SRA Code of Conduct for Solicitors, RELs and RFL	6
	para 1	9
	para 1.2	27
	para 1.3	9, 10
	para 1.4	9, 27, 29
	para 6	6
	para 6.2	7, 9
	para 6.2(a)	7
	para 6.2(b)	7
	para 6.2(i)–(iii)	81
	para 6.3	8-9, 29
	SRA Financial Services (Conduct of Business) Rules	11
	SRA Financial Services (Scope) Rules	11
	SRA Principles	6
T	Taxation of Chargeable Gains Act 1992	15
	Town and Country Planning Act 1990	
	s 55	19, 20, 23, 30
	s 55(2)	19
	s 57(1)	19
	s 192	21
U	UK Finance Mortgage Lenders' Handbook for Conveyancers	
	Pt 1	82
	Pt 2	82
	Pt 3	82
V	Value Added Tax Act 1994	16, 136

1 The Key Elements and Structure of a Freehold Property Transaction

1.1	Introduction	2
1.2	Key elements and structure of freehold property transactions	2
1.3	Professional conduct issues in a property transaction	6
1.4	Sources of finance for a property transaction	10
1.5	Types of mortgage	11
1.6	Property taxation	12
1.7	Core principles of planning law	19
1.8	Taking instructions	25

SQE1 syllabus

This chapter will enable you to achieve the SQE1 Assessment Specification in relation to Functioning Legal Knowledge concerned with the following:

- Key elements and structure of freehold property transactions
- Law Society Conveyancing Protocol
- Professional conduct
- Sources of finance for a property transaction
- Types of mortgage
- Taxation - property
- Core principles of planning law

Note that for SQE1, candidates are not usually required to recall specific case names or cite statutory or regulatory authorities. Cases and statutory or regulatory authorities are provided for illustrative purposes only unless otherwise indicated.

Learning outcomes

By the end of this chapter you will be able to apply relevant core legal principles and rules appropriately and effectively, at the level of a competent newly qualified solicitor in practice, to realistic client-based and ethical problems and situations in the following areas:

- The procedure for transferring a freehold property from a seller to a buyer
- The significance of exchange and completion
- Professional conduct issues that may arise in a property transaction

- Financial aspects of a property sale and purchase transaction, including legal costs, sources of finance and property taxation
- When planning permission is required and whether a property is subject to breaches of planning control
- Taking a client's initial instructions in a property sale and purchase transaction.

1.1 Introduction

Land and buildings come in all shapes and sizes, from flats and houses to fields, offices, factories, shops and even nuclear power plants. No two properties are the same. Property clients are also very varied: clients buy land and buildings for different reasons and a client who wants to occupy a house or business premises will have very different priorities from a client who wants to invest in or develop a property to raise income and a capital profit. Some clients want outright ownership and are prepared to pay the purchase price up front, some clients only want the building for a limited period and prefer a pay as you go rental arrangement. Nevertheless, whatever shape and size the property and regardless of how and why the client wants it, there are recognised procedures for buying, selling and leasing land and buildings in England and Wales which lawyers are expected to follow.

The process of transferring the ownership of a property is called 'conveyancing'. This chapter explains the basic conveyancing procedures involved in transferring a freehold property from one owner to another, together with some of the conduct, financial and planning issues specific to property practice. Some of these are preliminary issues that must be identified and resolved before the legal work on the transaction starts and some are issues that will occur throughout the transaction at different points. Leasehold property is dealt with in **Chapters 6–10**.

* The tax rates set out in this chapter are correct as at the date of publication. Please note that these tax rates may no longer be current as at the date of any future SQE assessment.

1.2 Key elements and structure of freehold property transactions

There are two milestones in a conveyancing transaction: exchange of contracts and completion. Completion is the stage when the bulk of the purchase money is paid to the seller and the transfer deed is completed to transfer the property to the buyer. Exchange of contracts is not compulsory, but is useful in the majority of cases because it fixes the completion date and gives the buyer time between exchange of contracts and completion in order to make their final preparations. It is also useful where the parties are agreed that conditions must be fulfilled before completion can take place. The contract records the agreed terms and can be relied upon if anything goes wrong in the period between exchange of contracts and completion. However, it is not always necessary to have a gap in time. Exchange of contracts and completion can take place simultaneously, or the parties can agree to proceed straight to completion without an exchange of contracts.

Around these two milestones are three stages in the transaction, the pre-contract stage, the pre-completion stage and the post-completion stage. During each stage the solicitors acting for each party will carry out various tasks so they can exchange and then complete.

Figure 1.1 Conveyancing milestones and stages

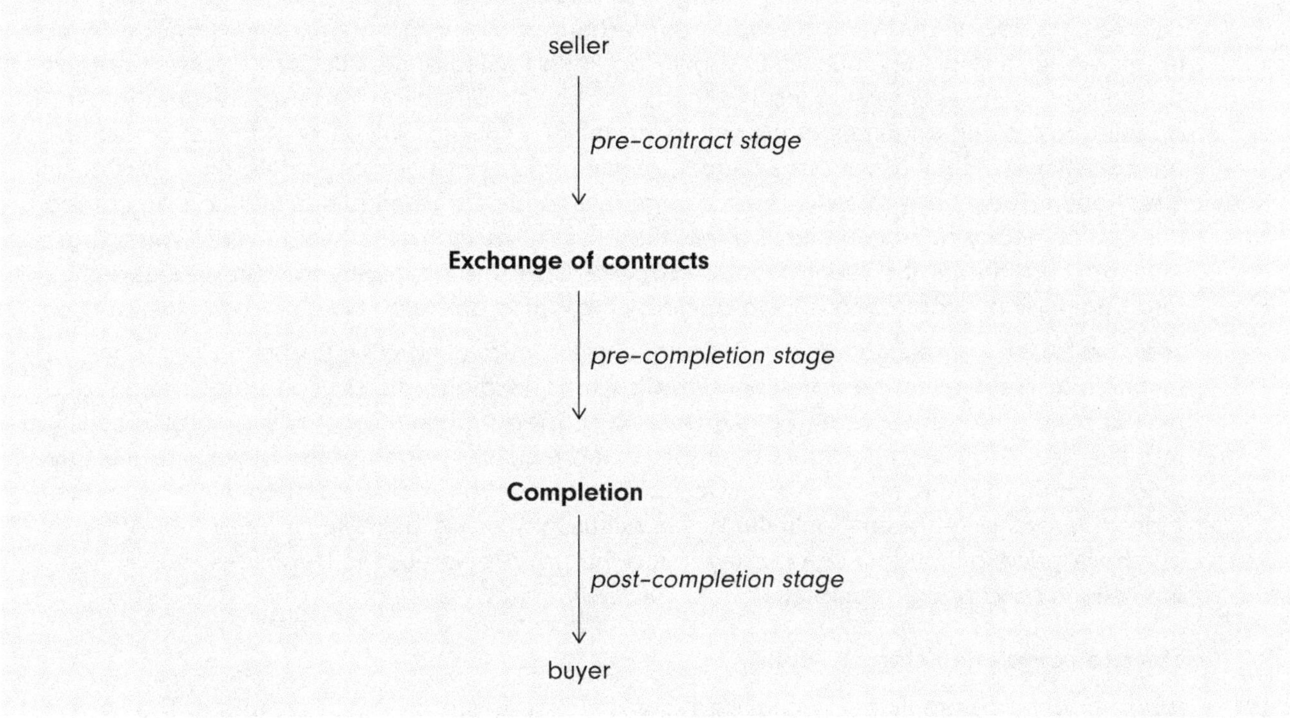

It is important to realise that the parties are not bound to the transaction until contracts are exchanged. Buyers sometimes have cause to complain when the seller pulls out of the transaction just before exchange of contracts, after the buyer has incurred considerable time and expense. The obvious solution for this problem would be for the buyer to exchange contracts as soon as they make an offer so that, for example, they are not gazumped by a new buyer offering a higher price. However, the buyer should not enter the contract until they have carried out numerous searches, enquiries and a survey of the property. This is because of the principle of 'caveat emptor', which is a Latin phrase meaning 'let the buyer beware'. Caveat emptor means that the seller is not obliged to disclose information about the property, other than about limited matters of title, and would not be liable for any defects in the property which later come to light. So, the onus is on the buyer to discover as much about the property as possible before exchanging contracts and committing to the purchase. Caveat emptor does not entitle the seller to give misleading answers to the buyer's enquiries.

1.2.1 The pre-contract stage

A conveyancing transaction starts with the solicitors for both parties taking instructions from their client. It is important to do this right at the start to establish the degree of consensus between the parties and identify any outstanding issues that may cause delay, frustration and additional costs later in the transaction. Thereafter the steps in the pre-contract stage reflect the caveat emptor principle. The seller's solicitor submits a pre-contract package of documents to the buyer's solicitor which includes a draft contract and evidence of the seller's title to the property being sold. The buyer's solicitor must check the documents of title very carefully to ensure that, firstly, the seller is entitled to sell the property, and secondly, there are no encumbrances, such as restrictive covenants, which would prevent the buyer from using the property as they intend. It is important that the buyer's solicitor is satisfied with the title before exchange of contracts because the contract will usually include a provision prohibiting the buyer from raising further queries on the title, known as 'requisitions', after exchange. **Chapter 2** explains how title is investigated.

The buyer's solicitor's concerns will not be limited to matters of title. They will also want to carry out additional searches and enquiries about such things as boundaries, access, disputes, outgoings and previous works carried out at the property. The seller is not obliged to answer such enquiries, but will probably do so to facilitate the sale. Any incorrect replies on the part of the seller could lead to the buyer having an action for misrepresentation. In addition to making enquiries of the seller, the buyer's solicitor will carry out what are known as pre-contract searches of various statutory, public and private bodies to help the buyer obtain information about the property. There are many searches and enquiries that can be carried out and as nearly all of them incur a fee, the buyer's solicitor must decide which ones are most appropriate for the client and the property. **Chapter 3** explains the range of searches and enquiries available and how to decide which ones are relevant.

The results of the investigation of title and the pre-contract searches and enquiries may necessitate changes to the draft contract. **Chapter 4** explains the structure and content of a typical contract for the sale and purchase of a property. Once the buyer's solicitor is satisfied that the necessary searches have been done, the results reported to the buyer and the buyer's lender, and that the contract is in an acceptable form, then exchange of contracts can take place. On exchange of contracts the buyer will usually pay a deposit, typically 10% of the purchase price, although it can be any figure the parties agree. The deposit is usually held by the seller's solicitor until completion.

1.2.2 The pre-completion stage

It is only when contracts are exchanged that the parties are bound to complete. The time in between exchange and completion, the pre-completion stage, is spent making sure all the correct documentation and the completion money will be available on the completion date. The transfer deed (the document which will transfer the legal title in the property) will need to be prepared and executed in readiness for completion. The buyer's solicitor will carry out pre-completion searches to check that the information obtained at the pre-contract stage remains valid and to ensure that there will be no problems registering the buyer's title at the Land Registry. On completion the buyer will pay the balance of the purchase money and the seller will hand over the keys to the property.

1.2.3 The post-completion stage

In the post-completion stage, both sides must finalise the administrative matters. The seller's solicitor must ensure that any mortgage the seller had on the property is paid off and removed from the title. They will usually have given an undertaking to do this. The buyer's solicitor must ensure that Stamp Duty Land Tax (England) or Land Transaction Tax (Wales) is paid on the transfer. Finally, the buyer's solicitor must register their client as the new owner of the property and register any new mortgage over the land. **Chapter 5** explains the conveyancing process from exchange to post completion.

1.2.4 The Law Society Conveyancing Protocol

The Law Society Conveyancing Protocol (the 'Protocol') applies to residential conveyancing only. The current version of the Protocol was issued in 2019 and replaced earlier versions, the first of which was issued in 1990. The Protocol is designed to standardise the residential conveyancing process; it is a set of instructions to conveyancers as to how to carry out a residential sale and purchase and is accompanied by a series of standard documents issued under the 'TransAction' brand. For example, where the Protocol is used, the form of standard pre-contract enquiries to the seller that the seller's solicitor will ask their client to complete for a freehold property is called a Property Information Form (TA06).

All firms that undertake residential conveyancing and want to be members of The Law Society's Conveyancing Quality Scheme ('CQS') are required to comply with the Protocol, a Client Service Charter and mandatory training and enforcement procedures. Membership of the CQS is essential for any firm wanting to be on the panels of solicitors approved by the residential mortgage lenders to act for lenders where the buyer is taking out a mortgage.

The text of the Protocol is available online and provides a useful checklist of the procedural stages in a straightforward residential transaction. The procedures set out in the Protocol reflect what standard practice is in residential conveyancing and, in the residential context, in this manual.

1.2.5 Summary of key elements and structure

The following chart summarises the procedure explained in **Chapters 1** to **5**. You should refer back to the chart while working through these chapters as you will need to maintain a sense of the overall structure of a conveyancing transaction while engaging with the detail.

CONVEYANCING PROCEDURE

SALE AND PURCHASE OF FREEHOLD PROPERTY

SELLER'S SOLICITOR	BOTH SOLICITORS	BUYER'S SOLICITOR
	PRE-CONTRACT STAGE	
Take instructions from the seller client	Check for conflicts of interest	Take instructions from the buyer client (and possibly the lender client)
Investigate title and produce evidence of title (deduce title) to the buyer		Investigate title
Reply to buyer's pre-contract enquiries		Raise pre-contract searches and enquiries (and check buyer client has commissioned survey)
Draft the contract		Approve draft contract
		Prepare pre-exchange report to client(s)
	Obtain client signature to the contract	
	Exchange contracts	Pay the deposit
	PRE-COMPLETION STAGE	
Approve the draft transfer deed		Draft the transfer deed*
		[Draft the mortgage deed if acting for the lender and] obtain client execution of mortgage deed

* Conventionally it is the buyer's solicitor that drafts the transfer deed but it is not uncommon for the seller's solicitor to do so (it would then be provided to the buyer's solicitor at the same time as the draft contract)

SELLER'S SOLICITOR	BOTH SOLICITORS	BUYER'S SOLICITOR
Reply to buyer's pre-completion enquiries, including giving undertaking to discharge seller's mortgage		Raise pre-completion searches and enquiries (updating and, if acting for the lender, checking buyer's solvency)
		Submit report on title/certificate of title to lender and request mortgage advance (if appropriate)
	Complete transaction	
	POST-COMPLETION STAGE	
Post-completion matters (including discharging existing mortgage if necessary)		Post-completion matters (including paying Stamp Duty Land Tax/Land Transaction Tax and registering the transfer of title with Land Registry)

1.3 Professional conduct issues in a property transaction

In any property transaction there will always be a number of preliminary matters to be considered once a solicitor receives instructions to act. If the solicitor does not obtain clear instructions and clarify these preliminary matters at the outset, the solicitor, and more importantly their client, may run into severe difficulties later in the transaction. These difficulties could lead to delay and expense for the client, as well as stress and a general feeling that the solicitor should have anticipated these matters much better.

The first question should always be 'Can we act on behalf of this client?' and then 'Can we carry out the client's instructions?'. For solicitors, the starting point and constant point of reference must be the professional conduct regulations laid down by the Solicitors Regulation Authority in the Code of Conduct for Solicitors. A firm's conduct will be governed by the Code of Conduct for Firms. Any breach of those regulations (collectively known as 'The Code of Conduct') may lead to disciplinary proceedings against the solicitor and/or the firm, and also a potential negligence claim.

The SRA Standards and Regulations contain 'SRA Principles', such as acting with integrity and acting in the best interests of each client. The SRA Principles underpin the whole of the SRA Standards and Regulations, including The Code of Conduct which sets out regulations describing what firms and solicitors are expected to achieve in order to comply with the SRA Principles. The regulations that are most relevant to property practice are contained in paragraph 6 in The Code of Conduct. Paragraph 6 deals with conflicts of interest and confidentiality.

1.3.1 Acting for seller and buyer

A solicitor may be asked to act for more than one party in a property transaction. Often the parties want this because they believe that it will result in cost and time savings. The problem is that when acting for more than one party in a transaction, a conflict of interest may arise between those parties. For example, a solicitor might be asked to act for both the seller and the buyer. The parties may not see a problem with this because, as far as they are concerned, they have already agreed the price and they both want the sale and purchase to go through as quickly and cost-efficiently as possible. However, the parties may argue later, perhaps if an issue is revealed in the searches and enquiries that causes the buyer to seek a reduction in the purchase price.

Acting for buyer and seller is governed by paragraph 6.2 in The Code of Conduct which states that, subject to certain exceptions, a solicitor cannot act for both parties if there is a conflict of interest or a significant risk of such a conflict. Acting for a buyer and a seller carries a high risk of conflict of interests where the land is being transferred for value. This is particularly the case where the clients do not have equal bargaining power (eg an experienced developer and a first-time buyer) or where there has to be a negotiation on price.

An exception set out in paragraph 6.2(a) allows a solicitor to act for more than one party, even if there is a conflict of interest, where the parties have a 'substantially common interest' in relation to the matter and provided that certain conditions are met. However, the Law Society has stated that:

> The SRA's exception for circumstances where the two clients have a 'substantially common interest' does not apply to a property purchase. Although both clients will have a common interest in completing the sale, they also have different interests, since one is buying and one is selling.

Another exception set in paragraph 6.2(b) allows a solicitor to act even if there is a conflict of interest where the clients are competing for the same objective. The conditions for so acting are as for paragraph 6.2(a) above. So, it might be possible, in theory, to act for two buyers who are competing against each other to buy a property, but this exception will not apply in a buyer and seller situation.

1.3.2 Acting for joint buyers

It is usually acceptable to act for joint buyers, provided that the solicitor can comply with paragraph 6.2 in The Code of Conduct. It may be necessary to advise residential buyers separately about how they want to hold the equitable interest in the property, particularly if they are not married or in a civil partnership (see **2.5.4**).

1.3.3 Acting for borrower and lender

Acting for more than one party in the same transaction is more common when the parties are the borrower and the lender. Acting for a lender and borrower is possible unless, under paragraph 6.2 of The Code of Conduct, there is a conflict of interest or a significant risk of such a conflict. The Law Society has stated that:

The risk of a conflict is high if:

- the mortgage is not a standard mortgage (such as one provided in the normal course of the lender's activities, where a significant part of the lender's activities consists of lending and the mortgage is on standard terms) of property to be used as the borrower's private residence
- the mortgage is a standard mortgage but you do not use the approved certificate of title

(See **4.10** for information about the approved certificate of title.)

In residential transactions, the lender will frequently instruct the borrower's solicitor to act for them as well as the borrower in connection with the grant of the mortgage. This is because, in the vast majority of cases, the mortgage is a standard mortgage and the approved certificate of title will be given to the lender.

It is also possible to act for more than one party under the exception in paragraph 6.2(a), even if there is a conflict of interest, where the parties have a 'substantially common interest' in relation to the matter and provided that certain conditions are met. These conditions are that both clients have given their informed written consent, effective safeguards have been put in place to protect any client confidential information and that the solicitor is satisfied that it is reasonable for them to act for both clients.

Where the solicitor is acting for the borrower and the lender, they must bear in mind the possibility that the duty of confidentiality under paragraph 6.3 of The Code of Conduct to one client may come into conflict with the duty of disclosure to the other client: see the **Ethics and Professional Conduct** manual at **6.4.3**.

In large commercial property transactions, the lender usually has its own solicitors, separate from those of the borrower. This is because the mortgage documents are likely to be subject to negotiation between the solicitors for the two parties, and so will not be on standard terms. However, it is common for the lender's solicitor to ask the borrower's solicitor to carry out the title investigation and the searches and enquiries and to report the results to the lender and the borrower as this avoids duplication of costs and time. The solicitors may feel that it is appropriate to agree this because the clients have a substantial common interest in wanting the borrower to obtain good title to the property and in ensuring that there are no problems adversely affecting the property's value.

1.3.4 Acting for joint borrowers

It is usually acceptable to act for joint borrowers, provided no conflict of interests exists or is likely to arise. However, a problem can arise where, for example, a matrimonial home is owned by a married couple jointly and one of them agrees to mortgage it as security for a business loan. If the spouse agrees to the loan and the business subsequently fails, the bank will enforce the security against the matrimonial home. In such circumstances the spouse may seek to have the mortgage set aside on the basis of undue influence. Although there is no rebuttable presumption of undue influence between married people, the lender is put on enquiry because the transaction is not to the spouse's advantage.

The House of Lords laid down detailed guidelines for solicitors acting in these circumstances. This guidance is commonly referred to as 'the *Etridge* guidelines'* as they derive from a 2001 case of the same name involving a business loan to a husband secured on a matrimonial home owned jointly by the husband and his wife. The lender is entitled to proceed on the basis that the solicitor advising the spouse has done so properly. The lender should, with the borrower's consent, provide the solicitor with the following information:

(a) the purpose for which the loan is being made available;

(b) the current amount of the borrower's indebtedness;

(c) the amount of the current overdraft facility;

(d) the amount and terms of the new loan; and

(e) a copy of any written application made by the borrower for the loan.

The solicitor should:

(i) explain to the spouse the purpose for which the solicitor has become involved;

(ii) explain that the lender will rely on the solicitor's involvement to counter any suggestion that the spouse has been unduly influenced or has not fully understood the nature of the transaction; and

(iii) obtain confirmation from the spouse that they wish the solicitor to act for them in the transaction, and to advise them on the legal and practical implications of the transaction.

The solicitor's discussion with the spouse should take place at a face-to-face meeting in the absence of the borrower and the advice should be given in non-technical language. The nature and extent of the advice given will depend on the facts of the case, but should include an explanation of the nature of the documents, the practical consequences to the spouse of signing them and a warning as to the seriousness of the risks involved. It must be clearly explained to the spouse that they have a choice as to whether or not to proceed with the transaction.

The solicitor must check if the spouse wishes to proceed. The spouse should be asked whether they want the solicitor to write to the lender confirming that matters have been explained to them. The solicitor must not confirm this to the lender unless they have received the relevant documents from the lender and have express instructions from the spouse to do so. If the solicitor thinks that the transaction is not in the spouse's best interests, they should give reasoned advice to that effect. If it is 'glaringly obvious' that the spouse is being 'grievously wronged', the solicitor should decline to act.

In the *Etridge* case, the House of Lords considered whether the wife should be advised by a different solicitor from the husband, but decided that the cost disadvantage outweighed the benefit. Therefore one solicitor can advise both parties, provided that the *Etridge* guidelines are followed and the solicitor is satisfied that they can comply with paragraph 6.2 of The Code of Conduct.

Although the *Etridge* case involved husband and wife, the same principles will apply to civil partners, cohabitees, parent and child and any other situation where property is being charged in return for a loan that is not being made to all of the property owners.

* *Royal Bank of Scotland v Etridge (no 2) and others* [2001] UKHL 44, often shortened to *Etridge*, is the case used in practice to consider issues of undue influence. You may be required to know and be able to use this term in the SQE1 assessments.

1.3.5 Contract races

Another situation that can cause difficulties for solicitors is where a seller client is selling a property using a marketing strategy known as a 'contract race'. In a contract race, a pre-contract package is sent to multiple buyers who then compete to be ready to exchange contracts first. This is regarded as a legitimate selling technique, so long as all the prospective buyers know that they are engaged in a race. However, problems arise when the seller instructs their solicitor that they do not want the prospective buyers to know.

Paragraph 1.4 of The Code of Conduct is relevant to this situation. Where a solicitor acts for a seller of land, they must not mislead or attempt to mislead the buyers, either by their own acts or omissions, or by being complicit in the acts or omissions of others. This means that the solicitor should inform all buyers immediately of the seller's intention to deal with more than one buyer. If the seller refuses to agree to such disclosure, the solicitor cannot disclose the contract race to the prospective buyers because they have a duty of confidentiality to the seller client under paragraph 6.3. Instead, the solicitor should immediately stop acting in the matter.

1.3.6 Undertakings

Paragraph 1 of The Code of Conduct is also relevant where a solicitor is asked to give an undertaking. An undertaking is a statement made by or on behalf of a solicitor, or the firm, to someone who reasonably places reliance on it, that the solicitor or firm will do something, cause something to be done, or will not do something. Paragraph 1.3 deals with undertakings and says that solicitors should perform all undertakings, and do so within an agreed timescale. Failure to honour an undertaking is professional misconduct so a solicitor should always ensure that anything they undertake to do is within their control.

Example

You act for John, the buyer of a house known as Manor Fields. The contract for the sale and purchase of Manor Fields was finally agreed last week. The seller's solicitor e-mailed you three days ago to confirm that he was holding a contract signed by the seller and was ready to exchange contracts. After some delay, you have now received John's signed contract. John has just telephoned to say that there has been a computer glitch at his bank and the deposit monies required for exchange will not now be transferred into your firm's bank account until tomorrow.

The seller is insisting that exchange of contracts takes place today and is threatening to pull out if it does not. John is anxious not to lose the property and has been told by the seller that the seller's solicitor will exchange today if you give the seller's solicitor an undertaking that the deposit money will be transferred to their firm by close of business tomorrow. John has instructed you to go ahead and exchange contracts on this basis.

Explain whether you should give such an undertaking.

Paragraph 1.3 in The Code of Conduct says that undertakings must be performed within an agreed timescale or within a reasonable amount of time. Failure to honour an undertaking is professional misconduct. If you do not receive the deposit money from John, you will be personally liable to pay it.

Undertakings are binding even if they are given in relation to something outside the solicitor's control. Therefore, the undertaking should make it clear that the deposit money will be paid only provided it is received from John, or the undertaking should not be given at all.

Other conduct matters

Mortgage fraud, property and title fraud and data protection issues are outside the scope of this manual and are considered in the **Ethics and Professional Conduct** manual. Money laundering is considered in the **Legal Services** manual.

1.4 Sources of finance for a property transaction

One of the most important considerations at the start of a property transaction is whether the client will have enough money to see it through. At first glance, this might not seem to be part of the solicitor's role. However, the client may not be aware of all the legal expenses and incidental costs involved in purchasing a property and they are almost certainly not going to be able to deal with the legal aspects of borrowing any money that is necessary.

One thing a solicitor is obliged to do is to provide the client with the best possible information about the likely overall cost of their matter, at the beginning and at appropriate points throughout the transaction. This involves clearly explaining the fees, when they are likely to change and warning the client about any other payments for which the client may be responsible. In a conveyancing transaction, this could include payments such as Stamp Duty Land Tax/Land Transaction Tax, Land Registry fees and search fees. The type of information and how it is given to clients will vary according to the needs and circumstances of the client and the type of work that is involved. For example, a commercial client who instructs the solicitor on a regular basis is unlikely to need the same information as an individual instructing the solicitor on a one-off residential conveyancing matter. A solicitor has to send a letter of engagement to their client setting out the costings at the beginning of the transaction.

Most clients, be they residential or commercial, will choose to finance the transaction by borrowing the majority of the purchase price. There are many sources of loan finance ranging from banks, insurance companies and finance houses to loans from trust funds and family members. For residential purchases, the normal source of finance is a bank or building society. Both offer long-term loans and commercially competitive rates. Some large employers (such as banks) offer mortgages at concessionary rates to employees, although an employee who has received a larger sum at a lower rate of interest than is available elsewhere may subsequently find that it is difficult to change jobs. Alternatively, a client may be able to arrange for a loan from a relative or a private trust fund, in which case the parties must be separately advised. Also, a residential buyer may be able to take advantage of a Government backed scheme, such as 'Help to Buy' (now only available for properties in Wales) where an equity loan of up to 20% of the value of a new-build home priced up to £300,000 is available.

Methods of finance for commercial property are more numerous and often more complex. One thing common to all lending on property, no matter where the finance comes from, will be the lender's concern to secure the loan against a valuable asset, principally the property itself. The most usual way of doing this is by a mortgage. The creation of the mortgage is something which will be dealt with by a solicitor, either a solicitor acting solely for the lender, or a solicitor acting for buyer and lender jointly.

Sometimes a solicitor is asked to advise on the most appropriate form of finance, both for that particular client and that particular transaction. A solicitor may not be in the best position to advise on such matters and there are restrictions placed on solicitors when they provide financial advice.

(a) Subject to (d) below, if the solicitor is carrying out a regulated activity in relation to a regulated mortgage contract, then they must be authorised to do so under the Financial Services and Markets Act 2000 (FSMA 2000).

(b) A regulated mortgage contract includes one where the borrower is an individual, the lender takes a first legal charge over property in the UK and at least 40% of the property is intended for occupation by the borrower or a member of their immediate family.

(c) Regulated activities include arranging or advising on a regulated mortgage contract (ie a specific mortgage product), but not giving generic advice such as the differences between types of mortgage, or arranging the execution of a mortgage chosen independently by the client or on the advice of an authorised person.

(d) If a regulated activity is involved and the firm is not authorised by the Financial Conduct Authority (FCA) to carry out regulated activities (which most firms will not be), the solicitor can still arrange or advise on a regulated mortgage contract by relying on the s 327 exemption for professional firms (often referred to as the 's 327 exemption' as it derives from s 327 FSMA 2000). The exemption allows solicitors to carry out regulated activities if they are incidental to the provision by the firm of professional services, ie services regulated by the SRA.

(e) Arranging or advising on a regulated mortgage contract under the exemption for professional firms is subject to the solicitor complying with the SRA Financial Services (Scope) Rules and SRA Financial Services (Conduct of Business) Rules. These rules do not allow a solicitor to recommend that a client enters into a regulated mortgage contract, except where the advice is an endorsement of a recommendation made to the client by an authorised person.

If the solicitor does not have the requisite knowledge to provide generic advice, or the client requires advice on a specific mortgage product, the solicitor should refer them to a person authorised by the FCA to provide that advice.

1.5 Types of mortgage

The two most common types of mortgage generally available in the market are repayment and interest-only mortgages.

1.5.1 Repayment mortgages

With this type of mortgage, the borrower will make monthly payments to the lender made up partly of instalments of the original amount borrowed and partly of interest chargeable on the loan. The borrower can choose to pay interest at the lender's standard variable rate ('SVR'), fix the interest rate for a set period or agree a 'tracker' rate of a certain percentage above the UK base rate set by the Bank of England. With a fixed rate or tracker rate, the interest will revert to the SVR at the end of the agreed period. The advantage of a repayment mortgage is that by the end of the mortgage term, the borrower will have paid off everything they owe.

1.5.2 Interest-only mortgages

With this type of mortgage, the borrower will also make monthly payments to the lender, but those payments will only comprise interest chargeable on the loan. The advantage is that the monthly repayments for an interest-only mortgage are likely to be lower than under a repayment mortgage, but at the end of the mortgage term the borrower will still owe the lender the whole of the original amount borrowed. The borrower must therefore find an alternative way to pay off the loan, such as a savings or investment product, if they want to be free of the mortgage at the end of the term.

It is possible to obtain a combined mortgage where part of the loan is interest only and part is repayment. The lender will usually want to see evidence as to how the capital will be repaid at the end of the term.

1.5.3 Other types of mortgage

For clients who are unable to enter into mortgages which charge interest, there are finance schemes that are Sharia compliant and avoid the payment of interest. For example, the bank buys the property and resells it to the buyer at a higher price. The buyer repays the excess to the bank by instalments over a period of years. Alternatively, the bank buys the property and leases it to the buyer in return for rent, and at the end of the lease the bank transfers the property to the buyer.

1.6 Property taxation

The taxes that will be charged on a property transaction will depend on whether the client is the buyer or the seller and whether the property is residential or commercial.

Taking a residential property first, the buyer may have to pay either Stamp Duty Land Tax ('SDLT') in England, or Land Transaction Tax ('LTT') in Wales, when they purchase the property. A seller, who makes a capital gain by selling the property for more than they bought it for, will probably not have to pay Capital Gains Tax ('CGT') on that gain if they have used the property as their only or main residence.

A buyer of a commercial property, such as an office block, will pay SDLT or LTT on the purchase just like a residential buyer, although there is no special concession for first-time buyers and the rates at which the tax is calculated are different. The main difference is that the buyer of a commercial property may have to pay VAT on the purchase.

A commercial property is likely to be owned by a company and companies pay Corporation Tax on their income and capital profits (rather than income tax and CGT). So, if the property is rented out the landlord will pay Corporation Tax on the rent. Corporation Tax will also be payable on any gain if the property is sold for more than its purchase price. Corporation Tax is not covered in this manual.

1.6.1 Stamp Duty Land Tax ('SDLT') in England and Land Transaction Tax ('LTT') in Wales

SDLT has only been in existence from 1 December 2003. Before that there was Stamp Duty, which was a tax paid on *documents*, the payment of which was evidenced by a stamp being impressed into or stamped onto the document. SDLT is a tax not on documents but on property *transactions*.

In Wales, SDLT was replaced with LTT with effect from 1 April 2018. LTT is similar to SDLT in many respects but the two are not identical. This chapter will outline the principles of SDLT in sections (a), (b) and (c) and return to LTT in section (d).

SDLT/LTT is charged using a separate rate of tax per portion of the purchase price. Exactly what is payable depends on the type of property (residential or commercial) and the value of the transaction.

(a) The basis of charge for residential freehold property (SDLT)

First-time buyers of residential property can claim relief from SDLT if they intend to occupy the property as their main residence and the purchase price is no more than £500,000. They do not pay anything on purchases up to £300,000 and pay 5% on the portion from £300,001 to £500,000.

The SDLT rates for residential buyers who are not first-time buyers are as follows:

Part of consideration	SDLT Rate
So much as does not exceed £125,000	0%
So much as exceeds £125,000 but does not exceed £250,000	2%
So much as exceeds £250,000 but does not exceed £925,000	5%
So much as exceeds £925,000 but does not exceed £1,500,000	10%
The remainder	12%

So, the SDLT payable on the purchase of a £275,000 home by a second-time buyer is £3,750 (0% on £125,000, 2% on £125,000 and 5% on £25,000).

Note that SDLT is payable on 'land' (which includes fixtures) but not chattels, so if the sale involves valuable chattels (such as carpets and curtains and freestanding white goods) it may be possible to save SDLT by apportioning part of the purchase price to the chattels. However, any apportionment must be a fair value or a fraud on HMRC is being committed.

Example

Priya is intending to sell her current house and buy a new house. The purchase price for the new house is £575,000, but Priya has asked you to apportion £10,250 to the carpets and curtains.

What information will you need to obtain from Priya before you can advise her on the tax she will have to pay on her purchase?

In relation to her purchase, Priya will pay £18,750 in SDLT if the purchase price for the house is £575,000, but only £18,237 if the price is reduced by £10,250 because the carpets and curtains are 'chattels' and not part of the land. The price apportionment will therefore save Priya £513 in SDLT. However, you will need to be sure that the £10,250 is a fair reflection of the value of the carpets and curtains, because if it is not, the apportionment could be treated as a fraud on HMRC and result in criminal sanctions.

There are higher rates of SDLT if the buyer already owns a property and is buying an additional property or if the buyer is not a UK resident.

(b) The basis of charge for non-residential or mixed use freehold property (SDLT)

The SDLT rates for non-residential or mixed use freehold properties are as follows:

Part of consideration	SDLT Rate
So much as does not exceed £150,000	0%
So much as exceeds £150,000 but does not exceed £250,000	2%
So much as exceeds £250,000	5%

So, the SDLT payable on the purchase of a £275,000 commercial property by a buyer is £3,250 (0% on £150,000, 2% on £100,000 and 5% on £25,000).

If VAT is charged, SDLT is payable on the VAT-inclusive sum.

There is an online SDLT calculator on the Gov.UK website that calculates SDLT for both residential and commercial properties.

(c) How SDLT is paid

SDLT is paid to HMRC, usually online by bank transfer, accompanied by a form called an SDLT1 which provides the necessary details of the transaction. It must be paid within 14 days of completion and if it is not paid, the transfer of the property to the buyer will not be registered by the Land Registry. Failure to file and pay on time will also attract penalties and interest.

(d) LTT

There are a number of key differences between SDLT and LTT. The first is that there is no relief for first-time residential buyers from LTT. The rates at which the tax is charged are also different.

The LTT rates for those who are buying residential freehold property are as follows:

Part of consideration	LTT Rate
So much as does not exceed £225,000	0%
So much as exceeds £225,000 but does not exceed £400,000	6%
So much as exceeds £400,000 but does not exceed £750,000	7.5%
So much as exceeds £750,000 but does not exceed £1,500,000	10%
The remainder	12%

So, the LTT payable on the purchase of a £275,000 home is £3,000 (0% on £225,000 and 6% on £50,000).

There are higher rates of LTT if the buyer already owns a property and is buying an additional property or if the buyer is not a UK resident.

The LTT rates for non-residential or mixed use freehold properties are as follows:

Part of consideration	LTT Rate
So much as does not exceed £225,000	0%
So much as exceeds £225,000 but does not exceed £250,000	1%
So much as exceeds £250,000 but does not exceed £1m	5%
So much as exceeds £1m	6%

So, the LTT payable on the purchase of a £275,000 commercial property by a buyer is £1,500 (0% on £225,000, 1% on 25,000 and 5% on £25,000).

If VAT is charged, LTT is payable on the VAT-inclusive sum.

There is an online LTT calculator on the Gov.UK website that calculates LTT for both residential and commercial properties.

The other key difference between SDLT and LTT is that a land transaction return for LTT must be submitted to the Welsh Revenue Authority within 30 days of completion, rather than 14 days.

1.6.2 CGT and private residence relief

(a) The basis of charge

Capital gains tax ('CGT') is charged on gains made on 'chargeable assets' within the meaning of Taxation of Chargeable Gains Act 1992. This includes freehold and leasehold property, and the interests of co-owners in the case of jointly-owned property. Some transactions that are incidental to the sale of land also give rise to a charge to CGT, for example where a separate payment is made for the release or modification of an easement or covenant. Gifts also fall within the meaning of 'disposal' for the purpose of CGT.

The gain on a sale of property is calculated by deducting the purchase price of the property (or its base value in 1982 if purchased earlier than this) from its current sale price. Certain forms of expenditure incurred in acquiring or improving the property can also be deducted in appropriate cases. The gain is chargeable at a rate set by the Government after allowing for the individual's annual exemption.

(b) Private residence relief

A seller of a residential property is likely to be able to claim the benefit of private residence relief ('PRR') if it is the sale of an individual's dwelling house used as their only or main residence. To qualify, the seller must have occupied the dwelling house as their only or main residence throughout the period of ownership. If an individual has more than one residence, they can choose which of their residences will qualify for PRR by making an election to HMRC. PRR will also be available to trustees if the property is occupied by a beneficiary as their principal residence.

Certain periods of absence are allowed, for example if the owner is an employee and has to live abroad or in service accommodation as part of their job, but there are very specific conditions attaching to each of these periods of time if they are to be disregarded.

If the seller has a garden of more than 0.5 hectares, the gain on the excess is chargeable to CGT unless the seller can demonstrate to HMRC that the extra garden was necessary for the reasonable enjoyment of the house. The relief may be lost on any part of the house used exclusively for business use.

Example

It is 2025 and you act for Priya who is selling the house she bought back in 2009 for £138,000. The agreed sale price is £410,000.

What information will you need to obtain from Priya before you can advise her on the tax she will have to pay on her sale?

If her sale completes, Priya will have made a capital gain of £272,000. However, she will not have to pay CGT on the gain if she can claim the private residence relief. You will need to know whether:

- Priya lived in her house continuously from 2009
- She owned and/or lived in more than one house during this time
- The garden is more than 0.5 hectares
- She used any part of the house for a business use

1.6.3 VAT

Value Added Tax, although an important and sometimes tricky concept, is uncomplicated in most property transactions. However, it is important to understand the basics of what VAT is and how it is charged and collected.

(a) Basis of charge

VAT is a tax on 'taxable supplies', ie some goods and services provided by a taxable person in the course or furtherance of a business. It is ultimately borne by consumers, but it is charged by the supplier who adds it to the price of the goods or service, so it is an example of an 'indirect' tax. The current relevant legislation is the Value Added Tax Act 1994 and various regulations and EC Directives.

To charge and collect the VAT, the supplier must be a 'taxable person'. A taxable person is a person whose turnover over the past 12 months has exceeded the registration limit, currently £85,000.

VAT is collected by HMRC from each supplier. It is collected at the end of each VAT period (usually every three months) by the supplier completing a VAT return to HMRC online.

- Output tax is the VAT charged by the supplier on its goods or services (ie its output).
- The supplier delineates this output VAT separately on its invoices when charging its customers.
- The customer, the recipient of the goods or services, pays the VAT. In a customer's business this is called input tax.
- To calculate the VAT due to HMRC, the supplier deducts input tax it has paid against the output tax it has charged and only the net amount is sent to HMRC.
- In other words, the supplier accounts to HMRC for the value added by its business; input tax paid by the supplier is recovered.

Input tax is only recoverable if attributable to a taxable (or output) supply and there must be an immediate and direct link between the two. Most businesses make taxable supplies of goods and services and so have no difficulty in recovering their input tax; the only issue is one of cash flow because of the quarterly accounting mechanism. However, some types of business, such as insurance companies, banks, building societies, make exempt supplies to customers. If you only sell or supply exempt goods and services, then your business is exempt, you cannot register for VAT and you cannot recover any input tax.

(b) Differences between standard, exempt and zero-rated supplies

VAT is charged at different rates depending on the type of supply.

- Standard rated supplies attract VAT at the standard rate, currently 20%.
- There is a reduced rate of 5% for items such as domestic fuel supplies and certain construction, conversion and renovation services.
- Zero-rated supplies are still taxable supplies, but are charged at a zero rate
- Exempt supplies are non-VATable. However, sometimes a supplier of land has the option to charge VAT ('the option to tax').

(c) What constitutes a taxable supply in property transactions

The vast majority of residential transactions do not involve the payment of VAT. The sale of a new build house by a developer is zero rated so the buyer will not pay any VAT, and the subsequent sale of a residential property by a private individual will not be in the course of a business, so the seller will not be charging VAT to the buyer in addition to the purchase price.

The situation is more complicated with commercial properties. There is a difference between 'old' and 'new' commercial properties for VAT purposes. A new commercial property is one which is within three years from completion of the building. Supplies of interests in, rights or licences to occupy commercial land or buildings are generally exempt. However, the following supplies are taxable supplies, or can be made into taxable supplies by the seller exercising the 'option to tax' (ie to charge VAT):

- The sale of a greenfield site is exempt, subject to the option to tax.
- The supply of construction services is standard rated.
- Professional services, provided by an architect or surveyor for example, are standard rated.
- The sale of a new freehold building is standard rated.
- The sale of an old freehold building is exempt, subject to the option to tax.
- The grant of a lease is exempt, subject to the option to tax.

(d) Reasons why a client would make an option to tax and the effect that it has

The seller of a new commercial building has no choice but to charge the buyer VAT. The seller of an old commercial building does have a choice. The effect of that seller opting to tax is to turn what would have been an exempt supply into a taxable supply. A seller of an old building may want to do this to enable recovery of the input tax incurred in relation to the building, for example on building work costs and professional fees incurred in renovating the building to get it ready to sell.

A possible disadvantage of opting to tax the supply of an old building is that the seller has to charge VAT on the purchase price. This will not be a problem if the buyer makes taxable supplies and is therefore able to recover its input tax VAT. However, if the buyer cannot recover its input tax VAT, or can only make a partial recovery, then the purchase price is, in effect, increased; there will be a real cost to the buyer's business and the building will be unattractive. Thus, if the target market for the building includes 'VAT-sensitive' financial buyers (as in the City of London), the seller will try very hard to avoid opting to tax the supply of the building. If it does so, there may be a detrimental effect on the sale price of the property that can be charged because the potential buyer will seek to claw back some of the irrecoverable input tax VAT by reducing its offer for the purchase price. Also, if the option to tax has been made before the date of transaction (or indeed if there is a VAT element in the price because the building is new), the VAT will count as chargeable consideration for SDLT/LTT purposes so there will be extra SDLT/LTT to pay, which is 'tax on tax'.

Example

You act for Bankridge Estates Limited ('Bankridge'), a developer that specialises in the renovation and conversion of former industrial buildings into offices. In 2018 Bankridge purchased Victoria House, a 1930s warehouse which had been vacant for a number of years and was in a poor state.

Bankridge has now completed its planned works to renovate Victoria House and has decided to sell the freehold in order to raise capital for other projects. It has found a buyer, Fidelity Insurance plc. Bankridge wants to ensure that it recoups as much of the cost of the renovation works as possible, including the VAT paid.

What are the VAT implications of this scenario?

Answer

For VAT purposes, this is a sale of an 'old' freehold commercial property. 'Old' in this context means one that was completed more than three years prior to the sale. Accordingly, the sale is exempt, subject to the option to tax. Bankridge therefore has a choice as to whether or not to opt to tax, but only by doing so can they recover any of the VAT paid to the construction team during the refurbishment.

The problem with opting to tax is that VAT will have to be charged on the purchase price on the sale and as an insurance company, the buyer will probably not be able to recover any of this (because it does not make VATable supplies in the course of its business). The buyer might therefore object to Bankridge opting to tax, or seek a reduction in the purchase price to compensate it for the irrecoverable VAT. The client will have to weigh up the benefit of recovering the refurbishment VAT against the potential loss of sale proceeds, or even the sale itself.

(e) VAT summary

(i) Most real estate transactions are exempt from VAT.

(ii) VAT is not usually paid on residential transactions.

(iii) VAT is only compulsory on 'new' commercial properties.

(iv) VAT is not always charged on 'old' commercial properties.

(v) The seller has an option to tax the supply of 'old' commercial properties.

(vi) The seller needs to opt to tax only if it has paid VAT that it wants to recover.

(vii) If the seller opts to tax, the buyer will usually be able to recover the VAT paid.

(viii) If the buyer makes only exempt supplies, such as insurance or financial supplies, it may be unable to recover fully VAT it has to pay.

(ix) So, a buyer that makes exempt supplies will resist the seller's option to tax, or seek a compensatory reduction in the purchase price.

A solicitor dealing with commercial property transactions must understand the VAT status of the transaction so they can advise a seller client as to whether or not VAT must be charged, or if not, whether it is advisable to opt to do so. Then the solicitors for both parties must make sure that the contract for the sale and purchase of the property accurately reflects the agreed position and, in particular, whether VAT is to be charged in addition to the purchase price (see **4.7**).

1.7 Core principles of planning law

Planning law affects whether a building can be built, altered or extended and also specifies the particular use to which property can be put. It is therefore important for a buyer to be satisfied that the property which they are buying has permission to be on the site where it has been built, and also that it is being used for its authorised purpose. Planning permissions will normally be subject to conditions, so a buyer will need to check any conditions are acceptable and have been complied with. As planning matters generally run with the land, any breach of planning would be the responsibility of the owner of the property and any enforcement action could be against the buyer of that property. The buyer should also bear in mind that if they wish to carry out any works to, or change the use of, the property after purchase, they may need to apply for planning permission.

At one time there was no organised planning control of development. Generally, the only restrictions on what people could do with their property were those imposed by way of restrictive covenants. Even today, this is still an important way of preventing someone building on land or using buildings in a way that is considered inappropriate. However, after the Second World War some central control of development became necessary and this need has become more acute as the population has grown and the urban areas in which people increasingly live have become more congested. England is now one of the most densely populated countries in the world, with over 90% of the population living in urban areas covering just 8% of the land area.

1.7.1 Statutory definition of 'Development'

Section 57(1) of the Town and Country Planning Act 1990 ('TCPA 1990') states that planning permission is required for carrying out any development of land. 'Development' is defined by s 55* of the TCPA 1990 as the carrying out of building, engineering, mining or other operations in, on, over or under land, or the making of any material change in the use of any buildings or other land. So there are broadly two strands of controlled development, firstly operational development (building, engineering, mining or other operations) sometimes referred to as 'BEMO', and material change of use.

* The definition of development in s 55 of the TCPA 1990 is a key definition in planning law. You may be required to know and be able to use this statutory reference and definition in the SQE1 assessments.

1.7.2 Matters that do not constitute 'Development'

Some things are specifically excluded from the definition of development, such as the carrying out of the maintenance, improvement or other alteration of any building or works which affect only the interior of a building, or do not materially affect the external appearance of a building.

In addition, some material changes of use are excluded from the definition of 'development', so do not require planning permission. Section 55(2) of the TCPA 1990 excludes a change of use within the same class of use as specified in the Town and Country Planning (Use Classes) Order 1987 (the 'Use Classes Order')*. The Use Classes Order contains lists of uses grouped together into use classes denoted by a letter of the alphabet and, in most cases, a number (thus B2 and B8 are each separate use classes, whereas E(a) and E(b) are in the same class E). In England, the uses are divided into the following main groups:

B2 - general industrial

B3 - storage and distribution

C - residential uses: hotels (C1), dwelling houses (C3), houses in multiple occupation (C4)

E - commercial, business and service

F - local community and learning: learning and non-residential institutions (F1) and local community (including shops selling essential goods in premises not exceeding 280m^2 with no other such facility within 1,000m) (F2).

Class E was introduced on 1 September 2020 and contains a large number of different uses, of which the following are the most common:

E(a) - retail sale of goods, other than hot food

E(b) - sale of food and drink for consumption on the premises

E(c) - financial and professional services

E(g) - uses which can be carried out in a residential area without detriment to its amenity, including offices to carry out any operational or administrative functions and research and development.

In Wales, the uses are divided into the following main groups:

A1 - shops

A2 - financial and professional services

A3 - food and drink

B1 - business

B2 - general industrial

B8 - storage and distribution

C - residential uses: hotels (C1), residential institutions (C2), dwelling houses sole or main residence (C3), homes in multiple occupation (C4), dwelling houses not sole or main residence (C5), short term lets (C6)

D - non-residential institutions (D1), assembly and leisure (D2).

In addition, there are a number of uses that are classified as 'sui generis', which is Latin for 'the only one of its kind' or 'in a class of its own'. These are uses which could potentially have adverse effects on their locality and include entertainment establishments (such as cinemas and bingo halls), drinking establishments (such as pubs and wine bars) and hot food takeaways (for the sale of hot food for consumption off the premises).

Changes of use to another use, or mix of uses, within the same use class will not require planning permission. For example, in England, a change of use from a clothes shop to a restaurant will not require planning permission as both are within class E. In Wales, a change of use from a clothes shop to a stationers will not require planning permission as both are within class A1.

A change of use from one class to another will require planning permission (although see **1.7.4** for the possibility that planning permission will be granted automatically without the need for a planning application and an express planning permission).

Changes to and from a sui generis use will always require planning permission (although see **1.7.4** for the possibility that changes from a sui generis use will be granted automatically without the need for a planning application and an express planning permission).

* The Uses Classes Order is a key piece of legislation in planning law. You may be required to know this statutory reference in the SQE1 assessments.

1.7.3 The effect of planning permission

Once a planning permission has been obtained, it continues to exist for the benefit of the land and of all persons for the time being interested in it (unless otherwise specified in the planning permission itself). A planning permission will usually state that it has to be *implemented* within a certain time and will lapse if not implemented in that time. In England, this is usually within three years of the date of the permission; in Wales this is usually within five years of the date of the permission. Planning permissions do not generally impose a time limit by which the authorised development must be *completed*, but if the Local Planning Authority ('LPA') decides that completion will not take place within a reasonable time, it can serve a completion notice stating that the permission will cease to have effect if completion has not taken place by the expiration period stated in the notice. However, completion notices are rare and as a general rule, a planning permission, once implemented, runs with the land forever and any conditions attached to it will burden the relevant land. The grant of a planning permission is effective for planning purposes only; it does not obviate the need for other types of approval that may be necessary (see **1.7.6–8** below) or confer the right to breach an enforceable covenant affecting title to the land (see **2.5.5**)

1.7.4 Matters that do not require express planning permission

Even if development within the definition of s 55 is proposed, it is not always necessary to apply *expressly* for planning permission as, in some cases, it is automatically granted. In England, permitted development rights are set out in the Town and Country Planning (General Permitted Development) Order 2015 ('GDPO 2015'). In Wales, permitted development rights are set out in the Town and Country Planning (General Permitted Development) Order 1995 ('GPDO 1995'). The GPDO 1995 originally applied to both England and Wales but was revoked in England by the GPDO 2015. Where the term 'GPDO'* is used in this chapter, it refers to both the GPDO 2015 and the GPDO 1995.

The most common categories of development which are granted automatic planning permission under the GPDO (often described as 'permitted development') are developments within the curtilage of a dwelling house (such as extensions below a certain size) and minor operations (such as painting the exterior of a building or installing a CCTV camera). The GPDO also grants automatic planning permission for specified changes between use classes, and for changes from certain sui generis uses, although the current Use Classes Order should be checked on each occasion that a change of use is proposed as it is amended fairly frequently.

It is possible for the Secretary of State in charge of Town and Country Planning, or the LPA, to exclude the effect of the relevant GPDO by issuing an Article 4 Direction*. So before relying on the automatic planning permission granted by the GPDO, the solicitor should check the latest version of the GPDO and make sure that there is no Article 4 direction negating the relevant concession. Enquiries of the LPA, such as those usually carried out as part of the local search before exchange of contracts when buying property, will reveal this (see **Chapter 3**).

As it can be a very complex issue deciding if proposed works or a change of use amount to development or come within the GPDO, in cases of doubt it is possible to apply for a Certificate of Lawfulness of Proposed Use or Development under s 192 of the TCPO 1990. An application can be made to the LPA before the works are commenced, specifying the proposed works or change. The LPA must issue a certificate if they are satisfied the proposals would not constitute development, or would be granted permission as permitted development under the GPDO, otherwise it must refuse the application. If the development does not come within the GPDO and there is no Certificate of Lawfulness, then express planning permission must be obtained.

* The GPDO and Article 4 Directions are key pieces of legislation in planning law. You may be required to know these statutory references in the SQE1 assessments.

1.7.5 Enforcement: time limits and the range of the LPA's enforcement powers

The LPA has a range of action it can take if someone develops property in contravention of planning control. To find out if there has been a breach, an LPA can exercise a right of entry to the property or serve a planning contravention notice, which requires the recipient to provide information about operations, use, or activities being carried out on the land and any matter relating to the conditions attached to a planning permission. If the LPA decides to take action, it has the following options.

Enforcement notice

This can be issued where it appears to the LPA that there has been a breach of any type of planning control and it is expedient to issue the notice in the light of its planning policies for the area. The enforcement notice must be served on the owner, occupier and any other person having an interest in the land, such as a mortgagee, and will become effective 28 days after service. The enforcement notice must specify the alleged breach and the steps to be taken, or the activities to be discontinued, in order to remedy the breach and the timescale for this. It is possible for any person interested in the land to appeal an enforcement notice.

In Wales, an LPA can serve an enforcement warning notice where it appears to the LPA that there has been a breach of planning control and there is a reasonable prospect that planning permission would be granted if an application was made. The warning notice must give details of the breach and warn that further enforcement action may be taken if an application for planning permission is not made within the period specified in the notice.

In England, from 25 April 2024, LPAs have the power to issue enforcement warning notices when it appears that there has been a breach of planning control. The enforcement warning notice is an invitation to the recipient to regularise the breach by applying for a retrospective planning permission.

Stop notice

An enforcement notice cannot become effective until 28 days after it has been served and its effect is suspended if the recipient appeals it, so the LPA can serve a stop notice to bring activities in breach of planning control to an end before the enforcement notice takes effect. A stop notice cannot be served as a method of enforcement in its own right; an enforcement notice must be served first. However, an LPA can serve a temporary stop notice, effective for 56 days (England) or 28 days (Wales) only, which gives time for further investigation. In extreme cases, the LPA can apply to court for an injunction.

Breach of condition notice

This is very similar to an enforcement notice but can only be served where the breach of planning control is a breach of a condition attached to a planning permission. Unlike an enforcement notice, there is no right of appeal against the service of a breach of condition notice.

Injunction

The LPA can apply to court for an injunction to restrain an actual or apprehended breach of planning control. Since this is a discretionary remedy, the LPA must show that an injunction is expedient and necessary and that the remedy is appropriate in the circumstances.

Time limits

If there is a breach of planning control, the time limit for enforcement action will depend on whether the property is in England or Wales.

In England, the LPA must take enforcement action within 10 years of the alleged breach. However, for breaches involving operational development (such as building works) or changing the use of a building to use as a single dwelling house that took place before 25 April 2024, the time limit is the one that applied before this date, which is within four years of the alleged breach.

In Wales, for breaches involving operational development (such as building works) or changing the use of a building to use as a single dwelling house, the time limit for enforcement action is within four years of the alleged breach. The time limit for all other breaches of planning control is within 10 years of the alleged breach.

An LPA can apply to a magistrates' court for a planning enforcement order to enable enforcement action to be taken when the statutory time limits have expired and the breach of planning control has been concealed.

If the LPA fails to take enforcement action within the relevant time period, then no further action can be taken in respect of the breach.

Failure to comply with one of these planning control notices is an offence punishable with a fine.

The important thing to remember is that it is the current owner of the property who is held responsible and not necessarily the person who, for example, obtained the planning permission, or failed to obtain it. This is why it is very important for the buyer's solicitor to carry out the necessary searches and enquiries at the pre-contract stage to discover the planning history of the property (see **Chapter 3**).

Example

Your client, Sheila, lives in a detached property in Fowey in Cornwall overlooking the harbour. In 2023 she built a bungalow at the end of her large garden. She has been renting this out to a friend. Her friend has now moved out and Sheila has decided to sell the bungalow. The buyer has asked to see a copy of the planning permission for the bungalow. Sheila has admitted that she did not obtain planning permission.

Should you be concerned about this situation?

Answer

The building of the bungalow would fall within the definition of 'development' set out in s 55. As such, it would require express planning permission unless it fell within the GPDO. This is unlikely and so Sheila will be in breach of planning control. If there has been a breach of planning control, there are time limits within which the LPA must take enforcement action. In England, enforcement action for building works must take place within four years of the alleged breach (because it took place before 25 April 2024). Here, the breach occurred within the four years and, as such, the LPA can bring enforcement proceedings. The most likely method of enforcement is an enforcement notice requiring the breach to be rectified. Failure to comply with the enforcement notice is a criminal offence punishable by a fine.

1.7.6 Building regulation control

A separate issue, but one which often needs to be considered at the same time as planning issues, is building regulations control. Building regulations are concerned with the health and safety aspects of buildings being constructed or altered and they control the materials and construction methods used. It is necessary to apply for building regulations consent for many works carried out to buildings, even where the changes themselves do not require an application for planning permission.

Following an application to the building control authority for building regulations consent, the work will be inspected by a building control officer. Depending on the extent of the work carried out there could be several inspections. After the final inspection, the building control authority should issue a certificate of compliance. In addition there are self-certification schemes regulated by trades and professions (eg plumbing and installation of windows), which do not require a separate application to the building control authority. The person who does the work can self-certify their work and their relevant body sends notification to the building control authority.

Building control authorities can prosecute for breach of building regulations control. In Wales, a prosecution must be brought within two years of the offence. In England there is now no time limit for bringing a prosecution: prior to 1 October 2023 the prosecution had to be brought within six months of the breach being discovered and within two years of completion of the building work. A building control authority can also serve an enforcement notice requiring the work to be altered or removed. In Wales, an enforcement notice must be served within one year of completion of the work. In England, the time limit is within 10 years of completion of the work. They can also take out injunctions, which are not time limited, if the work is unsafe. A prospective buyer, and their lender, would be concerned about the structural soundness of a building which had not been granted building regulations consent, even after the risk of prosecution or enforcement has passed. A lender may be reluctant to lend without a full structural survey and/or retain some of the mortgage advance until remedial works are carried out.

A buyer can check that building regulations have been complied with using the searches and enquiries usually carried out before exchange of contracts. For example, the pre-contract enquiries of the seller will ask about any works carried out to the property and any consents obtained and the CON29, part of the local search, will reveal details of building regulations consents and certificates granted (see **Chapter 3**). If a consent has not been granted, the buyer can ask the seller to obtain a regularisation certificate from the building control authority which lists the work required to bring the building up to standard. Alternatively insurance can be obtained, but this usually only covers the cost of compliance with the regulations should the building control authority bring enforcement proceedings; it will not cover personal injuries or business interruption caused by a defective building.

1.7.7 Listed buildings

A listed building is one that has been included in a list of buildings of special architectural or historic interest by the relevant government department. In England, this is currently the Department for Culture, Media and Sport with the assistance of Historic England. In Wales, the Welsh Ministers are responsible for drawing up the list with the assistance of Cadw. There are three grades of listing (Grade 1, Grade 2* and Grade 2) and the listing includes the building and any object or structure fixed to the building or within the curtilage of the building that forms part of the land and has done so since before 1 July 1948.

Once a building has been listed, the owner will probably require listed building consent to demolish, alter or extend the building in addition to planning permission. The higher the listing, the harder it will be to obtain listed building consent from the local authority. Listed building consent may be required even when planning permission is not required, for example for internal alterations. Moreover, there are a number of classes of permitted development under the GPDO that do not apply to listed buildings, so if this type of work is to be carried out to a listed building, express planning permission from the local authority will be required.

1.7.8 Conservation areas

LPAs are obliged to designate as conservation areas any parts of their own area that are of special architectural or historic interest, the character and appearance of which it is desirable to preserve or enhance. Designation of a conservation area gives broader protection than the listing of individual buildings. All the features, listed or otherwise, within the area are recognised as part of its character.

What this means for the clients is that it will be more difficult to make changes to the property than would normally be the case. For example:

- Changes to the external appearance of a building in a conservation area may require planning permission from the LPA that is not required elsewhere, as some permitted development rights are curtailed.
- Demolition or substantial demolition of a building within a conservation area will require planning permission from the LPA.
- Any work planned to a tree in a conservation area must be notified to the LPA six weeks in advance so that the LPA may determine whether or how the work to the tree should take place.

1.7.9 Planning summary

A solicitor acting for the buyer of a property will need to ask the following questions:

(a) Is there a planning permission for the construction of the building or was planning permission not needed?

(b) Is the building currently being used for its authorised planning purpose?

(c) Are there any planning conditions which would prevent the buyer's future use or any proposed alterations?

(d) Are there any existing breaches of planning law for which action could be taken against the buyer after completion?

(e) Have any works been done which would have required building regulations consent?

(f) Is the building listed or in a conservation area?

The answers to these questions will come from a variety of different sources. This will be further discussed in **Chapter 3**.

Example

A buyer client is intending to buy a detached residential property. The buyer has noticed that the seller has built a conservatory on the back of the property. The buyer would like to carry out some internal alterations after they have purchased the property.

What are the planning implications of this scenario?

Answer

The building of a conservatory would fall within the definition of 'development' and so would have required planning permission. However, the GPDO automatically grants planning permission for certain types of specific development without the requirement to obtain express planning permission. One example of such development is the erection of small extensions (including conservatories) to an existing residential property. These extensions are, however, subject to restrictions on size and position.

LPAs can exclude the effect of part or all of the GPDO if they think fit. They do this by way of an Article 4 Direction which will restrict the GPDO in part or in full in relation to its area. This permits the planning authority to control all aspects of development in great detail and would be appropriate, for example, in a conservation area. Therefore, before you can definitively state whether the conservatory required express planning permission, you would need to check that the size and position of the conservatory fits within the requirements of the GPDO. If it does, and there is no Article 4 Direction in place, then the conservatory would not have required express planning permission – it would have been granted automatically under the GPDO.

Buildings regulations set standards for design and construction that apply to most new buildings and alterations to existing buildings in England. This is an entirely separate requirement from planning permission. Building regulations consent would have been required for the conservatory even if no express planning permission was required and planning permission had been granted automatically under the GPDO.

In relation to the proposed internal alterations, certain matters which would otherwise fall within the definition of 'development' are specifically excluded and these include works for the maintenance, improvement or other alteration which affect only the interior of a building. The proposed internal alterations would therefore not require planning permission.

The buyer will require building regulations consent for the proposed internal alterations. The buyer will need to make an application for consent to the building control authority before starting the work. Once the work is completed, the building control authority will carry out an inspection and issue a certificate of compliance if it is satisfied that the work has been carried out safely and using appropriate materials.

1.8 Taking instructions

It is important that the solicitors for both parties to a sale and purchase transaction take instructions from their clients at the start. Firstly, they will need to check what has been agreed at the marketing stage and that the buyer has been provided with an Energy Performance Certificate ('EPC') for the property. An EPC is produced by an accredited energy assessor and the seller must make one available to the buyer, free of charge, at the earliest opportunity, preferably within 7 days of first marketing and in any event within 28 days.

Secondly, it is important to establish the degree of consensus between the parties and identify any outstanding issues that may cause delay, frustration and additional costs later in the transaction. If important issues are missed, the seller client may lose the sale, or the buyer client may end up with a property that has a defective title, or which cannot be used for the purposes the client intended, or one that is not worth what the client paid for it.

Firms will have their own checklist for taking instructions; the checklist below takes account of the issues raised in this chapter.

Initial Instructions Checklist

1. **Full names, addresses and contact details of buyer(s) and seller(s)**

2. **Name, address and person to contact at estate agents**

3. **Name and address of other party's solicitors**

4. **Full address of the property to be bought**

5. **Fixtures and fittings being bought?**

6. **Tenure**

7. **Price**

8. **Deposit agreed?**

10. **Mortgage**
    Seller: existing mortgage?
    Buyer: sources of funding and mortgage required/arranged?

11. **Anticipated completion date?**

12. **Synchronisation of a related sale?**

13. **The present and intended use of the property?**
    Any recent alterations to the property?

14. **Situation of the property (proximity to railways, industrial premises, rivers, open land)**

15. **Property survey commissioned/done?**

13. **Is anyone other than the seller in occupation of the property?**

15. **Have any terms (other than price) have been agreed between the parties?**

Summary

- A typical conveyancing transaction has two milestones, exchange of contracts and completion, and is broken down into three stages - pre-contract, pre-completion and post-completion.
- The Law Society Conveyancing Protocol standardises the residential conveyancing procedure for those firms that adopt it.
- A solicitor cannot usually act for more than one party in a property transaction if there is a conflict of interest or a significant risk of conflict of interest.
- Acting for buyer and seller in the same transaction carries a high risk of conflict of interest.
- It will often be possible to act for both buyer and lender in a residential transaction if the mortgage is on standard terms. In commercial property transactions, the lender will usually be separately represented.

- A solicitor acting for more than one buyer in a contract race must comply with paragraphs 1.2 and 1.4 of The Code of Conduct
- Undertakings are frequently given in property transactions, but failure to comply with an undertaking constitutes professional misconduct.
- A buyer may obtain finance for the purchase from a bank, building society, employer or relative.
- A buyer will usually choose from a repayment mortgage or an interest-only mortgage. The interest rate may be variable, fixed or track the base rate set by the Bank of England.
- SDLT (England) and LTT (Wales) is charged on freehold transactions at different rates depending on the type of property and the purchase price and is payable by the buyer.
- A liability to CGT may arise for the seller on the disposal of an interest in land.
- Gains made on the disposal of a principal private dwelling house are exempt from CGT.
- The sale of a residential property by a private individual will not give rise to VAT.
- The sale of a commercial building less than three years old is standard rated for VAT.
- The sale of a commercial building more than three years old is exempt, subject to the seller's option to tax.
- Planning permission is required for an activity that constitutes 'development'. This includes building, engineering, mining or other operations ('BEMO') and a material change of use.
- The GPDO automatically grants planning permission for certain types of development.
- A failure to obtain necessary planning permission, or to comply with any conditions contained in a planning permission, may result in enforcement action by the local authority.
- You will need to check the time limit for enforcement action as it will vary according to whether the property is in England or Wales and the time at which the alleged breach of planning control took place.
- Additional controls exist if the building is listed or the property is in a conservation area.
- Building regulations consent is needed for building works. A failure to obtain the consent casts doubt on the safety of the works and may result in enforcement action.
- Once a sale is agreed, full instructions on the transaction should be taken at an early stage.

Sample questions

Question 1

A solicitor acts for a client who has been ready to exchange contracts on the purchase of her new house for several weeks. The purchase is being funded by a new mortgage and the proceeds of the sale of her current flat. The plan is to exchange on the sale of the flat and the purchase of the house simultaneously. The client has phoned, in a very distressed state, to say that the buyer of the flat has just said that he can only proceed if the price of the flat is reduced by £5,500 as his surveyor says that the flat needs to be rewired.

Which of the following statements best describes the client's position following the buyer's demand to reduce the sale price of the flat?

A The client will have to agree to the price reduction on the flat and proceed with the purchase of the house even though she may not have enough money to complete the purchase of the house.

B The client cannot recover any of her wasted conveyancing costs if the sale of the flat and the purchase of the house does not proceed.

C The client is not obliged to agree to the price reduction on the flat and can recover her wasted conveyancing costs from the buyer of the flat.

D The client will have to agree to the price reduction on the flat because she should have told the buyer of the flat that the flat needed rewiring.

E The client was not obliged to tell the buyer of the flat that the flat needed rewiring, but she will have to reimburse him for his wasted conveyancing costs if he decides not to proceed.

Answer

Option B is correct. Neither party has any legal rights against the other unless and until contracts are exchanged, so the buyer is at risk of being 'gazumped' (where the seller raises the price at the last minute) and the seller is at risk of being 'gazundered' (where the buyer reduces the price at the last minute). This is what lies behind much of the criticism of the conveyancing system in England and Wales.

So, in this situation, the client cannot force the buyer of the flat to proceed, but she is not obliged to accept the price reduction (so options A and D are wrong). Nor can she sue him for wasted costs. Similarly, the client cannot be forced to complete the purchase of the house (option A is also wrong for this reason), or be sued by the seller of the house for wasted costs. The client may not have known anything about the state of the wiring, but in any event, she is not obliged to tell the buyer of the flat anything about it because of the principle of 'caveat emptor' (option D is also wrong for this reason). Therefore, she is not obliged to reimburse the buyer of the flat for his wasted costs and option E is wrong.

Question 2

A solicitor acts for the buyer of a new-build flat from a residential development company ('the seller') and has a received a pre-contract package from the seller's solicitor. The estate agent acting for the seller has told the buyer that there is another person interested in buying the flat and that this other person viewed it yesterday. The estate agent has also told the buyer that the seller has instructed its solicitor to send a pre-contract package to this other person. Neither the solicitor nor the buyer has heard anything from the seller or its solicitor about this yet.

Which of the following statements best describes the position of the seller's solicitor having received the seller's instruction to send a pre-contract package to the other person interested in buying the flat?

A The seller's solicitor does not need to say anything to the buyer's solicitor. It does not matter that there is another person interested in buying the flat as it was the estate agent that allowed them to view the flat, not the seller or the seller's solicitor.

B The seller's solicitor has already breached The Code of Conduct by failing to inform the buyer's solicitor that another interested person viewed the flat yesterday.

C The seller's solicitor will probably breach The Code of Conduct if, having obtained their client's consent to the disclosure, they fail to inform the buyer's solicitor that a pre-contract package is being sent to another interested person.

D The seller's solicitor should disclose to the buyer's solicitor that they are sending a pre-contract package to the other interested person, even if their client does not agree to this disclosure.

E The seller's solicitor must immediately cease to act for the seller.

Answer

Option C is correct.

Once the solicitor receives the instruction from the seller to send the additional pre-contract package, then the obligation not to mislead described in paragraph 1.4 of The Code of Conduct is relevant. However, the seller's solicitor also has a duty of confidentiality to the seller client in paragraph 6.3; they cannot disclose the contract race to prospective buyers without their seller client's consent, so option D is wrong.

Option B is not the best answer as a mere viewing may never result in an offer for the flat.

Option A is not the best answer as the duty not to mislead arises regardless of how the other person was introduced to the property.

It is only when the seller refuses to consent to the disclosure that the seller's solicitor must decline to act, so option E is not the best answer. So long as the seller consents to the disclosure, and that disclosure is made, then the contract race can proceed.

Question 3

A solicitor is acting for the buyer of a freehold property in England. The pre-contract searches and enquiries have revealed that the designated planning use for the property is use as offices within use class E of the Town and Country Planning (Use Classes) Order 1987. Following completion, the buyer wishes to open a wine bar at the property, which is a sui generis use. Investigation of title has not revealed any restrictive covenants related to use of the property.

Does the buyer need to apply for express planning permission in order to be able to use the property as a wine bar?

A No, because there is nothing on the title restricting the use of the property.

B No, because a change of use never constitutes development.

C No, because whilst the proposal constitutes a material change of use, planning permission is automatically granted under the Town and Country Planning (General Permitted Development) Order 2015 ('GPDO').

D Yes, because any change of use requires express planning permission.

E Yes, because the proposal constitutes development and will not be covered by the GPDO.

Answer

Option E is correct.

Planning permission is a separate issue to restrictive covenants on title, so option A is wrong.

Planning permission is required for any activity which constitutes 'development.' Under s 55 of the Town and Country Planning Act 1990, 'development' includes the making of any material change in the use of any buildings or other land. A change between a use within use class E and a sui generis use is a material change of use, so option B is not the best answer.

Express planning permission is therefore required, unless planning permission is automatically granted under the GPDO. This change of use will not be covered by the GPDO as it is a change of use from use class E to a sui generis use; therefore planning permission is not automatically granted and express planning permission will be required, so option C is not the best answer.

Option D is not the best answer because a 'material' change of use will constitute development.

2 Investigation of Title

2.1	Introduction	32
2.2	The distinction between registered and unregistered land	32
2.3	How to investigate title to freehold registered land	32
2.4	How to investigate title to freehold unregistered land	36
2.5	Issues that might be revealed in an investigation of title and the further action required	42

SQE1 syllabus

This chapter will enable you to achieve the SQE1 Assessment Specification in relation to Functioning Legal Knowledge concerned with the following:

- Investigation of a registered and unregistered freehold title
- Process of analysing Land Registry official copy entries
- Process of analysing an epitome of title and deducing ownership
- Issues that could arise from an investigation of title and further action required.

Note that for SQE1, candidates are not usually required to recall specific case names or cite statutory or regulatory authorities. Cases and statutory or regulatory authorities are provided for illustrative purposes only unless otherwise indicated.

Learning outcomes

By the end of this chapter you will be able to apply relevant core legal principles and rules appropriately and effectively, at the level of a competent newly qualified solicitor in practice, to realistic client-based and ethical problems and situations in the following areas:

- The distinction between registered and unregistered land
- The way in which the seller deduces title to the buyer in registered land
- How official copies are set out in registered land
- The way in which the seller deduces title to the buyer in unregistered land
- The requirements of a good root of title for unregistered land
- How to analyse the title deeds listed in an epitome of title
- Issues that might be revealed in the investigation of title and the further action required.

2.1 Introduction

Investigation of title is the process of establishing who owns the property and whether there are any rights or rules which could affect the owner's use and enjoyment of it. When a property is being sold, the solicitor acting for the buyer will need to check firstly that the seller owns the property, so is in a position to sell it to the buyer, and secondly whether there is anything that burdens the seller's title which would deter a buyer, such as restrictive covenants against the intended use or rights of way in favour of a neighbour. A bank or building society considering lending money and taking security over a property will have similar concerns to those of a buyer. The lender will want to ensure that if the borrower defaults on the loan, the property can be sold on the open market for at least as much as is outstanding on the loan. The seller's solicitor will also need to investigate their client's title: they will be keen to anticipate any problems with the title and deal with them in advance. Moreover, the seller's solicitor will need to investigate the seller's title in order to produce the first draft of the contract of sale. Under a typical sale contract the seller promises to sell the property 'free from incumbrances' (ie third party rights that bind the property and may be a problem for the buyer and/or the lender) unless the seller states otherwise, so any incumbrances need to be identified and specified in the contract at the earliest possible stage.

2.2 The distinction between registered and unregistered land

Historically, title to land was all unregistered and was proved by parchment or paper title deeds. The Land Registration Act of 1925 introduced a system in England and Wales which was designed to ensure that ownership of land was registered in a central database: the Land Registry.

Since 1 December 1990 it has been compulsory in every part of England and Wales to register an unregistered title on a change of ownership and about 85% of land and property is now registered. However, much of the land owned by the Crown, the aristocracy and the Church has not been registered because it has never been sold and historically few landowners have voluntarily registered their land. The Government aims to have the whole of England and Wales registered by 2030 but, for the time being, property lawyers can expect to encounter unregistered titles on a fairly regular basis, particularly where property has been in the same hands for a long time.

2.3 How to investigate title to freehold registered land

In order to investigate a registered title, the seller's solicitor needs to obtain copies of the register of title for the property, which are called 'official copies'. They will also need to get a copy of the Land Registry plan for the property, which is known as the 'title plan'. The firm is likely to have an account with the Land Registry which allows the solicitor to order these documents by telephone or online and receive them the following day. A number of law firms have an arrangement with the Land Registry which allows them to request official copies electronically and also view the register and title plans online.

2.3.1 The way in which the seller deduces title to the buyer in registered land

'Deduction of title' is the expression used for the seller's obligation to prove to the buyer their ownership of the property they are trying to sell. This ownership is proved by producing documentary evidence of title to the buyer. Modern practice is for title to be deduced before exchange of contracts and for the buyer to be prevented from raising any objections to that title after exchange of contracts. With registered land, the seller should supply to the buyer, at their own expense, official copies that are less than six months old.

The buyer's solicitor will also need to investigate whether there are any overriding interests affecting the property; this information will come through various searches and enquiries (see **Chapter 3**).

2.3.2 How official copies are set out in registered land

The official copies show the title number to the property and an 'edition date', which is the date on which the Land Registry last updated the title (probably on a previous sale or mortgage). They also show the date which is often referred to by conveyancers as the 'search from date', the specific date of the official copies showing the entries subsisting on the register at a certain time. In the example below, the edition date is 16 September 2004 and the search from date is 14 October 2024.

<table>
<tr><td rowspan="2">Official copy of register of title</td><td>Title number HA145672</td><td>Edition date 16.09.2004</td></tr>
<tr><td colspan="2">- This official copy shows the entries subsisting on the register on 14 October 2024 at 16:05:23.
- This date must be quoted as the 'search from date' in any official search application based on this copy.
- The date at the beginning of an entry is the date on which the entry was made in the register.
- Issued on 14 October 2024.</td></tr>
</table>

The official copies show the entries on three registers:

(a) the Property register

(b) the Proprietorship register

(c) the Charges register.

(a) The Property register

The Property register will always contain a description of the land by reference to the postal address and the title plan and also indicate whether the title is freehold or leasehold. The Property Register may, amongst other things, indicate that:

(i) there are easements or rights benefiting the land and, if so, that those easements/rights are subject to obligations

(ii) that certain things one might usually expect to come with the land (eg rights of light and air over adjacent land) have been excluded from the title.

(b) The Proprietorship register

The Proprietorship register will always identify the current owners and their address. It will also always identify the class of title. The State guarantees the title and compensation is payable in certain circumstances if a defect is found in a registered title. The class of title is determined by the Land Registry when the property is first registered and there are three possible classes of title for freehold land:

(i) **Absolute title**: the most common and best class, the registered proprietor has vested in them the legal estate subject only to the entries on the register, overriding interests and where the proprietor is a trustee, minor interests of which they have notice, such as the interests of the beneficiaries under the trust.

(ii) **Possessory title**: granted where the proprietor is in possession of the property but has lost the title deeds or is claiming through adverse possession, this means that the proprietor is also subject to all adverse interests existing at the date of first registration.

(iii) **Qualified title**: granted where there is a specific identified defect which the Registrar feels cannot be overlooked or 'cured' by the grant of absolute title.

Although it is sometimes possible to upgrade a possessory or qualified title, the buyer will be concerned if the class of title is not absolute as this may affect their ability to obtain a loan to purchase the property and/or sell it in future.

The Proprietorship register may also indicate the price paid for the land by the current owners (but only if the land has been sold since 1 April 2000) and it will also show if the owners gave an indemnity covenant when they bought the land, which will be evidence of a chain of indemnity covenants (see **2.5.6** below).

The Proprietorship register will also contain any restrictions on the owners' ability to sell. Since 13 October 2003, the Land Registry has provided only two types of entry for the protection of third party interests - notices and restrictions. Prior to LRA 2002 it was possible to apply for two other types of entries known as cautions and inhibitions and it is still possible to come across these types of entry on the Register, although with the passage of time they are becoming increasingly rare.

The presence of a restriction in the Proprietorship register is an indication that the proprietor's ability to deal with the property is limited or that a prior condition must be satisfied in order for a disposition to be registered. The protection afforded by the restriction may be permanent or for a specified period; it may be absolute or conditional (for example, a restriction requiring the consent of another party to a disposition). A restriction is therefore a more powerful type of entry than a notice. Examples of restrictions are given in **2.5.4** below (a co-ownership restriction) and **2.5.8** below (a lender restriction). Another example is where a court makes an order requiring a restriction to be entered; this can be in the course of litigation or family proceedings to prevent the property being sold.

(c) The Charges register

The Charges register will identify the incumbrances. In particular, the solicitor will be looking out for:

(i) covenants affecting the property, which can be restrictive or positive

(ii) easements affecting the land, such as a right of way over the property

(iii) charges over the land, most commonly mortgages

(iv) leases granted over the whole or part of the property

(v) notices registered by third parties claiming an interest in the property.

Some of these incumbrances may not present a problem for the buyer, but others will. So the buyer's solicitor needs to be able to identify them to advise the client on what action to take in respect of the different entries (see **2.5** below).

An example of an official copy for 10 Bladen Road, Warrington, Cheshire WA1 1SL is set out below. This title will be referred to in later chapters of this manual.

Official copy of register of title

Title number LM6042 Edition date 30.04.202X

- This official copy shows the entries subsisting on the register on 14 September 202X at 10:55:50
- This date must be quoted as the 'search from date' in any official search application based on this copy.
- The date at the beginning of an entry is the date on which the entry was made in the register.
- Issued on 14 September 202X.
- Under s.67 of the Land Registration Act 2002 this copy is admissible in evidence to the same extent as the original.
- For information about the register of title see Land Registry website www.landregistry.gov.uk or Land Registry Public Guide 1- *A guide to the information we keep and how you can obtain it.*
- This title is dealt with by Land Registry Hull Office

A: Property Register

This register describes the land and estate comprised in the title.

COUNTY	DISTRICT
Cheshire	Warrington

1. (18 December 2000) The freehold land shown edged with red on the plan of the above title filed at the Registry and being 10 Bladen Road, Warrington, Cheshire WA1 1SL.
2. (18 December 2000) The property has the benefit of a right of way granted by deed of grant dated 19 April 1969 and made between (1) Ivan Walton and (2) Jonathan Hartley.

NOTE: Copy filed

[see 2.5.1 below]

B: Proprietorship Register

This register specifies the class of title and identifies the owner. It contains any entries that affect the right of disposal.

Title absolute

1. (18 December 2000) PROPRIETOR(S): LEONARD HOLMES of 10, Bladen Road, Warrington, Cheshire, WA1 1SL.
2. (18 December 2000) The price stated to have been paid on 3 December 2000 was £180,000.
3. (18 December 2000) The transfer to the proprietor contains a covenant to observe and perform the covenants referred to in the Charges Register and of indemnity in respect thereof.

[see 2.5.6 below]

C: Charges Register

This register contains any charges and other matters that affect the land.

1. (18 December 2000) A conveyance of the land in this title dated 1 April 1968 and made between (1) Ivan Walton and (2) Jonathan Hartley contains the following covenants:

   'The Purchaser with the intent and so as to bind the property hereby conveyed and to benefit and protect the retained land of the Vendor lying to the west of the land hereby conveyed hereby covenants with the Vendor that he and his successors in title will at all times observe and perform the stipulations and conditions set out in the schedule hereto.'

   THE SCHEDULE ABOVE REFERRED TO

   '1. Not to use the property other than as a single private dwelling house;

   2. Not to build or allow to be built any new building on the property nor alter or allow to be altered any building currently erected on the property without the written consent of the Vendor or his successors in title; and

   3. To erect and maintain a good and substantial wall on the western boundary of the property.'

[see 2.5.5 and 2.5.6 below]

2. (18 December 2000) CHARGE dated 30 November 2000 to secure the monies including the further advances therein mentioned.
3. (18 December 2000) PROPRIETOR - NORTHERN WEST BUILDING SOCIETY of 54 Maine Road, Manchester, M2 3ER.

[see 2.5.8 below]

END OF REGISTER

Note: A date at the beginning of an entry is the date on which the entry was made in the Register

Note: These official copies should be accompanied by an official copy of the title plan. This has not been reproduced for the purposes of this example.

2.4 How to investigate title to freehold unregistered land

In all cases appearing to involve unregistered land, the first step is to check whether the land is already registered or is the subject of a pending application for first registration. It is also possible that a third party has lodged a caution against first registration, warning any person attempting to deal with the land that they have an interest in the land, such as an easement. When the application for first registration is lodged, the Land Registry will 'warn off' the cautioner, ie give them a limited period to establish their rights over the land and if they cannot do so, the registration will proceed and the cautioner will lose their rights. These checks can be done by an Index Map search at the Land Registry, on Form SIM (Search of the Index Map) accompanied by a plan of the property.

If the title has not been registered, then title is proved by the title deeds. The seller provides the buyer with copies of the title deeds (usually before exchange of contracts) and, if the sale is a sale of the whole of the property, hands over the originals to the buyer on completion. If the sale is a sale of part, the seller will keep the original title deeds and hand over certified copies to the buyer on completion. At completion, the buyer's solicitor examines the original title deeds against the copies that they received prior to exchange of contracts to check they are the same; this process is referred to as 'verification of title'. A memorandum of the sale of part is marked on the original deed.

2.4.1 The way in which the seller deduces title to the buyer in unregistered land

Deducing title in unregistered land involves examining the parchment or paper deeds which have been used to transfer ownership of the property in the past. These typically include conveyances, mortgages, assents (between personal representatives and a beneficiary under a will), deeds of gift and land charges searches. The seller's solicitor will usually be able to obtain the title deeds from the client, if the property is mortgage free, or from their mortgage lender, if it is subject to a mortgage.

Having obtained the title deeds, the seller's solicitor must consider whether any transaction in the property's history should have triggered first registration of title. The detail of the events that trigger first registration are beyond the scope of this book, but if the title should have already been registered, the seller will be required to register it before any other transactions can proceed. The buyer's lender is likely to insist that this defect in title is remedied before completion of the buyer's purchase. The next task is to look through the title deeds and find the document that will be the 'root of title', the document from which to begin the title investigation. While a number of documents in a set of title deeds might be capable of being a good root of title, the seller's solicitor must pick the single document that will be the root of title for that particular sale. This will usually be the most recent document that satisfies all of the requirements of a good root of title (see **2.4.2** below).

Once the root of title is identified, subject to some exceptions, any older documents that pre-date the root can be ignored. One exception is where the root document refers back to a third party right created in an earlier conveyance. The buyer is entitled to call for the earlier conveyance as the third party right will probably be binding on them and they will need details of it.

The seller's solicitor will then prepare what is known as an 'epitome of title', a schedule of all the documents from and including the root up until the present day. The documents should be numbered and listed in chronological order. Attached to the epitome are copies (rather than originals) of each of these documents.

Epitome of Title

relating to freehold property known as:

56 Black Horse Drive, Dorking, Surrey RH4 5SJ

No.	Date	Description of Document including parties and event	Evidence supplied	Original to be handed over at completion?
1	25/05/1955	Conveyance by (1) Mark Philip to (2) Simon Andrew	Photocopy	Yes
2	25/05/1955	Mortgage Deed between (1) Simon Andrew and (2) Mitford Bank Limited	Photocopy	Yes

Before epitomes of title became common, the practice was for a seller's solicitor to prepare an 'abstract of title', a precis of all the documents comprised in the title. In practice a solicitor may encounter both forms of presentation in relation to the same property, particularly with older properties that have not often changed hands.

2.4.2 The requirements for a good root of title

Under s 44 of the Law of Property Act (LPA) 1925, a root of title must:

- deal with or show who owns the entire interest (legal and equitable) that is being sold by the current owner
- contain a recognisable description of the relevant land
- do nothing to cast doubt on the seller's title
- be at least 15 years old.

A conveyance on sale or legal mortgage which satisfies the above requirements is generally acknowledged to be the most acceptable root of title, because it effectively offers a double guarantee. The current buyer will be investigating the seller's title back for a minimum period of 15 years, and the buyer under the root conveyance should similarly have investigated title over a period of at least 15 years prior to when they bought the property. Thus the current buyer is provided with the certainty of the soundness of the title over a minimum period of at least 30 years. A conveyance is generally considered preferable to the mortgage as it is more likely to contain a detailed description of the property by reference to a plan and more details of the incumbrances affecting the property and deal expressly with the legal and equitable interest in the property.

If neither a conveyance nor mortgage are available, then a deed of gift or an assent can be used, but as these transactions were gifts and not for value, title investigation is unlikely to have taken place and therefore they do not provide the double guarantee which is given by the conveyance on sale or legal mortgage. For this reason they are less satisfactory to a buyer when offered as roots of title.

To establish whether a conveyance deals with both the legal and equitable interests in the land, the solicitor should look for a paragraph beginning with the word 'WHEREAS' stating that the Vendor (seller) is *'seised of the property ... for an estate in fee simple and is selling the same to the Purchaser'* (buyer). The conveyance should also state that the Vendor conveys the land as *'beneficial owner ... unto the Purchaser'.* Such a conveyance is dealing with the entire legal estate and equitable interest in the land.

2.4.3 Checking each title deed listed in the epitome of title

Once the root of title has been identified, that root and all subsequent title deeds must be checked in a systematic and thorough manner. Many solicitors start by reading through all the title deeds a number of times, focusing on the following matters:

- the chain of ownership
- description of the land
- stamp duties
- incumbrances
- execution
- land charges searches

The chain of ownership

There should be an unbroken chain of ownership from the owner indicated in the root of title up to the present seller. Since legal estates can only be transferred by a deed, there should be documentary evidence of every change of ownership. So the person who acquired the property in the root of title should be the same person who is transferring title in the next document.

Sometimes it is not the same person. If the owner has died, the property will vest in their Personal Representatives (PRs), in which case the grant of probate identifying the PRs must also be produced to check it was them who transferred title in the next document in the chain.

Description of the land

The title deeds need to be checked to ensure the description of the property is consistent throughout. Frustratingly, plans in different title deeds do not always tally with each other. This is particularly likely where the deeds include one or more conveyances of part, indicating the land was once part of a larger estate.

Stamp duty

Stamp duty was payable on many conveyancing documents prior to December 2003 and this was evidenced by embossed stamps being placed on the document, usually in the top margin. A conveyance on sale was liable to 'ad valorem duty', ie duty that varied according to the amount of the purchase price. Some low-value transactions were exempt or liable to a reduced rate, but only if the conveyance included a 'certificate of value' stating that the transaction did not form part of a larger transaction or series of transactions in which the value exceeded the relevant threshold.

Ad valorem stamp duty was not payable on mortgages executed after 1971, or on deeds of gift and assents after 30 April 1987 provided the deed contained a certificate stating that the transaction fell within one of the categories of exempt documents.

In addition to stamp duty, from 1931 Inland Revenue also required some documents, including conveyances on sale, to be sent to them, in which case they would get a 'particulars delivered' or 'PD' stamp on them. Without the PD stamp the conveyance was not properly executed and the original buyer could be fined.

The rules and rates of stamping were very complicated, so a practitioner's text should be consulted to establish whether the right amount of stamp duty was paid at the time of the transaction. Stamp duty on property transactions was largely replaced by SDLT on 3 December 2003 (see **1.6.1**).

Incumbrances

Each title deed should be checked for incumbrances such as easements and covenants. Easements will often appear in a conveyance beginning with the words 'EXCEPTING AND RESERVING'. These words indicate that on an earlier sale, the seller was reserving an easement of some kind over the land being sold, such as a right of way. The words 'SUBJECT TO' also are used to introduce an incumbrance, such as an obligation to pay towards the maintenance of a road. There might also be restrictive and positive covenants the buyers entered into on previous sales (see **2.5.5** and **2.5.6** below).

Execution

Each document should be checked to ensure that it was properly executed. Most documents in a conveyancing transaction will need to be executed as a deed (s 52 Law of Property Act 1925), so the formalities for execution as a deed must have been complied with. A deed is defined in s 1(2) Law of Property (Miscellaneous Provisions) Act 1989 and must:

(a) be in writing

(b) make it clear on the face of it that it is a deed

(c) be signed by the person granting the interest in the presence of a witness who 'attests' the signature (ie provides evidence of it)

(d) be delivered as a deed.

Before 31 July 1990, a deed had to be signed *and sealed* by its maker and delivered as a deed. The seal (usually a red circular piece of paper) had to be on the document before the maker signed; if the seal was never there, the document was not a deed and could not have conveyed a legal estate. For details of execution by an individual or a company after 31 July 1990, see **5.3**.

The seller will always execute a conveyance in order to pass the legal estate in the land. A buyer will not always execute a conveyance (or indeed a transfer of registered land). A buyer will only do so if they are giving a new covenant or they will be holding the land on trust, in which case they are required to make a declaration about the nature of that trust. So in the case of co-owners you would always expect the buyers to sign.

Land charges searches

Some incumbrances, notably restrictive covenants, will only bind unregistered land if they are correctly registered as a land charge at the central Land Charges Department in Plymouth.

Immediately after such an incumbrance was created, the solicitor acting for the person who owned the land that benefited from the incumbrance should have registered the land charge. The registration should have been against the name of the person (the 'estate owner') who owned the legal estate in the land bound by the incumbrance. The most common land charges protect the following interests:

Class of land charge	**Interest protected**
C(iv)	an estate contract
D(ii)	a restrictive covenant (see **2.5.5** below)
D(iii)	an equitable easement
F	a Home Right (see **2.5.11** below)

As part of an investigation of an unregistered title, a solicitor must ensure that valid searches have been made against the names of all the estate owners revealed in the epitome of title and the attached documents, even if their period of ownership pre-dates the root of title. The search, on form K15, should be against each estate owner for the period that they owned the land. Only the years need be entered onto the K15 form, not the precise dates. If there is uncertainty about the exact years someone owned the land, then the search should be for any years that the individual might have done so. So, if in doubt, the solicitor should search back to 1926, when the land charges system was introduced. It is possible to rely on valid searches done by others in the past, on previous sales.

Example

Epitome of Title

relating to freehold property known as:

132, North Street, Rochford, Essex RM1 1TE

No.	Date	Description of Document including parties and event	Evidence supplied	Original to be handed over at completion?
	15/06/1948	Conveyance by (1) Eileen Fowler to (2) James Wright	Photocopy	Yes
1	23/04/1975	Conveyance by (1) James Wright to (2) Frederick Bunhill	Photocopy	Yes
2	23/04/1975	Mortgage Deed between (1) Frederick Bunhill and (2) National Midland Bank Limited	Photocopy	No
	05/05/1979	Death certificate of Frederick Bunhill	Photocopy	No
3	09/08/1979	Grant of Probate to Julian Andrewes and Thomas Taverner	Photocopy	No
4	06/09/1979	Assent made by (1) Julian Andrewes and Thomas Taverner to (2) Kate Chambers	Photocopy	No

You act for the buyer of this unregistered property in Essex. The seller is Kate Chambers. You have established that the 1975 Conveyance is a good root of title, but you have been provided with the 1948 Conveyance as it grants a right of way that is referred to, but not reproduced in, the 1975 Conveyance.

You should carry out the following land charges searches against the estate owners for the period of their ownership:

- Eileen Fowler 1926–1948 (you need to go back to 1926 as you cannot tell when she acquired the property)
- James Wright 1948–1975
- Frederick Bunhill 1975–1979
- Julian Andrewes 1979
- Thomas Taverner 1979
- Kate Chambers 1979–the present year

You will need to check the title deeds to see that the names are spelled in this way and that there are no existing searches on which you can rely. You will not need to carry out a search on the National Midland Bank Limited as a lender is not an estate owner (unless it is in possession) and nothing can be registered against its name.

2.5 Issues that might be revealed in an investigation of title and the further action required

Sometimes a property will come with certain rights attached to it, such as a right of way over neighbouring land. Such rights benefit the property and the buyer's solicitor need only check that the rights are sufficient for the intended use of the property (eg that the right of way is for vehicles as well as pedestrians and is not restricted to certain hours) and whether a contribution is required for upkeep. Sometimes a third party has rights over the property which are a potential burden in that they restrict the owner's use and enjoyment of the property and/or involve the owner in additional expense. A solicitor who fails to advise the buyer on the nature and extent of these rights so that the buyer can take this information into account when deciding whether or not to proceed with the purchase is likely to be negligent.

2.5.1 Easements

The most common easements are rights of way, rights of drainage and rights of support. In registered land, easements that burden the property should appear in the Charges register, but they may also appear in the Property register if the Land Registry has extracted text from a conveyance and easements that burden the property are mixed in with easements that benefit it. Also appearing in the Property register will be financial obligations to contribute attached to easements that benefit the property, such as a right to use a driveway on a neighbour's property subject to paying one half of the maintenance costs.

In unregistered land, easements are usually granted or reserved immediately in the first operative paragraph of the conveyance, just after the words that convey the property to the buyer.

Example

A property is transferred with the benefit of the following easement:

> *TOGETHER WITH a right of way for the Purchasers and their successors in title to pass and repass over the land shown hatched brown on the plan attached hereto with or without vehicles during normal working hours for the purpose of gaining access to and egress from the rear of the property hereby conveyed SUBJECT TO the Purchasers and their successors in title paying a fair and reasonable proportion of the costs of maintaining the land shown hatched brown on the plan attached hereto.*

The buyer of the property with the benefit of this right of way should be advised that if they want to use the right of way, they will need to contribute to the costs of maintenance (by virtue of the rule in *Halsall v Brizell* [1957]*). The buyer's solicitor should ask the client whether the right of way, expressed in these terms, is sufficient for their needs; for example, will they need to gain access to the property after 'normal working hours'? An enquiry should be raised as to whether the seller has, in fact, been contributing to the maintenance costs and if so, how frequently and how much. The enquiry should include a request for details of any disputes about the use of the right and/or the sharing of maintenance costs. The client should also be advised to instruct a surveyor to inspect the land hatched brown to establish whether it is useable and in good condition, or is likely to give rise to substantial expenditure in the near future.

* *Halsall v Brizell* is a term used in practice to discuss the law relating to easements. You may be required to know and be able to use this term in the SQE1 assessments.

2.5.2 Mines and minerals exceptions and reservations

In the past, a seller may have sold a piece of land but excepted or reserved out of the sale the mines and minerals beneath the surface, together with a right to come onto the land to extract the valuable coal and other substances. In registered land this will be noted in the Property register, for example:

> *There is excepted from the registration the mines and minerals underneath the property together with ancillary powers of working thereof.*

In unregistered land, such a provision will appear in the conveyance itself.

A mining exception means that the seller does not own any mines and minerals underneath the surface of the property and cannot transfer them to the buyer. Any encroachment on to them by the buyer will constitute a trespass. A reservation creates an incorporeal right in the mines and minerals by way of a profit à prendre. This type of entry could indicate that mining has taken place in the vicinity in the past, so enquiries should be made as to the ground stability and whether there has been any subsidence. Although entries such as these are fairly common, the buyer should be informed and enquiries made as to who is able to exercise this right and if it has ever been exercised in the past. All interests in coal are now vested in the Mining Remediation Authority under the Coal Industry Act 1994 and a mining search should be carried out (see **3.3.2**). Regardless of whether the property is registered or unregistered, the buyer's solicitor should also conduct an Index Map search at the Land Registry, on form SIM, to check whether the mines and minerals are registered under a separate title; if they are, this will help to identify the owner of those mines and minerals and any associated rights.

2.5.3 Declaration as to rights of light and air

Sometimes a landowner will sell off a part of their land ('Part A') and retain the other part ('Part B') for their own purposes. In order to preserve the right to develop Part B in the future, they may have declared in the transfer of Part A that Part A does not enjoy the benefit of any rights of light and air over Part B. So there will be nothing to stop the owner of Part B building on that land and, for example, blocking off light to the windows in the building on Part A.

Example

The following entry appears in the Proprietorship register for a registered freehold property:

> *A Conveyance of the land in this title dated 21 July 2010 made between (1) BROWN LILLARD LIMITED (Vendor) and (2) MERLIN PROPERTIES LIMITED (Purchaser) contains the following provision:*
>
> *'IT IS HEREBY AGREED AND DECLARED that the Purchaser shall not acquire any right of light or air or other easement which would interfere with restrict or prejudicially affect the use of any part of the adjoining land owned by the Vendor for building or any other purposes'.*

In this example, enquiries about the extent and location of the adjoining land owned by the Vendor in July 2010 should be made and the buyer will need to be informed and asked whether this reservation of rights to light and air causes concern given their intended use of the property and the likelihood of development nearby.

2.5.4 Co-ownership

When two or more people co-own a property, the legal interest can only be held under a joint tenancy. However, there are two ways of jointly owning the equitable interest in a property; as joint tenants or tenants in common. Joint tenants have an equal interest in the property. If one of two joint tenants dies, the other one will automatically become the sole owner of the whole property. It will not be possible for either of them to leave their share of the property to anyone else by will. Tenants in common can own either equal or unequal shares. If one of them dies, their share will pass according to the deceased's will, or if there is no will, to close relatives (including a spouse) and will not pass automatically to the survivor. It can be left by will to anyone the tenant in common chooses.

In registered land, it can be assumed that the equitable interest is held as a joint tenancy unless a restriction appears in the Proprietorship register in the following terms:

> *RESTRICTION: No disposition by a sole proprietor of the registered estate (except a trust corporation) under which capital money arises is to be registered unless authorised by an order of the court.*

In unregistered land, the conveyance to joint buyers will state whether the equitable interest is to be held as joint tenants or tenants in common.

When the title investigation shows that a property is jointly owned but it is being sold by only one of the co-owners, it is necessary to find out what has happened to the missing co-owner. If they are alive, they must be a party to the contract and the transfer of the property.

If the missing co-owner has died, the seller's solicitor will need to provide a certified copy of the death certificate. The co-owners held the legal title to the property as joint tenants as this is the only way the legal title can be held by co-owners. If the equitable interest was also held as joint tenants, then the surviving co-owner can transfer the property alone. In registered land, the buyer can assume that the equitable joint tenancy was not 'severed' (turned into a tenancy in common) prior to the death of the deceased co-owner in the absence of the restriction in the Proprietorship register. In unregistered land, the buyer will be entitled to assume that the joint tenancy was not severed if the transfer by the surviving joint owner to the buyer contains a statement that the surviving joint owner is solely and beneficially entitled to the land and neither of the following has occurred before the date of the transfer:

(1) A memorandum (written record) of severance endorsed on the conveyance of the property to the joint tenants.

(2) Bankruptcy proceedings registered against either of the joint tenants at the Land Charges Registry.

Where there is only one surviving legal owner and the equitable interest was held by the co-owners as tenants in common, another legal owner (often referred to as a 'second trustee') needs to be appointed to overreach the equitable interest of the deceased co-owner. The appointment of the second trustee can be made in the transfer of the property or by separate deed of appointment. Provided the buyer pays the purchase price to at least two trustees on completion, the equitable interest of the deceased co-owner will be overreached and the buyer will take the property free of it. The contract should provide for the appointment of second trustee for the purposes of the transfer (see **4.5**).

Alternatively, the deceased co-owner's interest may have passed to the surviving co-owner by will or under the intestacy rules; this can be proved by producing certified copies of the grant of probate and the assent from the PRs to the surviving co-owner as beneficiary.

There is no need to appoint a second trustee where there are two or more legal owners remaining, as the purchase price will be paid to at least two trustees on completion so overreaching will take place.

2.5.5 Restrictive covenants

Restrictive covenants prevent land being used in particular ways and are usually binding on successors in title to the original parties. In registered land they appear in the Charges register. In unregistered land they appear in the conveyance, often in or immediately after the first operative paragraph conveying the property to the purchaser. If the property is unregistered, a post-1925 restrictive covenant will only be binding against the buyer if it was validly registered as a D(ii) Land Charge against the name of the original covenantor. This can be checked with a Land Charges search.

Example

The Purchaser with the intent and so as to bind the property hereby conveyed into whosoever hands the same may come and to benefit and protect the adjoining and neighbouring property of the Vendors or any part thereof HEREBY COVENANTS with the Vendors and their successors in title not to use any building erected on the property hereby conveyed other than as offices.

This covenant will be problematic to a client who intends to use the property for another purpose, such as a home or a shop.

The buyer's solicitor should consider the following options for dealing with the restrictive covenant:

(a) ask the seller if they know who currently owns the property with the benefit of the covenant and, if this information is available, ask that owner if the buyer can come to some arrangement with them over the proposed use, such as a permanent release of the covenant or a one-off consent. This solution may not be appropriate if, for example, the covenant is very old and the person with the benefit of the covenant cannot be easily identified because the land has been sold off in parts

(b) obtain a restrictive covenant insurance policy for the proposed breach of covenant. This is a commonly used and cost-effective solution, but may not be appropriate if the person with the benefit of the covenant is likely to know that they have the benefit of the covenant and object to the proposed use (such as the immediate neighbour)

(c) apply to the Upper Tribunal (Lands Chamber) for modification or discharge of the covenant under s 84 Law of Property Act 1925, on the grounds that the covenant is obsolete or confers no practical benefit of substantial value or advantage (or is contrary to the public interest) and the loss of the covenant can be compensated in money. This may not be a quick or cost-effective option and the outcome is at the discretion of the tribunal.

The options may be mutually exclusive, eg a restrictive covenant insurance policy is generally not available where an approach has been made to a person with the benefit of the covenant alerting them to their rights. If the covenant is old, the successor in title to the property with the benefit may not be aware of it, so an approach to them may not be in the client's best interests.

2.5.6 Positive covenants

A positive covenant is one that obliges the covenantor to carry out works or incur expenditure. In registered land they appear in the Charges register. In unregistered land they appear in the conveyance, often in or immediately after the first operative paragraph conveying the property to the buyer.

A positive covenant always binds the original covenantor, but the burden of a positive covenant does not run to a successor in title to the original covenantor. So at first sight, a positive covenant is not binding on a new buyer. However, when the original covenantor sold the property, it is likely that they required their buyer to give them an indemnity covenant, so that if their buyer breached the covenant and the original covenantor was sued directly for the breach, they could recover their losses from their buyer. This arrangement is likely to have been repeated each time the property changed hands, resulting in a 'chain of indemnity' from the original covenantor to the current seller of the property.

It is possible to check whether the current seller gave an indemnity covenant to their seller when they purchased the property. In registered land, there will be the following entry in the Proprietorship register:

The transfer to the proprietor contains a covenant to observe and perform the covenants referred to in the Charges Register and of indemnity in respect thereof.

An example of an indemnity covenant as it would appear in a conveyance of unregistered land is as follows:

THE Purchaser hereby COVENANTS with the Vendors to observe and perform the covenants contained in the Conveyance and shall indemnify the Vendors from and against all actions costs proceedings and claims in respect of any future breach thereof.

If the seller did give an indemnity covenant when they purchased the property, they will require their buyer to give an equivalent indemnity covenant in the transfer of the property, so the buyer will be liable to the seller in contract if they do not observe and perform the positive covenant. Provision for this must be made in the contract (see **4.5**).

Example

You act for the buyer of a freehold registered property. The seller has provided you with official copies and the following positive covenant appears in the Charges register:

1. *(29 April 2000) A Conveyance of the land in this title dated 12 February 1978 and made between (1) Peter Johnson (the Vendor) and (2) George Flewitt (the Purchaser) contains the following covenants:*

   The Purchaser covenants with the Vendor for the benefit of every part of the Vendor's Retained Land with the intent that the burden of the covenants shall run with every part of the Property hereby conveyed at all times hereafter to observe and perform the following covenants:

   (1) Not to alter the external appearance of the Property without the consent in writing of the Vendor or the Vendor's successors in title
   (2) To keep the wall to the rear of the Property in a state of good repair and condition.

The first covenant is a restrictive covenant so will bind the buyer (see **2.5.5** above). The second covenant is positive, so the first question is whether it will bind the buyer, because the burden of a positive covenant does not run with the property. If the covenant binds the seller, then the seller will require an indemnity covenant from the buyer. The covenant will bind the seller if the seller is the original covenantor, George Flewitt, or if the seller gave an indemnity covenant to their seller when they purchased the property, thus creating or continuing a chain of indemnity. This can be established by looking in the Proprietorship register.

If the covenant is binding on the seller and the seller is requiring an indemnity covenant from the buyer, the buyer's solicitor should inform the buyer of the obligation to maintain the wall and ask the surveyor to inspect the wall to establish its condition. They should also ask the seller if they have been complying with the covenant and if not, whether anyone has tried to enforce it. The covenant may involve the buyer in extra expense which they had not envisaged, but it is unlikely to be a big problem in this example as most buyers will want to maintain the wall in any event.

2.5.7 Unknown covenants

Sometimes a property is subject to covenants, but the nature of those covenants and the wording of them is unknown. Often this is because they were contained in an earlier deed which has since been lost.

In registered land, the entry in the Charges register will make it clear that the details were not available when the property was first registered:

Conveyance of the land in this title and other land dated 24 April 1939 made between STUART GRIFFIN (1) and HERBERT RHODE (2) contains covenants but neither the original conveyance nor a certified copy or examined abstract thereof was produced on first registration.

In unregistered land the existence of covenants may be apparent on the face of the conveyance. For example, in a 1983 Conveyance, the property is sold *'SUBJECT TO the covenant contained in a Conveyance dated the 18th July One thousand nine hundred and thirty and made between Harold Stephens (as vendor) of the one part and Gerard Howard (as buyer) of the other part'*, but the seller is unable to produce the original or a copy of the 1930 Conveyance.

The safest option is to assume that the covenants are restrictive and will be binding on the buyer, even though the details are unknown, and to consider the options for dealing with problematic restrictive covenants set out in **2.5.5** above. In practice, obtaining an indemnity insurance policy will often be the most cost-effective course of action. The seller should take care to disclose this defect in title in the contract so that the buyer cannot object to it and use it as a reason not to complete the purchase.

2.5.8 Mortgages

A mortgage is rarely a problem because the seller usually intends to discharge it using the proceeds of sale immediately after completion. Indeed, the buyer will not commit to buying the property unless they are satisfied that the seller's mortgage will be discharged on completion of the sale. It is possible to tell if a registered property is subject to a mortgage as there will be two entries in the Charges register, one giving the date and purpose of the charge and the other stating the identity of the lender. The following is an example:

1. *(1 March 2005) REGISTERED CHARGE dated 1 September 2005 to secure the moneys including the further advances therein mentioned.*
2. *(1 March 2005) Proprietor: THE ROYAL BANK OF SCOTLAND PLC of 109/109A Castle Street, Edinburgh EH2 4JW*

The lender may also have put a restriction in the Proprietorship register preventing the borrower from making a disposition of the property without the consent of the lender:

RESTRICTION: No disposition of the registered estate by the proprietor of the registered estate is to be registered without a written consent signed by the proprietor for the time being of the charge dated 1 September 2005 in favour of THE ROYAL BANK OF SCOTLAND PLC of 109/109A Castle Street, Edinburgh EH2 4JW referred to in the charges register.

In unregistered land, a mortgage will appear as one of the title deeds listed in the epitome of title. A buyer will only be concerned with a mortgage that has not been discharged (paid off): a mortgage that has been discharged will have, usually on the back page, a 'vacating receipt' in the following terms:

R E C E I P T

NATIONAL MIDLAND BANK LIMITED hereby acknowledges to have received from [THE BORROWER] all monies intended to be secured by the written deed.

If there is a subsisting mortgage on the property, the buyer will want this to be discharged on completion so that they do not take subject to it. The buyer's solicitor should check that the contract states that the seller is selling the property free of the mortgage and that the seller's solicitor gives an undertaking to discharge the mortgage immediately on completion (see **4.4.1** and **5.5**).

2.5.9 Leases

The existence of a lease affecting a freehold property will not be a problem if the buyer is expecting it. For example, the buyer may be purchasing the property as an investment and is relying on the rental income payable by the tenant of the lease. The existence of a lease will be a problem to a buyer who is expecting the property to be sold with vacant possession, as the tenant will have possession and control of the property for as long as the lease lasts.

In registered land, the grant of a lease for a term of more than seven years, or the disposition of a (previously unregistered) lease with more than seven years to run, requires registration in its own right with a separate title number, but such leases are also regarded as third party interests that should be registered against the landlord's title. Such leases are protected and will appear as notices in the Charges register of the landlord's title. If they are so protected by the date when the transfer of the property to the buyer is registered, they will bind the buyer. If a lease for a term of more than seven years is not so registered, it will not bind the buyer, but it might qualify as an overriding interest if the tenant is occupation. Legal leases for a term not exceeding seven years and equitable leases where the tenant is actual occupation may be enforceable as overriding interests.

In unregistered land, a legal lease (other than a parol lease for three years or less) will have been created by deed and should be one of the title deeds scheduled in the epitome of title. A parol lease (ie one complying with the criteria in s 54(2) Law of Property Act 1925) does not require any formalities and will be binding on the buyer whether they know about it or not.

If a lease is revealed by the title investigation (or through the searches and enquiries in **Chapter 3**), the buyer's solicitor should report it to the buyer and check that the existence of the lease and its terms are compatible with the buyer's proposed use of the property.

2.5.10 Notices (registered land only)

A notice is an entry in the Charges register in respect of the burden of an interest affecting a registered estate or charge. Notices can be agreed or unilateral: agreed notices are put on the register with the agreement of the registered proprietor, unilateral notices are used where the registered proprietor has refused to consent to the entry or has not been asked about it. The entry of a notice does not guarantee that the interest it is valid or that it even exists. The notice itself does not give the person who registers it any rights over the property as such. It merely serves to ensure that the priority of the interest referred to in the notice is protected against any subsequent interests.

Example

You act for the buyer of a freehold registered property. The seller has provided you with official copies and the following entries appear in the Charges register:

1. *(22.01.2015) UNILATERAL NOTICE in respect of an agreement dated 15 October 2014 made between (1) Anne-Marie Jones and (2) Jackson Darcey.*
2. *(22.01.2015) BENEFICIARY: Jackson Leslie Darcey of 56 High Street, Dorking, Surrey RH4 2DH.*

The first step is to ask the seller's solicitor to ascertain to what the unilateral notice relates. Then there are two courses of action available to the buyer. One is simply to walk away from the transaction and another is to refuse to proceed any further with the transaction until the seller deals with the unilateral notice. This buyer should require the seller to get the notice cancelled by the Land Registry before exchange of contracts. If Mr Darcey agrees to the cancellation or the unilateral notice was lodged in relation to an option that has now expired, this should not be much of a problem. However, if the notice is in respect of a valid interest such as a contract for sale, covenants or a lease over the property, this will be of greater concern.

2.5.11 Home rights

A home right is a statutory right created under the Family Law Act 1996 for a non-owning spouse or civil partner to occupy the matrimonial home. A home right does not create an interest in land. In registered land, a home right will bind a buyer if it is protected by a notice in the Charges register by the date when the transfer of the property to the buyer is registered. In unregistered land a home right must be protected as a Class F land charge in order to be binding on a buyer.

If the title investigation reveals a home right (or an occupier comes to light in the searches and enquiries referred to in **Chapter 3**), the seller should be required to obtain from the non-owning occupier a release of all rights in the property and agreement to vacate on or prior to completion. This is usually dealt with in the contract (see **4.5**).

Summary

- Investigation of title is undertaken by the solicitors for the seller, the buyer and the lender.

  The seller's solicitor investigates title to anticipate problems that may arise and obtain the necessary information to draft the contract for sale. The buyer's solicitor investigates title to check that the seller is able to sell what they are contracting to sell and to discover any defects in title or problematic incumbrances. The lender's solicitor investigates title to ensure the property is worth the money that will be advanced to the borrower.
- Deduction of title is the process by which the seller shows evidence of their right to sell a property. Typically title is deduced before the contract for sale is exchanged.
- Where registered land is being sold, the seller will supply official copies of the register of title.
- Where unregistered land is being sold, the seller will supply an epitome of title (and/or an abstract). The epitome should begin with a good root of title satisfying s 44 of the LPA 1925 and contain copies of all documents affecting ownership from the date of the root until the present day.
- In registered land the solicitor will review the official copies and title plan, and carry out searches and enquiries to discover any interests that override and are not recorded on the registers of title.
- In unregistered land the solicitor will review the documents attached to the epitome. They will also carry out an Index Map search and central land charges searches, and review the results.
- When reviewing the epitome the solicitor should check for a good root, an unbroken chain of ownership, correct stamp duties and proper execution. The description of the property should be consistent throughout the documents and should match the contract.
- In both registered and unregistered land, any restrictions on ownership and incumbrances revealed by investigation of title must be considered carefully. If they affect the property or the buyer adversely, they must be discussed with the buyer and any available solutions considered.

Sample questions

Question 1

A solicitor is acting for the seller on the sale of freehold property with an unregistered title. The solicitor is preparing for deduction of title to the property to the buyer's solicitor and has examined the deeds and documents relating to the property.

Which of the following documents is the best candidate for a good root of title?

A A Conveyance of the property dated 10 August 1982.

B A Mortgage of the property dated 10 August 1982.

C A Deed of Gift dated 25 December 1990.

D A Grant of Probate dated 30 July 2019.

E An Assent of the property dated 8 August 2019.

Answer

Option A is correct.

Under s 44 of the Law of Property Act 1925, a root of title must be at least 15 years old so the Grant of Probate and the Assent (options D and E) are too recent to be good roots of title.

Option C is not the best answer. The Deed of Gift is old enough and will probably fulfil the other criteria set out in s 44, but as it was not a transaction between third parties for valuable consideration, it will not offer the double guarantee like the Conveyance and the Mortgage (ie that title has been investigated for at least 30 years).

Both the Conveyance and the Mortgage are capable of being good roots of title and offer the double guarantee, but the Conveyance is preferable to the Mortgage as it is likely to contain a more detailed description of the property by reference to a plan and details of the incumbrances that burden the property and deal expressly with the legal and equitable interest in the property. Therefore, option B is not the best answer.

Question 2

A husband and wife are the registered proprietors of a freehold property. The husband died six months ago and the wife is selling the property. The Proprietorship register contains a restriction stating that no disposition by a sole proprietor of the land (not being a trust corporation) under which capital money arises is to be registered except under an order of the registrar or of the Court.

What is the best advice to the buyer as to whether the wife can sell the property on her own?

A The wife is the sole legal owner of the property and can sell it on her own as she and her late husband held the legal title as joint tenants.

B The wife is the sole legal and equitable owner of the property and can sell it on her own as she and her late husband held the legal and equitable title as joint tenants.

C The wife needs to appoint another person to act as a legal owner alongside her in the sale of the property.

D The wife cannot sell the property until probate has been granted and she can show that her late husband's equitable interest in the property has been transferred to her by an assent from her late husband's personal representatives.

E It is safe to buy the property from the wife on her own as long as the buyer is provided with a certified copy of her late husband's death certificate.

Answer

Option C is the best answer in these circumstances. The husband and wife held the legal title to the property as joint tenants because that is the only way the legal title can be held by co-owners. However, the restriction in the Proprietorship Register indicates that they held the equitable title as tenants in common. Consequently, the wife cannot sell the property alone. In the light of this, options A, B and E are not good advice, although it is the case that the husband's death certificate will need to be produced.

Where the equitable title to a property is held by co-owners as tenants in common and one of those co-owners dies, another legal owner (also referred to as a trustee) needs to be appointed to overreach the equitable interest of the deceased co-owner before completion.

In relation to option D, although it is possible that the husband's equitable interest has passed to the wife by will or under the intestacy rules, the buyer would not need to wait for confirmation of this as long as the second trustee is appointed, thereby satisfying the wording of the restriction.

Question 3

A solicitor acts for a buyer of a registered freehold property. The official copies have revealed that there is a covenant in the charges register not to use the property for any commercial purpose. The covenant was created in 2015 for the benefit of land then and now owned by the district council. The buyer wants to use the property as a cake shop.

What is the best advice to the buyer as to how to proceed with the purchase?

A The buyer should withdraw from the purchase immediately to save wasted conveyancing fees.

B The buyer should proceed with the purchase as it is unlikely that the district council will take any action if the covenant is breached.

C The buyer should not exchange contracts until there has been a successful application to have the covenant modified or discharged by the Upper Tribunal (Lands Chamber).

D The buyer should obtain a restrictive covenant insurance policy for the breach of covenant.

E The buyer should ask the seller to approach the district council to see if they will release the covenant or consent to the proposed use.

Answer

This is a difficult question as it is a matter of professional judgment.

Option A is not the best advice as the problem is relatively common and may have a solution. Unless the buyer feels very strongly on the matter, it is probably too early to withdraw from the transaction altogether.

Option B is a very high-risk strategy: the covenant is relatively new and imposed by a statutory body, presumably for a good reason. It is unlikely that a breach of this covenant will go unnoticed.

Option C is also high risk in that the application will take some time and may not be successful as a covenant imposed so recently may be addressing a current and valid concern.

That leaves option D and E, which are mutually exclusive. Given that the covenant is very recent and imposed by a statutory authority, the chances of enforcement must be high so a restrictive covenant insurance policy may not be available at a reasonable cost. Therefore, in these particular circumstances, option E is the best advice.

3 Pre-contract Searches and Enquiries

3.1	Introduction	54
3.2	Who makes the searches and raises the enquiries	54
3.3	The range and type of searches and enquiries available	54
3.4	Deciding which searches and enquiries are relevant for a particular property	62
3.5	Matters commonly revealed in search results and replies to enquiries	63

SQE1 syllabus

This chapter will enable you to achieve the SQE1 Assessment Specification in relation to Functioning Legal Knowledge concerned with the following:

- Range and purpose of making searches and raising enquiries
- Who would make the searches and raise enquiries
- Results of searches and enquiries

Note that for SQE1, candidates are not usually required to recall specific case names or cite statutory or regulatory authorities. Cases and statutory or regulatory authorities are provided for illustrative purposes only unless otherwise indicated.

Learning outcomes

By the end of this chapter you will be able to apply relevant core legal principles and rules appropriately and effectively, at the level of a competent newly qualified solicitor in practice, to realistic client-based and ethical problems and situations in the following areas:

- Why searches and enquiries are made
- Who makes the searches and raises the enquiries
- The range and type of searches and enquiries available
- Deciding which searches and enquiries are relevant for a particular property
- Matters commonly revealed in search results and replies to enquiries

3.1 Introduction

Pre-contract searches and enquiries are necessary because when a person buys a property, the principle of 'caveat emptor' or 'let the buyer be aware' applies. In the contract, the seller only has a very limited duty to disclose certain matters affecting the title of the property. Although the seller cannot provide a misleading reply to any specific questions, the seller does not have a duty to disclose, for example, physical defects in the property or to admit to problems with the neighbour over who owns and maintains the boundary fences. The seller does not even need to disclose whether there is planning permission for the extension they have built on the rear of the property. The principle of caveat emptor has always been, and remains, a cornerstone of conveyancing in England and Wales, so the solicitor acting for the buyer must carry out a due diligence process to ensure that the buyer has as much information as possible and can enter into the transaction fully aware of any problems with the property.

3.2 Who makes the searches and raises the enquiries

The buyer's solicitor is at the heart of a conveyancing transaction to carry out the due diligence process. It is their responsibility to find out as much about the property as possible before the buyer enters into a binding contract to buy the property. At this stage the buyer can withdraw from the transaction if they discover something about the property they do not like; if something is discovered after exchange, the buyer may not be able to withdraw without being in breach of contract.

In advising the buyer, the solicitor must make a judgement as to the relevant searches and enquiries to make for the particular property. Failure to make the correct searches and enquiries can give rise to a claim of negligence from a buyer if the buyer should suffer a loss. The buyer's solicitor must then obtain all the relevant information from the results and replies to the searches and enquiries and then analyse it in order to provide clear, concise and coherent advice to the buyer. The buyer can then make an informed decision whether or not to proceed with the purchase, fully aware of any problems or liabilities which affect the property.

The information revealed as a result of the searches and enquiries will be of equal importance to a lender who is intending to make a loan to the buyer secured by a mortgage over the property. In residential transactions, the buyer's solicitor will often be acting for the lender as well. In commercial property transactions, the lender may be separately represented on all aspects of the transaction, or may ask the buyer's solicitor to carry out the title investigation and process the searches and enquiries (so as to avoid duplication of legal costs) and report to the lender and the lender's solicitors on these limited aspects of the transaction only.

3.3 The range and type of searches and enquiries available

There are a number of searches and enquiries that are carried out on virtually every conveyancing transaction, regardless of the type, location and value of the property. There are others that will only be relevant to properties in a certain location or of a particular age and type, or which would not be cost-effective given the value of the property.

3.3.1 Searches and enquiries relevant to every property

(a) Survey and personal inspection

A professional survey should always be strongly recommended to a client. Indeed, if the buyer is relying upon a mortgage to finance the transaction, the lender will require a survey of some sort.

A survey is obviously not something that a solicitor can carry out, but the solicitor may be asked to advise on the most appropriate type of survey. There are various types and which one is most appropriate in any given case really depends on the age and location of the property.

A lender will always require the borrower to pay for a 'valuation': this type of survey is to assess whether the property is adequate security for the loan and it will not necessarily tell the borrower much about the state of the structure of the property. If the buyer has concerns about the state of the property, or intends to carry out alterations to it after their purchase, they may wish to consider a full structural survey, which provides a detailed commentary on the structure. A less expensive alternative is a 'homebuyers' valuation and survey', which is less detailed than a structural survey but still contains advice on necessary repairs and maintenance requirements.

A personal inspection of the property by the buyer's solicitor is advisable as it will reveal more than is evident from the plan of a property. For example, the solicitor may find that the plan is inaccurate, or that there is a cable, drain, pathway or occupier that has not shown up on the plan. Unfortunately, the buyer may not be prepared to bear the cost of a personal inspection as well as a survey; personal inspections are very rare in residential conveyancing and tend to be confined to high value commercial transactions.

(b) The local search

A local land charges search and standard enquiries of the local authority should be raised on every sale and purchase of property. Together with the optional enquiries, these three are known collectively as the 'local search'.

The local land charges search, in form LLC1, provides details of any financial charges or restrictions on land that have been imposed by public authorities under statute, for example planning consents, tree preservation orders and conservation area designation orders.

The standard enquiries, in form CON29, reveal lots of information such as planning permissions, any restrictions on permitted development (such as an Article 4 Direction), whether the land has been designated as contaminated land, etc. The CON29 standard enquiries will also raise questions of liability for road repair. For the buyer, this can be important because it can lead to considerable expense if the road is not maintained at the local authority's expense (**see 3.5.2 below**).

In addition to the standard enquiries, there may be a number of optional enquiries that ought to be raised depending on the locality of the property. These are raised in a separate CON29O form and cover a range of diverse matters, including environmental and pollution notices and rights over common land.

The local search only relates to the property itself and not adjoining land. So, for example, if the attraction of a particular house is the view across a field, the solicitor should consider making specific enquiries to see if there is any proposed development on that field.

(c) Water and drainage search

Liability for the costs of drain and sewage repairs is another major concern for a buyer. However, the question of drain and sewer maintenance is not one for the local authority. Instead a separate set of enquiries known as the standard drainage and water enquiries should be raised with the statutory undertaker, usually a water company. Forms of of standard enquiries commonly used are called CON29DW (residential properties) and CommercialDW (commercial properties). The main purpose of the enquiries is to establish whether the drains and sewers serving the property are 'adopted' and therefore the responsibility of the statutory undertaker rather than the owner of the property. The search will reveal whether or not the property is connected to a public sewer for both foul and surface water drainage and whether the property is connected to a public water supply. If the property does not drain into a public sewer, the buyer will be liable for the costs of maintaining the drains and sewers and may be liable for the costs of bringing them up to adoption standard if the water authority decides to adopt them.

(d) Pre-contract enquiries of the seller

These are questions that the seller is required to answer. They are generally referred to as 'preliminary enquiries', or 'pre-contract enquiries'. They are the sort of standard questions that most solicitors acting for a buyer would raise at the pre-contract stage of the transaction. The enquiries can be very wide-ranging. What is included may depend on the solicitor raising them and their past personal experience in acting for buyers, but typical enquiries include whether the seller has had any disputes regarding the property, whether there are any third parties occupying the property, compliance with any covenants contained within the title, any planning permissions, issues about boundary maintenance and in the case of commercial properties, the VAT status of the transaction (see **1.6.3**).

(e) Environmental searches

With the impact of the Environmental Protection Act 1990 ('EPA 1990'), there has been a heightened awareness of the potential cost of cleaning up sites that are contaminated, particularly since the cost can rest with the owner or occupier of the property and not just the original polluter. As a result, environmental searches and enquiries should be carried out since there is a good chance that a solicitor will be found negligent if they do not advise on the risk and liability where the property is found to be contaminated land for the purposes of the EPA 1990. Both the CON29 standard and the CON29O optional enquiries of the local authority contain some questions relating to entries and notices made under the EPA 1990. However, reliance on these is not sufficient to identify the environmental risks which may exist. For example, the enquiry in the CON29 form asks whether a notice has been served designating the property as contaminated land, but a negative reply may just mean that the local authority has not inspected the property yet.

As with building surveys, there are different types of environmental search, each one differing in scope and the depth of detail given. The most common type of environmental search is commonly called a 'desktop' search. This type of search, usually carried out by a specialist environmental search company, looks at all plans of the area, information published by local authorities and the Environment Agency. If the local search, survey or desktop search identify a risk that the land may be contaminated, the buyer may consider commissioning a physical survey of the land to be carried out by a specialist environmental surveyor. The surveyor will take soil samples at selected points in the land, analyse them for evidence of contamination and recommend what action should be taken to clean up the land to avoid contamination. Alternatively, the buyer's solicitor can consider with the buyer whether insurance against environmental liability is the best way to manage the risk.

(f) Flood search

A flood search is indicated where the property is close to a river or the coast. However, most damage is caused by surface water flooding, which can occur anywhere when heavy rainfall has no other means of escape. Insurance for flooding is available for most residential properties thanks to a Government-backed reinsurance scheme known as 'Flood Re', but commercial properties (including buy-to-let properties) are not covered by Flood Re and insurance may only be available with very high premiums, or may not be available at all. Although standard pre-contract enquiries of the seller usually ask for details of any flooding affecting the property, the seller will often decline to reply under the caveat emptor principle. Accordingly, most firms will recommend a flood search on every property transaction.

Some information is available online. For example, there is a free screening search for river, coastal, surface water and reservoir flooding offered by the Environment Agency and a river and coastal flood risk indicator on the Land Registry website. However, neither of these searches is property-specific and neither shows groundwater flooding. Property-specific flood risk searches are available from commercial providers and these vary in their cost and coverage. The interpretation of results is a specialist area which should be referred to the buyer's surveyor and/or the consultant who produced the report, but a key thing to look for is whether the property can be insured at normal rates. If a flood risk is identified, a specialist report can be obtained to advise the buyer on flood risk and possible flood damage mitigation measures.

3.3.2 Searches and enquiries for particular properties and transactions

(a) Chancel repairs search

The owners of certain properties in a Church of England parish where there has been a medieval church with a vicar could be liable to pay the cost of repairing the chancel of the parish church. Liability for chancel repairs was highlighted when in 2003, Mr and Mrs Wallbank were ordered by the House of Lords to pay £186,000 for repairs to the nearby church of St John the Baptist in the village of Aston Cantlow under the provisions of the Chancel Repairs Act of 1932. In registered land, chancel repair liability lost its overriding status on 13 October 2013, but continues to bind a buyer if the previous transfer for value occurred prior to that date. In unregistered land, the buyer will only be bound if the chancel repair liability is referred to in the title deeds or protected by a caution against first registration lodged prior to first registration, but such a caution could be lodged after completion but prior to first registration (in the 'registration gap'). For these reasons, and even where there is no obvious Church of England Church nearby, some firms continue to carry out chancel repair screening searches on all property transactions, even though no liability will exist where the property is registered and the previous transfer for value occurred after 13 October 2013. Indeed, many firms consider that obtaining insurance against the liability is a more cost-efficient way of protecting the buyer than incurring legal costs in investigating the issue and obtaining the screening search.

(b) Mining searches

The Mining Remediation Authority website states that one in four properties in Britain sit on the coalfield. Since it is not always clear from the surface whether there has been any underground mining, it makes sense to carry out a mining search of every property in a coal mining area. Coal mining areas are identified in the Mining Remediation Authority's interactive map viewer. A mining search of the Mining Remediation Authority, on a CON29M form, will confirm if the property is in an area where mining has taken place in the past or is likely to take place in the future, whether there are shafts on the property, the existence of underground workings which may cause problems with subsidence and whether any claims for subsidence damage have been paid in the past or are pending. Subsidence occurs when the ground under a building collapses, or sinks lower, damaging the foundations and causing cracks in the structure above. It is important to find out whether a claim for subsidence has already been paid as if so, this may prevent a future claim being made.

There are other areas which have been affected by mining activity in the past; for example, tin in Cornwall, Devon and Somerset, clay in Cornwall, Devon and Dorset, limestone in parts of the West Midlands and brine and salt in Cheshire. It is possible to do specific searches, similar to the CON29M, in these areas.

Mining searches may also be indicated where there is a mines and minerals reservation revealed in the title investigation (see **2.5.2**).

(c) Canal & River Trust search

If the property is adjacent to a river or a canal, the buyer needs to be made aware of any liability for repairs to the maintenance of the waterways, banks and tow paths, as well as whether the property has been affected by flooding in the past. This information can be obtained from the Canal & River Trust.

(d) Commons search

Properties on green-field sites or adjoining an open space such as a village green may be affected by common rights, such as the right to pasture, that have been protected under the Commons Registration Act 1965. Councils in England and Wales are required to maintain a register of common land and a register of town and village greens. Such rights and designations may affect either the current enjoyment of the land, or the intended use/development of the property. In such circumstances, the buyer's solicitor should raise optional enquiry 22 in the CON29O form in the local search.

(e) Railways

A buyer of land adjoining a railway line will want to know whether there are any obligations to maintain the boundary features separating the property from the railway line and whether there are any restrictions on carrying out building work next to the line. Unfortunately Network Rail will not answer such enquiries, so the buyer's solicitor will have to raise additional pre-contract enquiries of the seller, which may not reveal much information. The buyer's solicitor can advise the buyer that there may be issues with future works near the railway line and that an approach should be made to Network Rail about any specific proposal.

It is possible (and advisable) to do searches on specific existing and proposed railway undertakings, such as Crossrail, HS2 and the Newcastle Metro. Also, the reply to enquiry 22 in the CON29 form in the local search will reveal if the property might be affected by a proposed rail scheme.

(f) Highways

The replies to enquiry 2 of the CON29 form in the local search will provide certain information about the roads adjoining the property (see **3.5.2** below), but verges and pavements will not be covered. This information may not be detailed enough where, for example, the property is going to be redeveloped and there is a grass verge in third party private ownership between the road and the title boundary of the property forming a possible 'ransom strip'. In such circumstances, the buyer's solicitor can send a plan to the relevant highways authority, asking for the boundaries of the publicly maintainable highways (including verges) to be marked onto it.

(g) Unregistered land searches

An Index Map Search ('SIM') and a Land Charges Department search against the seller and previous estate owners will be necessary in any purchase of unregistered land (see **2.4**).

(h) Company search

Where the seller is a company, the buyer's solicitor should carry out a company search at Companies House. This will confirm whether the seller has the capacity to enter into the contract, confirm the identity of the current officers of the company (to check the documents are signed by the right people) and to see if there are any fixed or floating charges secured on the property that will need to be discharged on completion. The search will need to be repeated just before completion to check for insolvency issues (see **5.4.3**).

Where the property is unregistered land, company searches should also be carried out against any corporate estate owners revealed in the epitome of title.

Bankruptcy/insolvency search

A solicitor acting for a lender should make a search against the borrower (who may also be their buyer client) to ensure that there are no bankruptcy or insolvency proceedings affecting them. These searches must be made just before completion (see **5.4.2**), but some firms will also make them prior to exchange of contracts so that any problems can be sorted out in good time. Where the borrower is an individual, the search is done by sending a K16 form to the Land Charges department in Plymouth. Where the borrower is a company, a company search will be needed.

3.3.3 Summary of the range and type of searches and enquiries available

Type of search	Standard Search Form?	Sent to?	Purpose	Particularly indicated where?
Survey/personal inspection			To assess the physical condition of the property	All transactions, but the type and level of detail required will vary
Local search	LLC1, CON29 and CON29O	The local authority	To identify matters imposed by or known to the local authority	All transactions, but CON29O enquiries should only be raised where appropriate
Water and drainage search	CON29DW, CommercialDW	The statutory undertaker, usually a water company	To establish connection to a public sewer and public water supply	All transactions
Pre-contract enquiries of the seller		The seller	To seek information that the owner/occupier of the property can be expected to know	All transactions: usually a standard set of enquiries, but additional specific enquiries can be raised
Environmental searches		Various sources of information available	To identify contaminated land	Desktop/risk screening searches for all transactions; enviro surveys where risk identified
Flood search		Various sources of information available	To identify whether the property is at greater than normal risk of flooding	Risk screening searches for all transactions; more detailed report where risk identified.

(*continued*)

(*continued*)

Type of search	Standard Search Form?	Sent to?	Purpose	Particularly indicated where?
Chancel repairs search		Search done by commercial provider	To identify potential liability to pay for repairs to the chancel of a Church of England Parish Church	Particularly relevant when the property is unregistered or where there has been no disposal for value of registered land since 13 October 2013
Coal mining searches Searches for other types of mining available for specific geographic areas	CON29M	Mining Remediation Authority	To establish whether the property is in a coal mining area and whether there has been a claim for subsidence	For properties in a coal mining area and/or with a mines and minerals reservation in the title.
Canal & River Trust search		Canal & River Trust	To establish liability for maintenance of waterways banks and towpaths	Where the property is adjacent to a canal or river
Commons search	CON29O, enquiry 22	Local authority	To check that the property is not protected as common land or a town and village green	Where the property is adjacent to open land
Railways search Specific searches available for proposed major rail undertakings		Network Rail	To establish liability for boundary maintenance and/or restrictions on use	No general search available, owner can raise a specific proposal with NR where a property adjoins a railway line
Highways search		Local highway authority	To establish whether verges and pavements are publicly maintainable	Where there appears to be land in private ownership separating the property from the highway

(*continued*)

Type of search	Standard Search Form?	Sent to?	Purpose	Particularly indicated where?
Index Map search	SIM	Land Registry	To see if the land is already registered, or registration is pending, or if there is a caution against first registration	Where the property appears to be unregistered land or where there is a mines and minerals reservation in the title
Land Charges search	K15	Land Charges Department in Plymouth	To see if certain types of incumbrance have been protected by registration against the relevant estate owner so as to be binding on the buyer	Where the property is unregistered land
Company search	Online application	Companies House	To check capacity, signatories and charges	Where the seller is a company (and against all corporate estate owners where the property is unregistered)
Bankruptcy/ insolvency search	Individuals: K16 Companies: Company search	Individuals: Land Charges department in Plymouth Companies: Companies House	To check there are no insolvency or bankruptcy proceedings	All transactions when acting for the lender

3.3.4 Online search providers

There is a great deal of information available from a wide variety of sources and the skill is in knowing which are the most appropriate searches and enquiries to raise in any given situation. It would be much easier if all the relevant information was held in one place. It would speed up the transaction overall and make the process of pre-contract searches and enquiries less risky and more certain. The National Land Information Service, known as NLIS, was developed by Government departments in conjunction with the Land Registry, local authorities and other bodies with the declared purpose of providing 'quicker and easier access to authoritative, accurate and comprehensive information on all land and property in England and Wales'.

NLIS is part of the development of e-conveyancing and the ultimate aim is to facilitate quick and efficient paperless property transactions by using the latest technology. NLIS is managed and regulated by Land Data, a separate company. To use the service, a firm must register with one of the 'channel' providers, certain channels that are licensed by NLIS to provide searches to solicitors and licensed conveyancers. The channels compete in the marketplace and differentiate their services by packaging and presenting information to suit their target audience.

The search is submitted by the solicitor via a secure internet connection to the chosen channel, which in turn passes it to the NLIS hub which acts as the gateway for information and services from NLIS data providers, such as the Land Registry, local authorities and the Mining Remediation Authority. The NLIS hub interrogates each of the appropriate data providers concurrently and reports back to the channel, which formats and presents the consolidated search results and replies which are returned electronically to the solicitor. In some cases, the whole process may take only a matter of hours, or even minutes, to complete. Some replies still come by post but these are diminishing in number. Using one of the channels through the NLIS hub, rather than sending a number of searches and enquiries to a variety of bodies, can save a solicitor a lot of time.

It is possible to order searches without using a licensed NLIS channel. There are other providers who obtain their underlying data from local authorities, land registry and other authorities in varying ways. An umbrella group, the Council of Property Search Organisations (CoPSO), publishes a list of its current members, all of whom agree to abide by code of conduct for the provision of property searches. These search providers compete on price and speed of delivery in order to secure their business.

3.4 Deciding which searches and enquiries are relevant for a particular property

It is not in the buyer's interests for all of the available searches to be made as the cost may outweigh the benefit, so choosing which searches to commission and which enquiries to raise is a key decision for the buyer's solicitor.

Example 1

You are acting for the buyer of Lavender House, a large, old Victorian property in North Cheshire that the buyer intends to live in. Lavender House is in a poor state of repair. The property is situated next to a small river and there is a disused warehouse on the opposite side of the river which is in the process of being converted into luxury flats. You have already made applications for a local search and a water and drainage search. You have also sent off your pre-contract enquiries to the seller's solicitor.

What other searches and enquiries should be made given the nature and location of Lavender House?

Answer

The following additional searches and enquiries would be appropriate in this case:

- Surveys should be carried out in all transactions. On the facts (the property is in a poor state of repair), the main thing to consider would be the condition of the property. A structural survey may be appropriate in this case.
- Canal & River Trust search – to check on responsibility for the riverbank.

- Flood search – the property abuts a river and so there is a risk of flooding.
- Environmental search – the land is near former industrial land: an environmental desktop search would reveal more information about the risks of contamination. This could be followed up by a specialist survey if necessary.
- Chancel repair search – the facts do not suggest that this might be near a church, but you have not seen a plan or been given any details about the last transfer for value so a chancel repair search should be considered.
- Mining Remediation search using form CON29M (and potentially a limestone search as well) as the property is within both a coal mining area and an area where limestone may have been mined. This will reveal whether there have been any workings which could cause subsidence and whether there is a compensation scheme in place.
- HS2 enquiry as the route will pass through parts of Cheshire.

Example 2

You act for the buyer of 25 Victoria Street. The seller has previously converted the property from residential use to use as a dental surgery and built an extension on one side of the property to use as a waiting room.

What specific searches and enquiries would be relevant on these facts?

Answer

The LLC1 search result will show details of planning permissions for change of use and any building operations, which the seller should have obtained.

The CON29 will also reveal details of any planning permissions granted, and any building regulations consents in respect of the building work. In addition, it will reveal any enforcement notice or stop notice that the local authority has if there has been a planning breach.

The CON29O will have details of any completion notice the local authority may have served in respect of any building work.

The pre-contract enquiries of the seller would ask the seller to supply planning permissions and building regulations consents. There will be standard enquiries about how the existence and use of the building is authorised, if there have been any works carried out on the property and a request for confirmation that necessary consents were obtained for such work. The seller should also supply any planning permissions, although these can also be obtained from the local planning authority for a fee.

A survey will provide information on the state of the building, including the extension.

3.5 Matters commonly revealed in search results and replies to enquiries

3.5.1 Planning permissions

As referred to in **Chapter 1**, a solicitor acting for the buyer of a property will need to check that there is a planning permission for the construction of any building on the property, unless planning permission was not needed (eg the building dates from before 1946). They will also need to check whether there are any planning conditions attached to the permission which would prevent the buyer's proposed alterations or future use of the property and whether there are any existing breaches of the planning conditions for which action could be taken against the buyer after completion.

Example

What information is revealed in this extract from the LLC1 search result?

Part 3 - Planning Charges
Reference - 2016/51709
Stage - Decision Made
Proposal - Single story rear extension
Approval sought - Full Planning Permission
Decision on - 31/01/2016 Approved with conditions

This reveals a conditional planning permission for erection of single storey extension granted in 2016. The buyer of the property will need to know whether the permission has been implemented, what the conditions are and if they have been complied with. The buyer's solicitor will therefore need to obtain a copy of the planning permission from the seller or the local authority. The local planning authority can still take enforcement action for breach of a planning condition for up to 10 years from breach of the condition. The buyer's solicitor will therefore need to check the rest of the CON29 results (for enforcement and stop notices) and the CON29O results (for completion notices) to check no enforcement proceedings have been taken. They will also need to ask the seller about compliance with the planning permission and any notices received about it from the local planning authority.

3.5.2 Road adoption

The CON29 part of the local search should be checked for information about roads and public highways adjacent to the property.

Example

What information is revealed in this extract from CON29 search result?

2	ROADS, FOOTWAYS AND FOOTPATHS	
2.1	Which of the roads, footways and footpaths named in the application for this search (via boxes B and C) are:	*Informative:* *If a road, footpath or footway is not a highway, there may be no right to use it. The Council cannot express an opinion without seeing the title plan of the property and carrying out an inspection, whether or not any existing or proposed highway directly abuts the boundary of the property.*
2.1(a)	Highways maintainable at public expense?	All the named roads are public highways maintainable at public expense except for Grange Road.
2.1(b)	Subject to adoption and, if so, is the agreement supported by a bond or bond waiver	Grange Road is to be adopted. There is no bond in place.

(*continued*)

2	**ROADS, FOOTWAYS AND FOOTPATHS**	
2.1(c)	To be made up by a local authority who will reclaim the cost from the frontagers	Yes
2.1(d)	To be adopted by a local authority without reclaiming the cost from the frontagers	No

Answer

In this example, it is revealed that Grange Road is not a public highway maintainable at public expense. This means there is no automatic right to use it and that the local authority is not paying for its maintenance. So the solicitor acting for the buyer of a property fronting onto Grange Road would need to establish how the buyer will have a right to use the road. For example, there may be an express easement in existence revealed in the title documents, or perhaps an easement could have arisen by long user. The solicitor would also have to ask the seller whether there are any current private arrangements for maintenance of the road and if so, what the recent contributions have been.

Entries (b) and (c) reveal that the road is to be adopted and made up at a cost to the frontagers (there being no bond in place from an original developer of the area to pay for these costs). In the long term, this is good news for the buyer. It means that Grange Road will become a public highway (so the buyer will not need an easement to use it) and the local authority will take over maintenance of the road. However, it also means that if the buyer proceeds with the purchase, they will have to contribute to the cost of bringing the road up to the standard where the local authority is prepared to adopt it, so a surveyor's opinion on the current state of Grange Road may be advisable. The buyer's solicitor will need to find out when the local authority intends to adopt the road and what the likely cost will be for the buyer.

3.5.3 Tree preservation orders

A tree preservation order ('TPO') will be revealed as a local land charge in the LLC1 result. TPOs are designed to protect trees of amenity value to local communities. The buyer will need to be told about any TPO as it is a criminal offence to lop or fell a tree subject to a TPO without the consent of the local planning authority. The solicitor should raise pre-contract enquiries of the seller to obtain a copy of the TPO, establish the location of the protected tree(s) and check the TPO has been complied with.

3.5.4 Smoke control orders

A smoke control order will be revealed as a local land charge in the LLC1 result. Its purpose is to restrict the use of non-smokeless fuels in domestic fireplaces and so might be a problem for the buyer if the property has an open fireplace which they intend to use.

3.5.5 Conservation areas

If the property is located within a designated conservation area, this will be revealed in either the LLC1 or CON29 results. The buyer should be informed as it will be more difficult to make changes to the property than would normally be the case (see **1.7.8**).

3.5.6 Occupiers

In certain circumstances, an occupier may be able to claim an equitable interest or a tenancy in the property. A non-owning spouse may have a protected home right under the Family Law Act 1996 and this will be revealed in the title investigation (see **2.5.11**). However, any adult occupier could potentially claim an interest or tenancy so the buyer's solicitor should ask the seller about occupiers in the pre-contract enquiries of the seller. If there is an adult occupier, the seller should be required to obtain from the occupier a release of all rights in the property and agreement to vacate on or prior to completion. This is usually dealt with in the contract (see **4.5**).

Summary

- The buyer's solicitor must carry out appropriate searches and enquiries to find out as much as possible about the property before the client contracts to buy it.
- There is a wide range of searches and enquiries available and the buyer's solicitor should carefully consider which ones are appropriate for the particular client, property and transaction.
- Some searches and enquiries will be appropriate for nearly every property transaction.
- Other searches and enquiries are only appropriate for when the property is of a particular type, location and/or value.
- The buyer's solicitor must consider the results of all searches, enquiries and surveys, make any necessary follow up enquiries and report appropriately to their client on them.

Sample questions

Question 1

A solicitor is acting for a client who intends to purchase a property. Contracts have not yet been exchanged. The boundary of the property adjoins a river. The client wants to know who is responsible to maintain the riverbank and who has maintained it in the past. The seller has owned the property for over 20 years.

Which of the following statements best describes the searches and enquiries the solicitor should carry out to address this specific issue?

A The solicitor should carry out a water and drainage search and raise specific pre-contract enquiries of the seller.

B The solicitor should carry out a desktop environmental search and a flood search.

C The solicitor should carry out a local land charges search (LLC1) and raise enquiries with the Canal & River Trust.

D The solicitor should raise enquiries with the Canal & River Trust and raise specific pre-contract enquiries of the seller.

E The solicitor should raise enquiries with the Canal & River Trust and carry out a flood search.

Answer

Option D is correct. The client is concerned about the maintenance of the riverbank. The solicitor must therefore raise enquiries with the Canal & River Trust who can provide specific information regarding liability for maintenance of the riverbank. In addition, the solicitor should also raise specific pre-contract enquiries of the seller to find out further information regarding the maintenance regime in place and the level of financial contribution incurred.

The other searches will not address the client's specific concern. The environmental search will only cover contamination risk and the flood search will only cover flood risk; accordingly options B and E are wrong. The water and drainage search will cover whether the property is connected to the public water supply and the use of a public sewer. Option C is wrong as the local land charges search (LLC1) only discloses financial charges or restrictions on land that have been imposed by public authorities under statute, none of which apply to matters concerning the maintenance of riverbanks.

Question 2

A solicitor is acting for the buyer in a conveyancing transaction. The seller's solicitor has provided official copies relating to the property. The buyer has instructed a surveyor to carry out a full structural survey. The solicitor is considering which additional pre-contract searches and enquiries should be raised in addition to the usual standard searches. The property register contains the following entry:

(2 July 1990) The conveyance of the land in this title dated 23 October 1919 referred to above contains the following provision 'EXCEPT AND RESERVING unto the Vendor his heirs and assigns all mines and minerals within and under the property hereby conveyed with all necessary and proper powers rights and easements for working and carrying away the same.'

Which of the following statements best describes the action required as a result of this entry?

A The solicitor should advise the client to instruct the surveyor to check for signs of subsidence at the property.

B The solicitor should advise the client to instruct the surveyor to check for signs of subsidence at the property and carry out an Index Map search on form SIM.

C The solicitor should conduct a search with the Mining Remediation Authority on form CON29M, carry out an Index Map search on form SIM and advise the client to instruct the surveyor to check for signs of subsidence at the property.

D The solicitor should conduct a search with the Mining Remediation Authority on form CON29M and advise the client to instruct the surveyor to check for signs of subsidence at the property.

E The solicitor does not need to carry out an Index Map search on form SIM as the property is registered land.

Answer

Option C is correct. This is an example of how investigation of title and searches and enquiries overlap. The entry shows that the property is subject to a mining exception and reservation. The solicitor should conduct a search with the Mining Remediation Authority on Form CON29M as the result of the search will reveal whether the property is in an area where mining has taken place in the past or is likely to take place in the future, the existence of underground workings which may cause problems with subsidence and whether compensation for subsidence damage has been paid in the past or any claim is pending. The solicitor should also conduct an Index Map search to check that the mines and minerals are not registered under a separate title (see **2.5.2**). In addition, the solicitor should advise the client to ask their surveyor to check for signs of subsidence at the property. So option E is wrong and options A, B and D are correct insofar as they go, but not the best answer as each one of them is incomplete.

Question 3

A solicitor acts for a buyer of a residential property fronting onto a road. The local search has revealed that the road is not a highway maintainable at public expense and there are no current plans for adoption by the local authority. Contracts have not yet been exchanged.

Does the buyer need to be concerned about this?

A Yes, the buyer should be advised not to purchase the property under any circumstances.

B Yes, further enquiries will be needed before the purchase can proceed.

C No, the buyer should proceed with the purchase of the property if the road is in good condition.

D No, the buyer should proceed with the purchase of the property if there is an express right of way over the road in the title documents.

E No, because the local authority will not be reclaiming the cost of adopting the road from the frontagers.

Answer

Option B is correct. The buyer does need to be concerned as there is no automatic right to use the road and the local authority is not paying for its maintenance. The solicitor will need to check the title deeds and raise pre-contract enquiries of the seller to establish whether the buyer will have a legal right to use the road and what arrangements are in place for maintenance. However, there are many properties that front on to roads that are not highways maintainable at public expense, including properties on new developments and high value houses on private developments, so option B is better advice than option A.

Options C, D and E are not the best advice as they imply that the buyer need not be concerned and each only address one aspect of the issue (right of way, maintenance and the possibility of adoption). Option E is also misconceived; just because the local authority has no current plans to adopt the road does not mean that they will not do so in the future. If they do so, they can require the frontagers to contribute to the costs of bringing the road up to adoption standard.

4 Preparation for and Exchange of Contracts

4.1	Introduction	70
4.2	The purpose of a contract	70
4.3	Standard Conditions of Sale and the Standard Commercial Property Conditions	71
4.4	Key conditions in the SC and the SCPC	72
4.5	The purpose of, and matters covered by, special conditions	76
4.6	Insurance and risk	78
4.7	Basics of VAT in a contract	79
4.8	The requirements of a lender	80
4.9	Acting for the lender	81
4.10	Purpose of, and timing for issuing, a certificate of title to the lender	82
4.11	Purpose and process of reporting to the client	83
4.12	Preparation for and exchange of contracts	83
4.13	The practice, method and authority to exchange	84
4.14	The consequences of exchange	85

SQE1 syllabus

This chapter will enable you to achieve the SQE1 Assessment Specification in relation to Functioning Legal Knowledge concerned with the following:

- Key conditions contained in the Standard Conditions of Sale and the Standard Commercial Property Conditions
- Methods of holding a deposit: stakeholder and agent
- Purpose of, and matters covered by, special conditions
- Insurance and risk
- Basics of VAT in a contract
- Acting for a lender
- Lender's requirements
- Purpose of, and timing for issuing, a certificate of title to the lender
- Purpose and process of reporting to the client
- The practice, method and authority to exchange
- Consequences of exchange

Note that for SQE1, candidates are not usually required to recall specific case names or cite statutory or regulatory authorities. Cases and statutory or regulatory authorities are provided for illustrative purposes only unless otherwise indicated.

Learning outcomes

By the end of this chapter you will be able to apply relevant core legal principles and rules appropriately and effectively, at the level of a competent newly qualified solicitor in practice, to realistic client-based and ethical problems and situations in the following areas:

- Drafting and negotiating a contract for the sale and purchase of a property
- Dealing with the buyer's deposit in the manner required by the contract
- Ensuring that the property is insured on the buyer's behalf immediately on exchange
- Ensuring that the contract contains appropriate provisions for VAT
- Ensuring the contract contains appropriate provisions to discharge the seller's mortgage
- Identifying the documentation that will be required where a property is to be mortgaged and the responsibilities of the solicitors for the lender and the borrower
- Reporting to the buyer and the lender prior to exchange of contracts
- Choosing the most appropriate method of effecting exchange of contracts
- Ensuring that the client is aware of the effect of exchange of contracts.

4.1 Introduction

The legal interest in the property passes from the seller to the buyer at completion. However, for the clients and their advisors, exchange of contracts is often the most significant moment in a property transaction. Prior to exchange there is no legally binding agreement and either of the parties is free to withdraw for any reason. At the moment of exchange, the parties should be ready to commit. The clients, estate agents and solicitors have put in a great deal of hard work getting to the point where the buyer client has enough information about the property and is satisfied with the price being paid for it. By exchange of contracts, the buyer should know exactly what they are getting and by exchanging contracts, both parties become bound to complete the transaction on the terms agreed. The formalities required to complete the transaction can then take place without the risk of the transaction collapsing. However, along with the relief and excitement comes anxiety; exchange of contracts is the point of no return. Once contracts are exchanged, the parties are committed to transferring the property at the agreed price, on the agreed date, and neither can change the terms of the deal without the co-operation of the other. So, there is a great burden of responsibility resting on the solicitors to ensure that the contract reflects the agreed terms and, so far as possible, anticipates problems that may occur before completion.

4.2 The purpose of a contract

A contract is not needed for every property transaction. The contract cannot transfer the land because a deed is needed to do that. A contract is merely an agreement to transfer the land at a later stage. Indeed, it is common when granting a lease to by-pass the contract and proceed straight to completion by granting the lease itself. There are, however, a number of reasons why the parties might want to have a contract. For example, perhaps the parties are satisfied with the property's title and the information revealed in the searches and enquiries, but there is going to be a delay before completion can take place. Usually this is because the buyer's financing arrangements are yet to be finalised, or the parties need more time to organise the practical aspects such as booking a removal company (particularly with a residential transaction where the parties may be in chain and the completion dates must be synchronised). There may also be certain matters not strictly to do with the transfer of the title to the property, such as an obligation on the seller to do certain building work to the property before the sale is completed, which still need a binding contract to make them enforceable.

In all these cases, rather than hoping the other party will not try to change the price or back out altogether, the parties can fix the terms of the transaction by exchanging contracts.

The contract provides both parties with certainty as to the nature and extent of the property, the financial terms, the timetable for completion and, most importantly, it prevents either party withdrawing from the transaction without being liable to the other for breach of contract.

4.3 Standard Conditions of Sale and the Standard Commercial Property Conditions

Once the parties have decided that they need a contract, there is a series of choices to make about which form to use. The contract is usually drafted by the seller's solicitor and sent to the buyer's solicitor as part of the initial pre-contract package. The first choice the seller's solicitor has to make is whether to use a pre-printed form supplied by law stationers, or to draft a contract in their firm's preferred style.

The pre-printed version and the firm's version may look very different, but they tend to include the same elements. In particular, whether the firm uses the pre-printed or its own version, they will need to incorporate a set of 'standard conditions'. Although there are what lawyers call the 'open contract rules' derived from statute and common law to assist where the contract is silent, these rules are not always satisfactory so it is better to have express conditions in the contract. Over the years the profession has devised 'standard conditions' which are designed to work for almost all transactions.

There are two sets of standard conditions commonly in use:

- The Standard Conditions of Sale (5th edition - 2018 Revision)
- The Standard Commercial Property Conditions (3rd edition - 2018 Revision)

The Standard Conditions of Sale ('SC') are used for all residential transactions and some simple commercial transactions, for example those involving properties which are empty, with a straightforward title and a relatively low price. The Standard Commercial Property Conditions ('SCPC') are more suitable for use with high value commercial properties and contain more detailed provisions for the management of occupational leases with which the property is being sold.

Taking the pre-printed versions of the contract first, both the SCs and the SCPCs are divided into three parts.

1. On the front page, there are headings relating to the description of the property and the terms of the sale. These details are unique to the property and the particular transaction and are sometimes referred to as 'the particulars of sale'.
2. In the middle of both versions are what is called the standard conditions, designed to apply to all transactions. These are either the SC or the SCPC, which contain much of the detail. These are the terms that will govern the transaction unless the parties specifically agree something different. The SCPC has two parts, the longer Part 1 which will apply unless excluded and the shorter Part 2 which only apply if specifically included.
3. On the back page are the special conditions - special in the sense that they are specifically drafted to meet the particular requirements of this transaction. There are some pre-printed suggestions at the top of the page and then a blank space into which the parties can insert any requirements of their own.

In firm-specific contracts, each firm's version will be slightly different but each will contain similar details about the property, the financial terms and appropriate special conditions, though perhaps in a different order to the pre-printed versions. In particular, there will usually be a clause incorporating one of the two sets of standard conditions.

4.4 Key conditions in the SC and the SCPC

The front page of a pre-printed contract contains the information about the parties, the property and the financial terms of the transaction. The example below is the front page of a pre-printed contract incorporating the SCs. The seller's solicitor will have obtained information about the buyer, the price, the deposit and the fixtures and fittings when they took instructions (see **1.8**). They should also have information about the seller, which they need to cross-check with the information in the proprietorship register in the official copies for a registered property, or the title deeds for an unregistered property. The title documents will provide the details of the property, including the address and whether the property is freehold or leasehold. The title documents will also reveal whether the property has the benefit of any rights over adjoining properties, such as a right of way. Some practitioners include these in the description of the 'Property', although it is not necessary to do so.

For a registered property, the contract will need to state the title number and the class of title, which is found in the proprietorship register of the official copies. The class of title can either be incorporated into the address by the 'Property' heading or typed in brackets after the 'Title Number' (see **2.3.2**).

Example

CONTRACT

Incorporating the Standard Conditions of Sale (Fifth Edition - 2018 Revision)

For conveyancer's use only

Buyer's conveyancer: ___________________

Seller's conveyancer: ___________________

Law Society Formula: [A/B/C/Personal exchange]

The information above does not form part of the Contract

Date	:	
Seller	:	Leonard Holmes of 10 Bladen Road, Warrington, Cheshire WA1 1SL
Buyer	:	Samira Ahmed of 46 Hales Rise, Liverpool L2 5SH
Property (freehold/~~leasehold~~)	:	10 Bladen Road, Warrington, Cheshire WA1 1SL
Title number/~~root of title~~	:	LM6042 (Absolute Title)
Specified incumbrances	:	The restrictive covenants referred to in entry 1 of the charges register of title number LM6042
Title guarantee (full/~~limited~~)	:	Full
Completion date	:	
Contract rate	:	The Law Society's interest rate from time to time in force
Purchase price	:	£380,000

(*continued*)

Deposit	:	£38,000
Contents price (if separate)	:	Nil
Balance	:	£342,000

The seller will sell and the buyer will buy the property for the purchase price.

WARNING	**Signed**
This is a formal document, designed to create legal rights and legal obligations. Take advice before using it.	Seller/Buyer

An unregistered property is defined in the contract by reference to the root of title. For example:

'56 Blackhorse Drive, Dorking, Surrey RH4 5JS more particularly delineated and edged red on a plan annexed to a Conveyance dated 25 May 1955 between (1) Mark Phillip and (2) Simon Andrew ("The Conveyance")'

The root of title will need to be inserted and can be used to define the Specified incumbrances. For example:

~~Title number~~/root of title: The Conveyance

Specified incumbrances: The covenant contained and referred to in the Conveyance

4.4.1 Specified incumbrances

It is necessary to specify in the contract all the burdens on the property against the heading 'Specified incumbrances'. Incumbrances are third party rights which will survive the transfer of the property to the buyer, such as restrictive covenants, easements and obligations to contribute to shared facilities. If these are not specified, the seller could be in breach of SC 3.1.1, which says that the seller sells free of all incumbrances other than those specified in the contract or of a type listed in SC 3.1.2. The SCPCs have equivalent conditions in SCPC 4.1.1 and SCPC 4.1.2.

SC 3.1.2 and SCPC 4.1.2 **both** list the following as incumbrances subject to which the property is sold:

- those specified in the contract
- those discoverable by inspection before the date of the contract
- those the seller does not and could not reasonably know about
- public requirements.

SC 3.1.2 also includes in its list:

- those, other than mortgages, which the buyer knows about
- entries made before the date of the contract in any public register, except for those maintained by the Land Registry, the Land Charges Department and Companies House.

SCPC 4.1.2 expresses the same concept slightly differently and includes in its list:

- matters, other than mortgages, disclosed or which would have been disclosed by the searches and enquiries which a prudent buyer would have made before entering into the contract.

The seller's solicitor must list as Specified incumbrances in the contract everything not covered by SC 3.1.2 or SCPC 4.1.2. Because the two sets of standard conditions are expressed differently, sellers' solicitors tend to list all incumbrances revealed by their title investigation (whether or not they think they are covered by SC 3.1.2 or SCPC 4.1.2) so as to bring them clearly within the category of 'those specified in the contract'. This is because non-disclosure of an incumbrance burdening the property might result in the buyer having a right to rescind the contract and/or claim damages.

The incumbrances will be revealed in the title documents but must be specified in the contract even though the seller will probably already have deduced title to the buyer at an earlier stage. For a registered property, incumbrances usually appear in the Charges register of the official copies, but the property register should also be checked as burdens are often hidden away there, perhaps where a right benefiting the property has been given subject to an obligation to pay for it.

Some solicitors do not refer to positive covenants as Specified incumbrances because the burden of a positive covenant does not run to a successor in title as a matter of land law. However, many solicitors will include them, particularly if positive covenants are mixed in with restrictive covenants in an entry in the Charges register.

The buyer's solicitor must make sure that the seller's mortgage is not included in the list of incumbrances to which the sale is subject. This is because the mortgage should be discharged shortly after completion (see **5.8.1**).

4.4.2 Title guarantee

A seller can sell with either full or limited title guarantee. A seller should sell with full title guarantee if they own the entire legal and equitable title to the property. Limited title guarantee is given where the seller has limited knowledge of the property, eg where the seller is an executor or trustee. Occasionally a seller will insist that no title guarantee is given at all, eg where the seller is a person appointed following the insolvency of the owner.

A full title guarantee implies more comprehensive implied covenants for title than would be the case with limited title guarantee. With both full and limited title guarantee, the seller will be impliedly covenanting in the transfer of the property that:

1. They have the right to dispose of the land
2. They will do all they reasonably can to transfer the title
3. In the case of leasehold land, the lease is subsisting at the time of disposal and there is no breach of covenant making the lease liable to forfeiture.

With full title guarantee, the seller will also impliedly covenant that the land is disposed free from incumbrances other than those the seller does not know about and could not reasonably know about. Section 6 of Law of Property (Miscellaneous Provisions) Act 1994 limits this covenant to exclude matters to which the disposition is expressly made subject, matters about which the buyer knows at the time of the disposition and matters which at the time of the disposal were entered on the registers of title. However, this is still a wider covenant than the one implied by giving limited title guarantee, namely that the seller has not incumbered the property and is not aware that anyone else has done so since the last disposition for value (so a seller who purchased the land for value will only be covenanting that incumbrances have not been created since they acquired the property).

Both sets of standard conditions provide that the seller will sell with full title guarantee (SC 4.6.2 and SCPC 7.6.2) so if the seller does not wish to sell with full title guarantee, a special condition amending the standard conditions will be needed.

4.4.3 Contract rate

The Contract rate is the rate of interest that will be charged if a party is late in completing. The interest is charged on the purchase price (less the deposit if it is the buyer in default as the buyer has already handed this over on exchange). The rate must be high enough to incentivise a potentially defaulting party to complete on time. Most conveyancers opt for 'the Law Society's interest rate from time to time in force', which is published weekly in the *Gazette* and is currently 4% above the base lending rate of Barclays Bank plc. This is, in fact, what the SCs and SCPCs already provide at 1.1.1(e), so if the parties are happy to use this rate, it is not necessary to fill in the gap on the front page of the contract, but it is common practice to do so. Sometimes the parties will specify a rate which is a specified percentage above the base rate of a different bank, often the bank used by the seller. The exact percentage above the relevant base rate is a matter for negotiation, with anything between 2–4% being considered within the normal range. See **5.9** for more detail on remedies for late completion.

4.4.4 Deposit: stakeholder and agent

A deposit is a pre-payment of part of the purchase price made by the buyer to the seller. It is evidence of the buyer's commitment to the transaction and if the buyer fails to complete, under SC 7.4 or SCPC 10.5 the seller may forfeit and keep the deposit. SC 2.2 and SCPC 3.2 provide that a deposit of 10% of the purchase price is payable on exchange of contracts and is paid to the seller's solicitor as 'stakeholder', which means that the seller's solicitor cannot hand it over to the seller until completion. However, if the SC are being used, SC 2.2.5 allows the seller to use the deposit as a deposit on a related purchase of a house for the seller.

The parties can agree to vary this arrangement:

- Sometimes the seller will agree to accept a reduced deposit, perhaps 5% instead of 10%, and this should be clearly stated on the front of the contract. This is a risk for the seller as there will be less of a fund to forfeit if the buyer fails to complete and the parties should consider incorporating a special condition requiring the buyer to top up the deposit to the full amount if completion is delayed.
- Sometimes the buyer will agree that the deposit can to be held by the seller's solicitor as 'agent' rather than stakeholder. This means that the deposit can be released to the seller immediately after exchange and can be used by the seller for any purpose whatsoever. This is a risk for the buyer because if the parties do not complete, the seller may not be a position to return the deposit, eg where the seller has become insolvent.

The deposit is paid on exchange of contracts. The SC provide that that the deposit can be paid by electronic means or by cheque drawn on the conveyancer's client account. The SCPC provide for payment by electronic means only. In both cases the funds must come from an account in the name of a conveyancer at a clearing bank. An electronic payment must be paid into the account in the name of the seller's conveyancer at a clearing bank, or in the case of the SC where SC 2.2.5 applies and the deposit is being used to fund the deposit on a related purchase, to an account at a clearing bank of a conveyancer nominated by the seller's conveyancer.

Example

Lui Chen is downsizing and has agreed to sell her large detached house to Paul and Wendy Blake. Lui has already found a new property to move into – a flat in the same neighbourhood. She has told the Blakes that she would like to use their deposit as soon as possible following exchange of contracts to fund the deposit she needs to provide on her purchase.

Will she be able to do this?

Answer

This depends what the contract says about what happens to the deposit between exchange and completion. If the contract incorporates the SC, then SC 2.2.5 allows Lui to put some or all of the deposit she receives from the Blakes towards the deposit she has to pay on her purchase as the facts indicate she is buying another property in England as her residence. As Lui is downsizing it is likely that the deposit on the house is larger than the deposit on the flat; any part of the house deposit not being used to fund the flat deposit must be held as stakeholder.

If the contract incorporates the SCPC, then SC 3.3.2 stipulates that the deposit is to be held by the seller's solicitor as stakeholder, which means it cannot be used for this, or any other purpose. A special condition would be needed to override SCPC 3.3.2.

It is unusual to have a simultaneous sale and purchase in a commercial context.

4.5 The purpose of, and matters covered by, special conditions

Special conditions relate to the individual characteristics of the property and the particular circumstances of the transaction. Special conditions appear on the back page of a pre-printed contract: the example below is the back page of a pre-printed contract incorporating the SCs.

Example

SPECIAL CONDITIONS

1 (a) This contract incorporates the Standard Conditions of Sale (Fifth Edition – 2018 Revision).

(b) The terms used in this contract have the same meaning when used in the Conditions.

2 Subject to the terms of this contract and to the Standard Conditions of Sale, the seller is to transfer the property with either full title guarantee or limited title guarantee, as specified on the front page.

3 (a) ~~The sale includes those contents which are indicated on the attached list as included in the sale and the buyer is to pay the contents price for them.~~

(b) ~~The sale excludes those fixtures which are at the property and are indicated on the attached list as excluded from the sale.~~

4 The property is sold with vacant possession.

(or)

4 ~~The property is sold subject to the following leases or tenancies:~~

5 ~~Conditions 6.1.2 and 6.1.3 shall take effect as if the time specified in them were rather than 2.00 p.m.~~

6 **Representations**

Neither party can rely on any representation made by the other, unless made in writing by the other or his conveyancer, but this does not exclude liability for fraud or recklessness.

7 **Occupier's consent**

~~Each occupier identified below agrees with the seller and the buyer, in consideration of their entering into this contract, that the occupier concurs in the sale of the property on the terms of this contract, undertakes to vacate the property on or before the completion date and releases the property and any included fixtures and contents from any right or interest that the occupier may have.~~

~~Note: this condition does not apply to occupiers under leases or tenancies subject to which the property is sold.~~

~~Name(s) and signature(s) of the occupier(s) (if any):~~

~~Name~~ ________

~~Signature~~

Space for incorporating special conditions

Notices may be sent to:

Seller's conveyancer's name: Johnson Bell LLP, 23 Victoria Street, Warrington, Cheshire WA1 2LN

E-mail address:* *tfallon@johnsonbell.co.uk*

Buyer's conveyancer's name: Dovedays LLP, 15 Albert Street, Nottingham NG1 4RX

E-mail address:* *kirsty.ryland@dovedays.co.uk*

*Adding an e-mail address authorises service by e-mail see condition 1.3.3(b)

There are some pre-printed special conditions, such as whether the sale includes any contents or excludes any fixtures (special condition 3) and whether the property is to be sold with vacant possession or subject to leases or tenancies (special condition 4). Special condition 5 will only be relevant where the time for completion has been altered by agreement and should be deleted if the parties have agreed that completion should take place by 2pm on the agreed day (see **5.9**). Special condition 6 is a standard clause that should be left in as it makes it clear to the parties that they should not rely on any representations that have not been made in writing, eg something said while viewing the property at the marketing stage. Special condition 7 will need to be completed where there is a non-owning adult occupier of the property; the occupier is agreeing to the sale and to give vacant possession on completion, and releasing any rights they may have in the property to allow the sale to take place (see **2.5.11** and **3.5.6**). These pre-printed special conditions need to be individually checked to decide which ones are relevant to a particular transaction.

There is also space to incorporate new special conditions. Because every property transaction is unique, it is impossible to describe everything that might require a special condition. However, as a starting point, the parties may require special conditions dealing with:

- the appointment of a second trustee for the purposes of the transfer (see **2.5.4**)
- arranging for the seller to obtain or pay for a restrictive covenant insurance policy (see **2.5.5**)
- disclosing a defect in title (eg see **2.5.7**)
- the seller selling with limited or no title guarantee (see **4.4.2** above)
- a deposit of less than 10% and/or for the deposit to be held as agent rather than stakeholder (see **4.4.4** above)
- the payment of VAT (see **4.4.7** below)
- the removal of fixtures by the seller (see example below)
- the inclusion of an indemnity covenant in the transfer to protect the seller from liability once they have lost physical possession of the property (see **2.5.6**).

An indemnity covenant is necessary when the title is burdened with covenants and the seller is either the original covenantor or has given an indemnity covenant to their seller when they acquired the property. This means they will have ongoing liability even after they part with the property and are no longer in a position to ensure compliance with the covenants. This is not so much of an issue with restrictive covenants as the burden will run with the land to the next owner. However, the burden of the positive covenant does not run with the land and so, if there is a breach of a positive covenant, the covenantee will sue the seller for any loss. Therefore SC 4.6.4 and SCPC 7.6.5 state that, where the seller has such an ongoing liability in relation to the property, the buyer must give the seller a personal indemnity covenant in the transfer, ie they will require a covenant from the buyer to observe the covenants affecting the title and, should the buyer breach them, to indemnify the seller should they be sued as a result under their original covenant. As this is covered by SC 4.6.4 there is no need to expressly insert a special condition to this effect but some solicitors do so to act as a reminder to check that this term has been included in the transfer.

Where the parties have agreed to something more unusual, their solicitors must consider what the contract already says about such matters in either the standard or pre-printed special conditions and whether that is good enough, or a new special condition should be drafted.

Example

You act for BGD Accountants Limited ('BGD'), the sellers of Manor House. In the entrance hall to Manor House there is a bronze statue by a famous sculptor which has been cemented to the floor. The statue is very valuable and has not been included in the purchase price as BGD wish to take it with them.

Do you need a special condition and what should it say?

The statue is likely to be a fixture and will automatically pass to the buyer with the land unless a special condition is included giving BGD the right to remove it. The contract should include pre-printed special condition 3(b), but should also have another special condition imposing a timetable for removal of the statue and making BGD responsible for making good any damage caused by its removal.

4.6 Insurance and risk

Under both sets of standard conditions, the risk of damage to the property passes to the buyer on exchange of contracts (SC 5.1.1 and SCPC 8.1). This means that the buyer must complete the purchase even if the property is damaged or destroyed between exchange and completion. The buyer may not be expecting this so will need prior warning so that insurance arrangements can be put into place at the moment of exchange. The buyer and any lender will need to be satisfied that the insurance is adequate in terms of the value of the property, the estimated cost of reinstatement and the type of risks covered. Where the buyer is financing the purchase with a mortgage the lender may insure the property on being requested to do by the buyer's solicitor, but if not, the buyer will have to take out a new insurance policy. Alternatively, buyers with several properties may already have a 'block policy' to which the new property can be added.

SC 5 and SCPC 8 provide that the seller is under no obligation to insure a freehold property unless required to do so by a special condition in the contract. It may be appropriate for the parties to agree that risk should remain with the seller, eg on a new build property in the course of construction. If this is agreed, then SC 5.1.3 and SCPC 8.1.2 require the seller to maintain the policy until completion and if the property suffers damage prior to completion, to hand the insurance proceeds over to the buyer or assign to the buyer all the seller's rights under the policy.

Even in those cases where risk does pass to the buyer on exchange, the seller will probably not cancel their policy in case the buyer fails to complete or because it is a term of their mortgage that the policy is maintained. Where there are two policies in place on the same property, there is a danger that when a claim is made, the buyer's insurer will reduce the proceeds because another policy exists. SC 5.1.5 and SCPC 8.2.4(b) therefore provide that if this happens and the buyer is unable to recover the full amount of the proceeds, the purchase price is reduced accordingly.

4.7 Basics of VAT in a contract

As explained in **1.6.3**, VAT is not normally chargeable in residential transactions. The seller's solicitor will usually choose to incorporate the SC, which provide in SC 1.4 that the purchase price and the contents price are inclusive of any VAT (because it is expected that no VAT will be charged or paid).

Contracts for the sale and purchase of commercial property should deal with whether the buyer will have to pay VAT in addition to the purchase price. VAT is payable when the property is less than three years old, or because the seller has exercised the option to tax. There are three possibilities:

(a) The purchase price is exclusive of VAT and VAT will be added on top.

(b) The purchase price is inclusive of VAT so that VAT, if any, cannot be added on top.

(c) The purchase price is exclusive of VAT, so VAT can be added on top in the unlikely event that the law changes to make an exempt supply chargeable at the standard rate, but the seller is contractually obliged not to opt to tax.

Taking each option in turn:

(a) The purchase price is exclusive of VAT and VAT will be added on top (SCPC 2)

This would be appropriate for the standard rated supply of a commercial building within three years of construction where seller has no choice but to charge VAT. It would also be appropriate for the sale of an old commercial property where the seller needs to opt to tax to recover VAT paid on refurbishment and/or professional costs and the buyer is not VAT-sensitive. In this case, SCPC 2 is the appropriate contract term:

2. VAT STANDARD RATED SUPPLY

    2.1 The seller warrants that the sale of the property will constitute a supply chargeable to VAT at the standard rate.

    2.2 The buyer is to pay to the seller on completion an additional amount equal to the VAT in exchange for a VAT invoice from the seller.

(b) The purchase price is inclusive of VAT so that VAT, if any, cannot be added on top (SC 1.4 or a special condition in an SCPC contract)

If the supply is standard rated, the supplier will have to account to HMRC for the VAT out of the purchase price. So this option would definitely not be appropriate for the sale of a new building or one where the seller has exercised the option to tax. It might be appropriate for the supply of an old commercial building where the seller does not have input VAT to recover (eg the seller has not carried out a refurbishment) and so has no reason to opt to tax. This is a popular option with VAT-sensitive buyers who cannot recover VAT paid on the purchase price. It is still a risk for the seller, as the law might change and a supply of land that used to be exempt becomes standard rated: the seller will have to take the VAT out of the agreed purchase price.

In this case, SC 1.4 (or an equivalent provision incorporated into an SCPC contract by a special condition) is the appropriate contractual provision:

1.4 VAT

1.4.1 The purchase price and the contents price are inclusive of any value added tax.

(c) The purchase price is exclusive of VAT, so VAT can be added on top if the law changes between exchange of contracts and completion to make an exempt supply chargeable at the standard rate, but the seller is contractually obliged not to opt to tax (SCPC Part 2, Condition A1)

This is appropriate for the supply of an old commercial building where the seller does not have input VAT to recover so does not need to opt to tax, but is not willing to take the risk that there will be a change in the tax regime between exchange and completion that would turn their originally exempt supply into a taxable supply, and the buyer is VAT-sensitive or would rather not pay VAT as there will be a cash-flow delay in recovering VAT on the purchase price. In this case, the parties should use the SCPC contract but incorporate one of the optional standard conditions in Part 2, condition A1. This disapplies SCPC 2 and provides instead that the seller will not opt to tax the supply of the property before completion, but will have the right to charge VAT in addition to the purchase price if, between exchange and completion, there is a change in the law making the sale of the property a supply chargeable to VAT.

Example

You act for Kerrier Property Investments PLC ('Kerrier'). Kerrier has agreed to buy Shaftesbury House from Cranbourne Properties Limited ('Cranbourne') as an investment property for a purchase price of £3,000,000 exclusive of any VAT. Cranbourne has not opted to tax the property for VAT purposes. The seller's solicitor has sent through a contract incorporating the Standard Commercial Property Conditions (3rd edition - 2018 Revision).

Cranbourne bought the site in 2011 and the construction of a retail building on the site was completed in 2014. The lease of the first tenant has expired and Shaftesbury House will be sold with vacant possession.

What is the VAT status of this transaction and what should the contract say about VAT?

Answer

This is the sale of an 'old' freehold property, as construction was completed more than three years ago (although the precise date of completion of construction in 2014 should be confirmed). This means that the sale and purchase transaction is exempt subject to the option to tax. We are told that Cranbourne has not opted to tax.

The purchase price is stated to be exclusive of any VAT. Further, SCPC 2 states that the buyer will be required to pay VAT in addition to the purchase price. From its name, Kerrier is unlikely to be a VAT-sensitive buyer and Cranbourne has not felt the need to exercise the option to tax. A fair position for the parties to agree is that Kerrier will not liable to pay VAT in addition to the purchase price, unless the VAT status of the transaction is changed between exchange and completion by a change in the law. This can be done by incorporating A1 of the Part 2 standard conditions into the contract.

4.8 The requirements of a lender

One of the most important parts of any property transaction is the funding of the purchase. For the vast majority of residential transactions, most of the finance will be by way of a mortgage. Even cash-rich buyers of commercial property will choose to borrow the money to purchase because the interest payable on the loan is a deductible expense for tax purposes and, for a large company, could be less than the return they will make by investing the cash or using it in other ways in the business operation.

Given their financial input for the transaction (which can be up to 95% of the value of the property), mortgage lenders seek to limit their exposure to the risks by setting out their own specific instructions and requirements for a conveyancer. For a potential buyer the important considerations in choosing a mortgage lender will be the amount that they can borrow, the interest rates available and the particular products on offer. They may not have considered whether the chosen lender has any specific requirements as to the nature of the property to be purchased, or the amount of control a lender has over decisions that need to be made in the conveyancing process. Most buyers appreciate that a lender will perform a basic valuation on a property to ensure it is suitable for securing the mortgage, but lenders also have requirements that they instruct the conveyancer to check specifically on their behalf and these instructions vary from lender to lender.

Once the lender is satisfied that the property is good security for the loan and that the buyer is creditworthy, the lender will issue a document to the buyer setting out the terms on which the lender is prepared to make the loan. This is in the form of a 'mortgage offer' for residential and simple commercial loans, or for more complex loans, a commitment letter with a term sheet attached followed by a facility agreement containing the detailed terms of the lending arrangement.

These documents give details of the loan amount, the interest rate, the term, the initial repayments and any other conditions eg that the buyer must carry out certain repair works. If so, there may be a retention from the mortgage advance until the works are done, which means that the borrower will have to find the sum retained from other sources in order to complete. The mortgage offer may allow the lender to withdraw the offer, even after the buyer has exchanged contracts. The solicitor acting for the buyer must ensure that the buyer has received, understood and, if required by the lender, accepted the mortgage offer prior to exchange of contracts.

In terms of further documents required by the lender, most lenders will want a first legal mortgage over the property owned by the borrower. Mortgages are legal if made by deed and completed by registration. This is important to a lender as a mortgage made by deed has implied into it a power of sale under s 101 of the Law of Property Act 1925, although a mortgage deed will usually have an express power. A lender will want a first legal mortgage so in the event that the borrower cannot repay the loan, it is paid first out of any proceeds of sale. The mortgage is likely to be a single mortgage deed in the lender's standard form, perhaps incorporating the lender's standard terms and conditions (a published booklet) and, if the lender is a Building Society, the Building Society Rules. The borrower's solicitor is under an obligation to explain to the borrower as to its obligations under the mortgage deed and, in particular, advise on the consequences of defaulting on the mortgage payments and the powers of the lender in the event of default.

4.9 Acting for the lender

Once it has sent the mortgage offer to the borrower, the lender will instruct solicitors to act on its behalf on the mortgage of the property. As discussed in **1.3.3**, under The Code of Conduct it is possible for a solicitor to act for a lender and a borrower on a property transaction under paragraph 6.2, even if there is a conflict of interest, provided that the clients have a substantial common interest and all the safeguards in para 6.2(i)–(iii) are in place. In residential conveyancing, the mortgage is likely to be on standard terms and it is common for the solicitor to act for both borrower and lender. However, a commercial mortgage is much less likely to be offered on standard terms and the terms of the mortgage documentation often have to be negotiated and agreed. It is much harder to act for more than one client when the solicitor may need to negotiate on matters of substance on their behalf.

Even where the lender is separately represented, it is common for the buyer's solicitor to report to the lender on the results of the title investigation and the pre-contract searches and enquiries. The lender needs to know the borrower will have good title to the property just as much as the buyer, because it wants to know it can sell the property in the future if it needs to enforce the security. The buyer's solicitor will be asked to prepare a certificate of title to disclose to the lender any problems with the property (see **4.10** below). The lender's solicitor can then help the lender decide what action it wants to take in relation to any problems disclosed. Alternatively, the lender's solicitor will obtain copies of title and searches etc. from the borrower's solicitor and report to the lender direct, with the borrower paying the costs.

The majority of UK mortgage lenders are members of UK Finance or the Building Societies Association. UK Finance collates and provides the instructions for individual member lenders and makes these available to view online in the UK Finance Mortgage Lenders' Handbook for Conveyancers. The Handbook provides comprehensive instructions for the conveyancer on a wide range of matters from covering the matters a specific lender will lend on, the type of searches required by the lender through to what circumstances indemnity insurance for defects in title can be accepted. Part 1 applies to all lenders using the Handbook, Part 2 is where individual lenders set out specific requirements that are different to Part 1. Part 3 sets out standard instructions to be used where a conveyancer is representing the lender but not the borrower. Although designed for the residential market, some lenders will use the Handbook for commercial loans or issue instructions that are very similar.

The lender's requirements must be met before the conveyancer will be in a position to request the release (draw down) of the mortgage funds and this will be the case irrespective of whether the buyer wishes to proceed to complete. Should a conflict of interest or instructions arise between the instructions of the buyer and the requirements of the lender the solicitor will be unable to proceed to purchase using the mortgage lender's funds until the conflict of interest is resolved to the lender's satisfaction.

4.10 Purpose of, and timing for issuing, a certificate of title to the lender

The lender will want to know that the property is adequate security for the loan. In particular, the lender will require a certificate from the solicitor acting for them that the property has 'good and marketable' title. In residential transactions, the lender will usually require a certificate of title in the form approved by the Law Society and UK Finance which aims to reduce the risk of a conflict of interest when a solicitor acts for both the lender and the borrower. The certificate confirms to the lender:

- there are no legal problems with the property (it has a 'good and marketable title') so the lender can safely lend against it
- who will own the property once the sale is completed
- the completion date when the funds are needed.

In commercial transactions, the lender is likely to require a more detailed certificate of title, such as the one produced by the City of London Law Society. This certificate is a report about a property, a summary of the information which has been ascertained by a solicitor in the title investigation and the pre-contract searches and enquiries. It is prepared by the buyer's solicitor based on information from their pre-contract investigations: sometimes it will be addressed to the buyer and the lender, sometimes just the lender. The benefit of the certificate is that it reduces the volume of paperwork to be reviewed and avoids the need for duplication of the title investigation and searches and enquiries. Therefore it saves time and expense for the borrower and the lender.

The certificate is structured as a series of statements about the property, eg 'There are no mortgages, charges or liens, legal or equitable, specific or floating, affecting the Property'. If this is not the case, then any such mortgages etc are disclosed immediately below the statement, eg 'The Property is subject to a mortgage dated 1 February 2013 in favour of Barclays Bank PLC'. If the information in the certificate is wrong, the lender can sue the firm which gave the certificate because there are warranties as to the correctness of the information contained within it. For example, the firm warrants that 'Subject to any Disclosures, in our opinion, subject to due registration at the Land Registry of the transfer of the Property from the seller to the Company, the Company has a good and marketable title to the Property...'

The certificate is given immediately prior to completion of the loan. Drafts will be provided to the buyer/lender's advisors at earlier stages in the transaction so they will have early warning of any major issues. The buyer's solicitors will not exchange contracts until they know the lender is satisfied with the certificate and any disclosures.

4.11 Purpose and process of reporting to the client

The parties have now reached a critical stage in the transaction. Both sets of solicitors have taken their client's initial instructions. The seller's solicitor has investigated their client's title, prepared the draft contract and deduced evidence of title to the buyer's solicitor. The buyer's solicitor has raised the pre-contract searches and enquiries and the results have been received and analysed. The buyer's solicitor has also investigated the seller's title and approved the draft contract. Any issues arising from investigation of title and/or the searches and enquiries will have been successfully resolved by the time the parties are ready to exchange contracts.

At this point the buyer's solicitor will send to the buyer a pre-contract report summing up the results of the pre-contract searches and the investigation of title. The report usually also explains the terms of the contract and the mortgage offer. The report will also include some disclaimers, eg that the solicitor cannot advise on the value or structure of the property.

4.12 Preparation for and exchange of contracts

The following steps should be taken in preparation for exchange of contracts:

(a) Report to client

The buyer's solicitor should report to the buyer in writing, explaining the results of title investigation, searches and enquiries and the terms of the contract and the mortgage offer.

(b) Report to lender

The buyer's solicitor should report to the lender, who will need to know the property is good security for the loan and has 'good and marketable title'.

(c) Ensure deposit funds are available

The deposit funds should be available to the buyer's solicitor in cleared funds, ready to send to the seller's solicitor at exchange of contracts.

(d) Check the mortgage offer is in place and that the client has sufficient funds to complete

The buyer needs to have the mortgage offer in place (and accepted it) and to have complied with any conditions attached to the mortgage offer (or be in a position to do so). The buyer's solicitor should also check that the buyer has the funds to proceed with the purchase at completion.

(e) Ensure arrangements are in place for insurance immediately following exchange

In most cases the contractual position is that risk passes to the buyer on exchange and therefore the buyer needs to have insurance in place from exchange. These arrangements need to have be made in advance of actual exchange so the insurance takes effect immediately.

(f) Contract signed

Both solicitors need to ensure that their client has signed their copy of the contract. In many cases a client will sign in 'wet ink', although a 2019 Law Commission report concluded that an electronic signature can lawfully be used to execute a document provided the person signing the document intends to authenticate it and any execution formalities are satisfied. A solicitor can sign the contract on their client's behalf if they have the client's express authority to do so.

(g) Completion date

Both solicitors will need to discuss this with their client and the other side in advance of exchange of contracts.

4.13 The practice, method and authority to exchange

Before exchanging contracts, both solicitors must obtain their client's authority to exchange. Authority should be obtained in writing and a note made on the file because a solicitor who exchanges contracts without their client's express or implied authority will be liable to the client in negligence. The clients should be made aware of the consequences of exchange, ie that they can no longer withdraw from the contract.

The main requirements for creating a binding contract for the sale of land are set out in s 2(1) of the Law of Property (Miscellaneous Provisions) Act 1989. These are that the contract must be in writing; it must incorporate all the agreed terms; these must be contained in one document, or where contracts are exchanged, in each copy of the contract; and, finally, the contract must be signed by the parties. It is usual in most transactions to exchange identical copies of the contract, rather than rely on a single document, so that each of the parties has something in their possession to which they can refer. Each copy is either signed by all the parties or, more commonly, each party signs only their own copy of the contract, which is then physically exchanged for the copy signed by the other party.

Exchange of contracts can be done in any one of three ways:

1. In person, by one solicitor attending the other's office and handing the contract over.
2. By post, with each solicitor sending their client's part of the contract by post to the other solicitor's office.
3. Over the telephone.

Exchanging contracts in person obviously has the great advantage of certainty as the solicitors can physically receive the contract. However, the solicitors rarely have the time to travel to the other solicitor's office to exchange contracts personally. They could instruct an agent to exchange contracts on their behalf but that adds to the cost of the transaction. Using the post saves them from having to personally travel to exchange contracts but the postal system can be unreliable.

The quickest, most cost-effective and reliable way to exchange contracts is to telephone the other solicitor and agree over the phone that contracts are exchanged. This only works if there are arrangements in place to ensure that each solicitor forwards their client's part of the contract to the other and the seller's solicitor receives the buyer's deposit. The Law Society has produced three protocols, known as Law Society Formulae A, B, and C, which can be followed by the parties' solicitors. The advantage of these formulae is that they all involve undertakings from the solicitors which, if breached, can result in disciplinary action against the offending party.

Law Society Formula A is used where one solicitor holds both parts of the contract duly signed. This means that one of the solicitors will have already sent their client's signed part of the contract to the other side prior to exchange of contracts. In Formula A, the undertakings are that the solicitor holding both signed parts of the contract will, that same day, send their client's signed part of the contract to the other side by first class post, through a document exchange, or by hand. The buyer's solicitor also undertakes, that day, to send to the other side a banker's draft or client account cheque for the agreed deposit, with their client's signed part of the contract if it is the buyer's solicitor who holds both parts.

Law Society Formula B is used where each solicitor holds their own client's signed part of the contract. It can be a quicker method of exchange because, unlike Formula A, it does not require one of the solicitors to send their client's signed part of the contract to the other side before an exchange can take place. The undertakings in a Formula B exchange are that each solicitor holds their own client's signed part of the contract; that each solicitor will, that same day, send the signed part of the contract that they are holding to the other side by first class post, through a document exchange, or by hand duly dated; and that the buyer's solicitor, together with the signed part of the contract, will that day also send to the other side a banker's draft or client account cheque for the agreed deposit. In practice, Formula B is by far the most common way of exchanging contracts.

Formula A and Formula B both contain the undertaking that the buyer's solicitor will send to the seller's solicitor a banker's draft or client account cheque. If the deposit is to be sent electronically (as permitted by the SC and required by the SCPC), the relevant formula will have to be varied accordingly by agreement between the two solicitors.

Formula C is the most complex of the three formulae and is used mainly in residential property work when there is a chain transaction. A chain transaction occurs where there are two or more properties being sold. The paramount aim is to synchronise all the exchanges in the chain so that nobody ends up owning two properties, their own and the one that they are buying, or no property at all. However, it is little used in practice because it is so complex.

In each case, the solicitors should record the exchange. Conventionally, details of the time of exchange and the formula used are often written by the respective solicitors in the top corner of the front page of the contracts being exchanged. This is done at the time of the phone call exchanging contracts. A file note is also made recording the fact of exchange with the following information:

- the date and time of exchange;
- the formula used and the exact wording of any agreed variation to the formula;
- the completion date;
- the deposit to be paid; and
- the identities of the solicitors involved in the exchange.

4.14 The consequences of exchange

Following exchange, a binding contract exists from which neither party may withdraw without incurring liability for breach. The seller retains the legal title in the property until completion, but holds the beneficial interest on behalf of the buyer. During this period, the seller is entitled to remain in physical possession of the property (although it is possible for the parties to agree that the buyer can occupy the property as licensee (see SC 5.2.2)). The seller must pay the outgoings, such as the community charge or business rates, until completion. Unless the contract provides otherwise, the buyer bears the risk of any loss or damage to the property, hence the need to ensure that insurance of the property is in place and effective from the moment of exchange.

Immediately after exchange, the solicitors should inform their respective clients and the estate agent that exchange has taken place and, if the exchange has taken place over the telephone, comply with the undertakings in the relevant Law Society Formula.

Summary

- It is important to resolve all outstanding queries and make sure appropriate financial arrangements are in place before exchange of contracts, because it is not usually possible for either party to withdraw from, or change the terms of, the contract after exchange.
- The seller's solicitor will draft the contract, which will then need to be reviewed by and agreed with the buyer's solicitor.
- A contract for sale must be in writing, contain all agreed terms and be signed by all parties. It will normally comprise the particulars of sale, the standard conditions of sale and the special conditions of sale.
- The particulars of sale should give a clear and concise description of the property and confirm whether it is leasehold or freehold.
- Most contracts will incorporate either the Standard Conditions of Sale (Fifth Edition) or the Standard Commercial Property Conditions (Second Edition). These have been produced by practitioners to deal with issues common to most property transactions.
- Special conditions will be needed to vary or supplement the position under the standard conditions, or to deal with matters specific to the transaction.
- The purpose of a deposit is to demonstrate the buyer's commitment to the purchase. The deposit is usually 10% of the purchase price.
- A deposit is usually held by the seller's solicitor in the capacity of stakeholder. There are risks associated with the deposit being held in the capacity of agent, and these risks must be explained to a buyer client.
- The contract will normally provide that the buyer must complete the purchase even if the property is damaged or destroyed between exchange and completion. Therefore the buyer's insurance must be in place immediately on exchange.
- If VAT is, or could become, chargeable on a property transaction, the contract must contain provisions to deal with it.
- In residential transactions, the solicitor may be instructed to act for the buyer as well as the lender. In commercial transactions, buyer and lender are usually represented separately.
- In residential (or straightforward commercial) transactions, a lender will issue a mortgage offer indicating the terms on which it is willing to lend. In more complex commercial transactions the offer will be in the form of a commitment letter with a term sheet attached, followed by a facility agreement containing the detailed terms of the lending arrangement.
- When acting for a lender in a residential transaction, the solicitor will usually have to carry out standardised instructions as set out in the UK Finance Lender's Handbook.
- The lender will require confirmation from its solicitor that the property has a good and marketable title.

- The borrower's solicitor must explain the nature and effect of the mortgage documentation to the borrower. They should also explain the key terms of the mortgage.
- The buyer's solicitor should report to the buyer on the results of the title investigation and the searches and enquiries. They should also explain the key terms of the contract.
- Contracts may be exchanged in person, by telephone or by post. Personal exchange is the safest method, postal exchange is the least safe method. Telephone exchange is the most common method.
- The Law Society has devised three formulae for telephone exchange, based on mutual undertakings. The choice of formula will depend on which parts of the contract each solicitor holds and whether there is a related sale or purchase.
- Each solicitor should explain the effect of exchange to the client and obtain their authority to exchange before doing so.

Sample questions

Question 1

A solicitor is acting for a buyer of a freehold property and exchanged contracts last week using the Standard Conditions of Sale (Fifth edition - 2018 Revision) with no relevant special conditions. Completion is to take place tomorrow. The seller's solicitor has just rung to say that there has been a fire at the property and it has been damaged.

Which one of the following best describes the advice the solicitor should give about the implications of the fire for the sale and purchase transaction:

A The buyer will have to complete the purchase, but the seller will have to repair the property and pay damages for the delay in completion.

B The seller is responsible for any damage which they cause, but not if the damage is caused by others.

C The buyer may rescind the contract and claim back their deposit.

D The risk passes from the seller to the buyer on exchange of contracts and so the buyer will have to complete the purchase. The buyer can claim on the insurance that they should have taken out on exchange.

E Completion will be delayed until the seller has received the insurance proceeds and used them to reinstate the property.

Answer

Option D is correct. Under SC 5, risk passes to the buyer on exchange, which means that that the buyer must complete the purchase even if the property is damaged or destroyed between exchange and completion. The buyer is unable to rescind the contract even if the property is destroyed (so option C is wrong). SC 5 also provides that the seller is under no obligation to insure a freehold property unless required to do so by a special condition in the contract and the facts tell us that there were no relevant special conditions in this case (so option E is wrong and option B is not the best answer). The buyer should have been advised to take out insurance on the property to come into effect on exchange, so they would be able to make a claim under the policy (as in option D), rather than look to the seller (as in option A).

Question 2

In which of the following circumstances should a solicitor acting on a sale and purchase of a commercial property recommend that in the contract the purchase price is expressed to be inclusive of VAT?

A The solicitor is acting for a buyer which is an insurance company.

B The solicitor is acting for a buyer which is a firm of accountants.

C The solicitor is acting for a seller and the property has been recently constructed.

D The solicitor is acting for a seller and the property is a 1950s office building.

E The solicitor is acting for a seller and the buyer is an insurance company.

Answer

Option A is correct. An insurance company is 'VAT-sensitive', ie it makes exempt supplies and may not be able to recover any VAT it has to pay on the purchase price. By contrast, a firm of accountants makes mainly standard rated supplies and is unlikely to object to paying VAT in addition to the purchase price since it will recover it (so option B is not the best answer).

A seller should never be advised by its own solicitor to make the purchase price inclusive of VAT (so options C, D and E are wrong). This is because if the supply is standard-rated (as with a new building), or it wants to opt to tax in order to recover VAT paid on refurbishment (as with the 1950s building), or the law changes the VAT status of the sale between exchange and completion, the seller will be unable to add the VAT to the agreed price. The sale proceeds will be reduced by the amount of VAT payable to HM Revenue and Customs.

Of course the seller may have to agree to a VAT inclusive purchase price as part of the commercial terms for the transaction, in which case, the seller's solicitor must draw their client's attention to the possible financial consequences of that decision.

Question 3

A solicitor acts for a buyer who is buying a property from the executor of a deceased owner. The title to the property is currently unregistered. The executor is described in the contract as the seller. The solicitor is explaining to the client the concept of 'limited title guarantee' referred to in the contract.

Which of the following is the best advice to the buyer about the seller selling with limited title guarantee?

A The seller should be selling the property with full title guarantee if the grant of probate appointing the executor has been granted, rather than limited title guarantee.

B Limited title guarantee means that there is an implied covenant that the seller has not incumbered the title to the property and the seller is not aware that anyone else has done so since the last disposition for value.

C Limited title guarantee means that once the title to the Property is registered, the class of title in the proprietorship register will be Possessory Title.

D Limited title guarantee means that there is an implied covenant that the property is disposed free from incumbrances other than those the seller does not know about and could not reasonably know about.

E Limited title guarantee means that once the title to the property is registered, the class of title on the proprietorship register will be Qualified Title.

Answer

Option B is the best answer as it is the correct definition of limited title guarantee. Option A is not the best answer as you would expect an executor to sell with limited title guarantee because they will have limited knowledge of the property. Option D describes full title guarantee. Options C and E are not the best answers as title guarantee for the purpose of the contract does not link to the class of title in registered land (see **2.3.2(b)**); the property may still be registered with Absolute Title even though it has been sold to the buyer by a seller only offering limited or no title guarantee. Title guarantee is about the seller; class of title is about the property.

5 Completion

5.1	Introduction	92
5.2	Pre-completion steps	92
5.3	Form of transfer deed and formalities for execution	92
5.4	Pre-completion searches	97
5.5	Practical arrangements for completion	103
5.6	Ensuring finances are in order for completion	103
5.7	Methods and effect of completion	104
5.8	Post-completion steps	105
5.9	Remedies for delayed completion	107

SQE1 syllabus

This chapter will enable you to achieve the SQE1 Assessment Specification in relation to Functioning Legal Knowledge concerned with the following:

- Pre-completion steps
- Form of transfer deed and formalities for execution
- Pre-completion searches
- Methods and effect of completion
- Post-completion steps
- Remedies for delayed completion
- Contractual compensation
- Common law damages
- Notice to complete
- Rescission

Note that for SQE1, candidates are not usually required to recall specific case names or cite statutory or regulatory authorities. Cases and statutory or regulatory authorities are provided for illustrative purposes only unless otherwise indicated.

Learning outcomes

By the end of this chapter you will be able to apply relevant core legal principles and rules appropriately and effectively, at the level of a competent newly qualified solicitor in practice, to realistic client-based and ethical problems and situations in the following areas:

- Drafting and agreeing a transfer deed
- Carrying out and analysing the results of pre-completion searches

- Making practical arrangements for completion
- Understanding the different methods of completion
- Carrying out post-completion steps
- Advising a client in the event of delayed completion or failure to complete.

5.1 Introduction

To get to this point in the sale and purchase of a freehold registered property, the buyer's solicitor will have taken instructions from the client, investigated the seller's title, carried out searches and enquiries, agreed the contract, reported to the client (and possibly the lender) and exchanged contracts. The bulk of the work on the transaction happens before exchange of contracts, but there are important steps which need to be carried out between exchange of contracts and completion, and after completion. This chapter will explain those steps and also consider what happens if there are problems and completion is delayed, or does not happen at all.

5.2 Pre-completion steps

Immediately after exchange the parties' solicitors must inform their clients that exchange has taken place and comply with any undertakings given in the course of any telephone exchange, which will usually involve sending their client's signed and dated part of the contract with the completion date inserted, to the other side.

Traditionally completion was four weeks after exchange of contracts, but now clients usually prefer to complete more quickly and so two weeks is common. In some cases exchange and completion takes place on the same day ('simultaneous exchange and completion').

The main tasks of the solicitors in the pre-completion stage are:

- Preparation of the transfer deed
- Pre-completion searches
- Making practical arrangements for completion
- Ensuring the finances are in order for completion

5.3 Form of transfer deed and formalities for execution

Section 52 of the Law of Property Act 1925 states that the transfer of a legal estate in land must be by deed. To be valid in law a deed must:

- make it clear that it is a deed
- be signed by the parties
- be delivered.

It is no longer compulsory to have the deed sealed.

Where the deed is executed by a private individual, the signature must be witnessed by an independent witness, to counter any potential allegation of undue influence (see panel 12 in the example transfer deed TR1 below).

A company may execute a deed in one of three ways:

(i) using the company seal in accordance with the articles of association

Executed as a deed by affixing the

common seal of [name of company]

in the presence of:

(ii) having it signed by a director and the secretary, or by two directors of the company, provided that the deed is expressed to be executed by the company

Executed as a deed by [name of company]

acting by [a director and its secretary]

[two directors]

(iii) having it signed by a single director in the presence of a witness who then attests that signature:

Executed as a deed by [name of company]

acting by a director

in the presence of:

signature of witness

Name

Address

The seller will always execute the transfer deed in order to transfer the land and the buyer will also do so if the buyer is entering into an obligation or making a declaration in the TR1, such as giving an indemnity covenant or declaring a beneficial interest under a trust.

In relation to delivery, a document which makes it clear on its face that it is intended to be a deed is presumed to have been delivered on execution, but this presumption can be rebutted by a contrary intention. So, if the client has signed the transfer but does not intend it to come into force yet, their solicitor needs to expressly say so in the covering letter when sending the deed.

The deed used to transfer the whole of registered freehold title is Land Registry Form TR1 (TP1 for transfers of part). If the land is unregistered, it will be subject to compulsory first registration so the solicitors will often choose to use a Land Registry transfer form, although it is possible to use a conveyance.

Conventionally, the transfer deed is completed by the buyer's solicitor and sent to the seller's solicitor for agreement immediately after exchange of contracts, but in straightforward residential transactions the transfer deed may be prepared by the seller's solicitor and sent to the buyer's solicitor in the pre-exchange package.

The transfer deed must reflect the terms of the contract and the title deeds. Below is TR1 for the sale and purchase of 10 Bladen Road, reflecting the official copies in **2.3.2** and the contract in **4.4**.

HM Land Registry
Transfer of whole of registered title(s) TR1

Any parts of the form that are not typed should be completed in black ink and in block capitals.
If you need more room than is provided for in a panel, and your software allows, you can expand any panel in the form. Alternatively use continuation sheet CS and attach it to this form.
For information on how HM Land Registry processes your personal information, see our Personal Information Charter.

Leave blank if not yet registered.	1	Title number(s) of the property: LM6042
Insert address including postcode (if any) or other description of the property, for example 'land adjoining 2 Acacia Avenue'.	2	Property: 10 Bladen Road, Warrington, Cheshire WA1 1SL
Remember to date this deed with the day of completion, but not before it has been signed and witnessed.	3	Date:
Give full name(s) of **all** the persons transferring the property. Complete as appropriate where the transferor is a company.	4	Transferor: Leonard Holmes <u>For UK incorporated companies/LLPs</u> Registered number of company or limited liability partnership including any prefix: <u>For overseas companies</u> (a) Territory of incorporation: (b) Registered number in the United Kingdom including any prefix:
Give full name(s) of **all** the persons to be shown as registered proprietors. Complete as appropriate where the transferee is a company. Also, for an overseas company, unless an arrangement with HM Land Registry exists, lodge either a certificate in Form 7 in Schedule 3 to the Land Registration Rules 2003 or a certified copy of the constitution in English or Welsh, or other evidence permitted by rule 183 of the Land Registration Rules 2003.	5	Transferee for entry in the register: Samira Ahmed <u>For UK incorporated companies/LLPs</u> Registered number of company or limited liability partnership including any prefix: <u>For overseas companies</u> (a) Territory of incorporation: (b) Registered number in the United Kingdom including any prefix:

(*continued*)

Each transferee may give up to three addresses for service, one of which must be a postal address whether or not in the UK (including the postcode, if any). The others can be any combination of a postal address, a UK DX box number or an electronic address.	6 Transferee's intended address(es) for service for entry in the register: 10 Bladen Road, Warrington, Cheshire WA1 1SL
	7 The transferor transfers the property to the transferee
Place'X' in the appropriate box. State the currency unit if other than sterling. If none of the boxes apply, insert an appropriate memorandum in panel 11.	8 Consideration
	x☐ The transferor has received from the transferee for the property the following sum (in words and figures): Three hundred and eighty thousand pounds (£380,000) ☐ The transfer is not for money or anything that has a monetary value ☐ Insert other receipt as appropriate:
Place'X' in any box that applies. Add any modifications.	9 The transferor transfers with x☐ full title guarantee ☐ limited title guarantee
Where the transferee is more than one person, place'X' in the appropriate box. Complete as necessary. The registrar will enter a Form A restriction in the register *unless*: – an 'X' is placed: – in the first box, or – in the third box and the details of the trust or of the trust instrument show that the transferees are to hold the property on trust for themselves alone as joint tenants, *or* – it is clear from completion of a form JO lodged with this application that the transferees are to hold the property on trust for themselves alone as joint tenants.	10 Declaration of trust. The transferee is more than one person and ☐ they are to hold the property on trust for themselves as joint tenants ☐ they are to hold the property on trust for themselves as tenants in common in equal shares ☐ they are to hold the property on trust:

(*continued*)

(*continued*)

Please refer to *Joint property ownership* and practice guide *24: private trusts of land* for further guidance. These are both available on the GOV.UK website.	
Insert here any required or permitted statement, certificate or application and any agreed covenants, declarations and so on.	11 Additional provisions The transferee covenants with the transferor to: 11.1 (by way of indemnity only) observe and perform the covenants referred to in entry 1 of the charges register of title number LM6042 ('the Covenants') so far as they are subsisting and capable of taking effect; and 11.2 indemnify the transferor against any liability incurred for any breach or non-observance of the Covenants occurring after the date of this transfer.
The transferor must execute this transfer as a deed using the space opposite. If there is more than one transferor, all must execute. Forms of execution are given in Schedule 9 to the Land Registration Rules 2003. If the transfer contains transferee's covenants or declarations or contains an application by the transferee (such as for a restriction), it must also be executed by the transferee. If there is more than one transferee and panel 10 has been completed, each transferee must also execute this transfer to comply with the requirements in section 53(1)(b) of the Law of Property Act 1925 relating to the declaration of a trust of land. Please refer to *Joint property ownership* and *practice guide 24: private trusts of land* for further guidance. Remember to date this deed in panel 3.	12 Execution Signed as a deed by Leonard Holmes in the presence of Signature of witness Name Address Signed as a deed by Samira Ahmed in the presence of Signature of witness Name Address

WARNING
If you dishonestly enter information or make a statement that you know is, or might be, untrue or misleading, and intend by doing so to make a gain for yourself or another person, or to cause loss or the risk of loss to another person, you may commit the offence of fraud under section 1 of the Fraud Act 2006, the maximum penalty for which is 10 years' imprisonment or an unlimited fine, or both.

(*continued*)

Failure to complete this form with proper care may result in a loss of protection under the Land Registration Act 2002 if, as a result, a mistake is made in the register.

Under section 66 of the Land Registration Act 2002 most documents (including this form) kept by the registrar relating to an application to the registrar or referred to in the register are open to public inspection and copying. If you believe a document contains prejudicial information, you may apply for that part of the document to be made exempt using Form EX1, under rule 136 of the Land Registration Rules 2003.

The following points should be noted:

Panels 1 and 2: the title number and the address of the property should be checked against the details in the contract and the official copies.

Panel 3: the transfer will only be dated upon completion.

Panels 4 and 5: the names of the parties should be checked against the details in the contract and, in the case of the transferor, the official copies.

Panel 6: the buyer is buying this property to live in and so they will want communications to go to their new address, not their old address. If the property will be tenanted, the buyer may want communications sent to another address, such as a registered office in the case of a company.

Panel 7: the operative part of the deed and it should not be amended.

Panel 8: the purchase price should be written in figures as well as words. VAT?

Panel 9: on the front page of the contract the seller has stated they are selling with full title guarantee. In addition, SC 4.6.2 states the seller is selling with full title guarantee.

Panel 10: there is only one buyer so none of these boxes apply. The purpose of this panel is for co-owners to declare how they are going to hold the equitable interest in the property, as tenants in common or joint tenants.

Panel 11: there should be an indemnity covenant to observe the covenants in the charges register. This is provided for in the contract by SC 4.6.4 as the seller will remain liable on the restrictive covenants in the 1968 Conveyance which will appear in the official copies following registration of the client's purchase

Panel 12: the signature of the seller, being an individual, must be witnessed

Panel 12: the buyer should also execute the transfer as they are entering into an indemnity covenant.

5.4 Pre-completion searches

Pre-completion searches are generally carried out by the buyer's solicitor and should be made as close to the completion date as possible. These pre-completion searches are carried out for four reasons:

1. To make sure that the seller has not further encumbered the title since investigation of title took place
2. To check the financial circumstances of the borrower when acting for the lender

3 To gain priority for the buyer, and the lender, over anyone else making an application before the buyer applies to register the change of ownership at the Land Registry

4 If the seller is a company, to check that the company has not gone into liquidation before the balance of the purchase price is paid over on completion.

5.4.1 Pre-completion search of the title

Checking the title for further encumbrances is necessary because there is usually a significant period between investigation of title and completion. During that period it is possible for the title to be further encumbered by the seller, eg by granting new easements over the property, entering into new covenants or even creating a new mortgage over the property. Pre-completion searches are therefore a way of updating the title position to check that nothing has happened and that the title is exactly as it was when title investigation last took place.

There are two types of pre-completion search depending on whether title to the property is registered or unregistered.

Registered land

If the title is registered, then a Land Registry search should be made against the title number to see if any new entries have been made since the 'search from' date, that is, the date on which the official copies were produced. Form OS1 is used if the whole property is being sold, or an OS2 if the sale is of part only. A plan will ordinarily need to accompany a request for an OS2 (unless a layout plan has been approved by the Land Registry, which is often the case in new housing developments). The application will give details of the title number, the address of the property, the names of the registered proprietors, the name of the applicant and the reason for the search, ie an intention to purchase, lease or charge the property.

The results of the search will be set out in Form OS1R or an OS2R as appropriate. The search result will reveal any new entry made since the 'search from' date and confer on the applicant a 'priority period' of 30 working days from the date of the search result. The priority period provides protection to the applicant against any subsequent entries which may be placed on the register after the date of the search but before the buyer is registered as proprietor. The buyer will take free from any such entries, provided that they submit their application for registration by 12 noon on the last day of the priority period.

If the buyer is financing the purchase of the property with the aid of a mortgage, then the application for a Land Registry search should be in the name of the lender and not the buyer. That way the results will confer priority upon both the buyer and the lender since the mortgage is deemed to take place slightly after the purchase by the buyer. A search made on behalf of the buyer will not protect the lender.

An example OS1 for 10 Bladen Road appears below. The buyer is purchasing the property with the aid of a mortgage from Barclays Bank PLC.

HM Land Registry

Application by purchaser for official search with priority of the whole of the land in a registered title or a pending first registration application

OS1

Use one form per title.

Any parts of the form that are not typed should be completed in black ink and in block capitals.

If you need more room than is provided for in a panel, and your software allows, you can expand any panel in the form. Alternatively use continuation sheet CS and attach it to this form.

HM Land Registry is unable to give legal advice, but you can find guidance on HM Land Registry applications (including our practice guides for conveyancers) at www.gov.uk/land-registry.

Conveyancer is a term used in this form. It is defined in rule 217A, Land Registration Rules 2003 and includes persons authorised under the Legal Services Act 2007 to provide reserved legal services relating to land registration and includes solicitors and licensed conveyancers.

For information on how HM Land Registry processes your personal information, see our Personal Information Charter.

HM LAND REGISTRY USE ONLY Record of fees paid
Particulars of under/over payments
Reference number Fees debited £

Where there is more than one local authority serving an area, enter the one to which council tax or business rates are normally paid.	1	Local authority serving the property: Warrington Borough Council
Enter the title number of the registered estate or that allotted to the pending first registration.	2	Title number of the property: LM6042
Insert address including postcode (if any) or other description of the property, for example 'land adjoining 2 Acacia Avenue'.	3	Property: 10 Bladen Road, Warrington, Cheshire WA1 1SL
Enter the full names. If there are more than two persons, enter the first two only.	4	Registered proprietor/Applicant for first registration SURNAME/COMPANY NAME: Holmes FORENAME(S): Leonard SURNAME/COMPANY NAME: FORENAME(S):

(continued)

(*continued*)

Guidance	Panel
	5 Application and fee
To find out more about our fees visit www.gov.uk/government/collections/fees-land-registry-guides	**Application:** Official search of whole with priority **Fee paid (£):**
	Fee payment method
Place'X' in the appropriate box.	☐ cheque made payable to'Land Registry'
The fee will be charged to the account specified in panel 6.	☐ direct debit, under an agreement with Land Registry
This panel must always be completed. A key number is only available to professional customers, such as solicitors. If you are paying by direct debit, this will be the account charged.	6 This application is sent to Land Registry by Key number (if applicable): Name: Address or UK DX box number: Email address: Reference: Phone no: Fax no:
Place'X' in one box only. For a search of a registered title enter a date falling within the definition of 'search from date' in rule 131 of the Land Registration Rules 2003. If the date entered is not such a date the application may be rejected.	7 Application and search from date x ☐ I apply for a search of the individual register of a registered title to ascertain whether any adverse entry has been made in the register or day list since 30.04.202X ☐ I apply for a search in relation to a pending application for first registration to ascertain whether any adverse entry has been made in the day list since the date of the pending first registration application.
Provide the full name(s) of each purchaser or lessee or chargee.	8 The applicant: Barclays Bank PLC
Place'X' in the appropriate box.	9 Reason for application I certify that the applicant intends to ☐ **P**urchase ☐ take a **L**ease x ☐ take a registered **C**harge
If a conveyancer is acting for the applicant, that conveyancer must sign. If no conveyancer is acting, the applicant (if more than one person then each) must sign.	10 Signature of applicant or their conveyancer: __________________ Date:

(*continued*)

WARNING
If you dishonestly enter information or make a statement that you know is, or might be, untrue or misleading, and intend by doing so to make a gain for yourself or another person, or to cause loss or the risk of loss to another person, you may commit the offence of fraud under section 1 of the Fraud Act 2006, the maximum penalty for which is 10 years' imprisonment or an unlimited fine, or both.

Failure to complete this form with proper care may result in a loss of protection under the Land Registration Act 2002 if, as a result, a mistake is made in the register.

Under section 66 of the Land Registration Act 2002 most documents (including this form) kept by the registrar relating to an application to the registrar or referred to in the register are open to public inspection and copying. If you believe a document contains prejudicial information, you may apply for that part of the document to be made exempt using Form EX1, under rule 136 of the Land Registration Rules 2003.

Unregistered Land

If the title to the property is unregistered then a land charges search is made on a form K15 (see **2.4.3**). The result of the K15 search will be on form K18 and confers a priority period of 15 working days from the date of the result, during which time the searcher will take free of any entries made on the register between the date of the search and the date of completion, provided that completion takes place during the 15 working day period. A land charges search will normally have been done as a pre-exchange search, but will need to be repeated against the current seller's name unless the transaction can be completed within the 15 working day priority period conferred by the pre-exchange search. It is not necessary to search again against the names of the previous estate owners as no entries can have been registered against them after they parted with the property.

In most cases the results of the pre-completion searches show no adverse entries, but if this is not the case, then the matter must be taken up with the seller immediately.

Comparison of Land Registry and Land Charges Department searches

	Land Registry	*Land Charges Department*
Form:	OS1 (or OS2)	K15
When to use:	registered land	unregistered land
Search against:	title number	owners' names
Fee:	standard fee for each search	fee for each name searched
Result form:	OSR1 (or OSR2)	K18
Priority period:	30 working days	15 working days

5.4.2 Checking for buyer's solvency on behalf of lender

A lender who is financing the purchase of the property will normally require some security, a mortgage or legal charge, over the property. So, the financial circumstances of the buyer are important to the lender as they will want to avoid lending money to a person who may be either bankrupt or in liquidation.

Where the buyer is an individual, there are numerous ways of checking financial standing but the method used when property is taken as security for a loan is to apply on behalf of the lender for a land charges search against the buyer.

- If the title is registered, the solicitor will apply for a land charges search against the name of the buyer (as well as carrying out the pre-completion Land Registry search against the property's title number). In these circumstances, it will be a special land charges search, known as a 'Bankruptcy only' search using a form K16. Using a K16 limits the search to the bankruptcy register at the Land Charges Department and will not reveal any entries on other registers as these will not be relevant to the lender.
- If title to the property is unregistered, the solicitor will already be making a land charges search against the seller (see **5.4.1** above), so the name of the buyer will be added to the name(s) to be searched against on form K15.

If the buyer is a company then it is not possible to do a bankruptcy land charges search against it; a company search will need to be carried out (see **5.4.3** below).

5.4.3 Company search against a company seller

In addition to carrying out the appropriate searches against the title, the solicitor acting for a buyer purchasing from a company should carry out a further company search prior to completion. A company search will reveal whether the seller is still in existence, whether it is solvent, and whether it has created any fixed or floating charges. This information cannot always be obtained from a Land Registry or land charges search.

A company search has no priority period. Therefore, it should be carried out as close as possible to the day of completion so it reveals the latest information. Where the transaction is of a particularly high value or where there is reason to be concerned about the solvency of a corporate seller or borrower, it is possible to do a telephone search at the Registry of Winding Up Petitions at the Companies Court on the day of completion.

Example

A solicitor acted for Rabinet plc ('Rabinet') on the purchase of a registered freehold property from Beckwith Limited ('Beckwith'). Completion took place on 12 December. The solicitor carried out an OS1 priority search prior to completion, which gave a priority period ending on 28 December. On 4 January the solicitor returned from a three-week holiday and submitted the application for registration of the transfer of the property to the Land Registry.

The solicitor has now discovered that a different firm acting for Beckwith had been in negotiations with the owner of a neighbouring property (Southwood Ltd) for the grant of a right of way over the property to Southwood Ltd. Due to a communication breakdown, the solicitor acting for Beckwith was unaware of the sale and completed the grant of the right of way on 10 December. This right of way would significantly interfere with Rabinet's plans for the property.

Will Rabinet be bound by the right of way?

Answer

The buyer client will take the property subject to the right of way because the solicitor did not submit the application to the Land Registry before the expiry of the priority period. The priority period simply gives a fixed time within which the applicant has first right to register a transaction, without worrying about any other transactions which may have taken place since the date of the OS1 search. If the application to register is not submitted in time to arrive by 12 pm on the last day of the priority period (28 December), this priority to any prior applications is lost. The Land Registry will therefore register the easement to Southwood Ltd in priority to the transfer to the buyer client if Southwood Ltd submitted its application before the Land Registry received the application on 4 January.

5.4.4 Bankruptcy search against an individual seller

In relation to a seller who is an individual, if the transaction relates to unregistered land, a Form K15 search against the seller as estate owner will reveal any entries relating to bankruptcy (see **2.4.3** and **5.4.1**). In the case of registered land, most conveyancing solicitors do not consider it necessary to do a bankruptcy check on an individual seller as s 86(5) of the Land Registration Act 2002 provides that where no notice or restriction relating to the bankruptcy appears on the registered title, a buyer for value acting in good faith without notice of the bankruptcy petition or adjudication will take good title from the bankrupt seller, even though legal title to the land has vested in the trustee in bankruptcy. However, the bankruptcy searches described at **5.4.2** can be done where the transaction is for a particularly high value or there is reason to be concerned about the solvency of the individual seller.

5.5 Practical arrangements for completion

The buyer and seller need to agree the practicalities for completion and this is done using a 'completion information form' which the buyer's solicitor sends to the seller's solicitor for them to complete. There are different versions of this form; the one most commonly used for residential properties is Form TA13 Completion information and undertakings. This asks the seller to confirm important information relevant to completion, including:

- arrangements for handing over the keys
- the place and method of completion
- the documents to be handed over at completion
- the exact amount payable by the buyer on completion

Importantly, the form also contains the undertaking the seller's solicitor gives to redeem the mortgage out of the completion money on completion. If there is an existing mortgage over the property, it is unlikely that the seller's solicitor will be able to discharge it before or immediately on completion since they will have only just received the completion money out of which the mortgage will be repaid. So, the buyer's solicitor asks the seller's solicitor to undertake to discharge any outstanding mortgage and to send evidence of discharge to the buyer's solicitor as soon as it is received from the lender. The form of undertaking should be agreed between the solicitors before the day of completion. Form TA13 does this by asking the seller's solicitor to list the mortgages and charges secured on the property and whether they 'undertake to redeem or discharge the [listed mortgages and charges] on completion and to send to us Form DS1, DS3, the receipted charge(s) or confirmation that notice of release or discharge in electronic form has been given to the Land Registry as soon as you receive them?'. The reply 'Yes' is treated as an undertaking.

5.6 Ensuring the finances are in order for completion

If the buyer is financing the purchase with the aid of a mortgage, before releasing the mortgage advance a lender will expect to receive:

- a certificate of title to confirm that the property is adequate security for the loan being advanced (see **4.10**)

- a solvency search against the borrowers (see **5.4.2** above)
- a clear OS1R in the name of the lender (see **5.4.1** above)
- an executed but not completed mortgage deed (see **4.8**).

The solicitor for the buyer will need to send a Financial Statement to the client advising the client of the funds needed to complete. This statement will show the amount to be forwarded by the buyer to its solicitor and will include the balance of the purchase price, any SDLT/LTT due, the registration fee, the amount outstanding for any other disbursements, usually the solicitor's fees and any other amount owing, eg a restrictive covenant insurance policy premium.

The buyer's solicitor should ensure that they have received both the mortgage advance from the lender and the balance of the purchase price from the buyer client. The balance of the purchase price should then be sent to the seller's solicitor to the bank account specified in the replies to the Completion information form (see **5.5** above). The solicitor should notify the seller's solicitor that the money is on its way. Once the money has been received, the seller's solicitor will contact the solicitor acting for the buyer and completion will take place.

5.7 Methods and effect of completion

At completion, the buyer's solicitor will send the balance of the purchase price and release the deposit paid on exchange to the seller. The buyer's solicitor will usually arrange for the completion money to be sent electronically: SC 6.7 and SCPC 9.7 require the completion money to be paid by direct transfer/electronic means in cleared funds from an account held in the name of a conveyancer at a clearing bank. On receipt of the completion money, the seller's solicitor will complete the transaction by dating the TR1. Once the TR1 has been dated, the lender's solicitor will need to date the mortgage deed. This cannot be done until after the TR1 has been dated, as technically, the buyer does not own the property until then and so would not be in a position to grant a mortgage over it.

The two most common ways to complete a property sale and purchase transaction are in person or by post.

5.7.1 Completion in person

Completion in person requires one solicitor, usually the buyer's solicitor, to attend the office of the other solicitor. The meeting usually takes place at the office of the seller's solicitor. All parts of the transfer should have already been executed by the parties in anticipation of formal completion and will usually be with the seller's solicitor since the seller normally executes the transfer last. The buyer's solicitor will usually arrange for the completion money to be sent electronically.

At the completion meeting the Buyer's solicitor will check any title documents against the evidence of title previously sent to them, which is only of real significance in unregistered land. In return for receiving the completion money, the Seller's solicitor will hand over title documents and other documents relating to the property, such as planning permissions, and guarantees or insurance policies. The Seller's solicitor will then arrange for the release of the keys to the property by whoever is holding them.

5.7.2 Completion by post

The disadvantage of completing in person is that it takes time. Friday was traditionally the day that lawyers would visit each other's offices to complete transactions, but the reality of modern life often makes it impractical to spend so much time away from the desk and it is much more common for completion to take place by post.

The biggest worry with the post is unreliability. The Law Society therefore introduced a Code for Completion by Post which again relies on undertakings given by the solicitors involved in order to be effective.

Law Society Code for Completion by Post

The Law Society's Code involves the seller's solicitor acting as the agent of the buyer's solicitor for the purpose of carrying out the completion procedure. The seller's solicitor does this at no cost to the buyer, on the basis the seller will be a buyer at some point and will likewise benefit from using the Code. It is important for the buyer's solicitor to set out in writing precisely what the seller's solicitor is to do on their behalf. The buyer's solicitor is asking the seller's solicitor to do whatever it is that they would have done if they could have attended the completion in person. On receiving the completion money, the seller's solicitor will then carry out the instructions and complete the transaction. The seller's solicitor should then contact the buyer's solicitor to inform them that completion has taken place. The documents which would have been handed over to the buyer's solicitor are instead sent by first-class post or document exchange.

Under the Law Society Code for Completion by Post the seller's solicitor gives an implied undertaking to carry out the buyer's solicitor's instructions. This undertaking may be enforced through the courts.

5.7.3 Effect of completion

The effect of completion depends upon whether the land is registered or unregistered. In unregistered land, legal title passes to the buyer on completion. In registered land, legal title does not pass to the buyer until the buyer is registered at the Land Registry as proprietor of the land. This is why it is important to protect the buyer from the creation of adverse third party rights in the intervening 'registration gap' using a Land Registry search which confers priority.

5.8 Post-completion steps

A number of steps will need to be carried out after completion, some of which have strict time limits attached to them.

5.8.1 Discharge of the seller's mortgage

Arrangements for the discharge of the seller's mortgage will have been agreed using the completion information form. In many cases, the buyer will have agreed to allow the seller's solicitor to discharge the mortgage after completion using the money received at completion, the buyer relying on the undertaking from the seller's solicitor (see **5.5** above). Alternatively, the seller's solicitor may ask the buyer's solicitor to send the amount required to redeem the mortgage direct to the lender on the day of completion, with only the balance being sent to the seller's solicitor.

Once the lender has received the amount required to redeem the mortgage from the seller's solicitor, they will either:

- complete Land Registry form DS1 and send it to the seller's solicitor for onward transmission to the buyer's solicitor; or
- submit an e-DS1 electronic discharge through the Land Registry portal; or
- use the Electronic Discharge (ED) system, sending an electronic message to the Land Registry which automatically removes the charge from the register.

If the ED or e-DS1 system is used, the seller's solicitor will not be sending a DS1 form to the buyer's solicitor. Instead, the seller's solicitor will send the buyer's solicitor confirmation that notice of release or discharge in electronic form has been given to the Land Registry.

5.8.2 SDLT/LTT

The seller's solicitor will send the TR1 to the buyer's solicitor who must then arrange for any SDLT (England) or LTT (Wales), to be paid (see **1.6.1**). SDLT must be paid to HMRC within 14 days of completion: LTT must be paid to the Welsh Revenue Authority ('WRA') within 30 days of completion.

The payment, together with the tax return (SDLT1 in England and Land Transaction Return in Wales), will need to be sent to the relevant authority. This can be done online or using a paper application.

HMRC will produce an SDLT5 form, and the WRA will return a WRA certificate, as proof that the tax has been duly paid on the transaction. Failure to pay SDLT/LTT can lead to fines and penalties and any application to the Land Registry to register the buyer as the new registered proprietor will be rejected unless the SDLT5/WRA certificate accompanies the application.

5.8.3 Registration of the new charge at Companies House

If the buyer is a company and has purchased the property with the aid of a mortgage, the lender's solicitor will have to register the charge at Companies House within 21 days of its creation (ie at completion) to ensure constructive notice of it is given to other creditors of the company. The time limit is absolute and cannot be extended without a court order. Failure to register renders the charge void against a liquidator or administrator of the borrower and the borrower's other creditors, so would seriously prejudice the lender's security.

5.8.4 Land Registry application(s)

Once SDLT/LTT has been paid (and, if relevant, the charge registered at Companies House), the buyer's solicitor will need to apply to have the buyer registered as the registered proprietor of the land in the title. The lender's solicitor (who may also be acting for the buyer) needs to apply to register the charge.

(a) Registered land

The applications to have the buyer registered as the registered proprietor of the land and the lender registered as the registered proprietor of the charge are made on Land Registry form AP1. If the seller had a mortgage which has been electronically discharged, the entries in the charges register protecting this mortgage will be automatically removed but if a DS1 has been used, the buyer's solicitor must apply for the mortgage to be discharged. All three of these applications can be made on the AP1 form.

A certified copy of the transfer (not the original) should be submitted with the application, along with the fee, the SDLT/LTT certificate and the DS1 (if used). As part of the policy to reduce the number of overriding interests, an applicant for registration must complete Form DI setting out any overriding interests that burden the title. These will then be entered on the register and thus cease to be overriding.

If the buyer has created a new mortgage, the following documents will also be needed:

- certified copy of the mortgage deed
- if the buyer is a company, certified copy of the certificate of registration issued by Companies House
- if the buyer is a company, the solicitor's /lender's written confirmation that the enclosed certified copy mortgage deed is the same as the one filed at Companies House and to which the certificate of registration relates.

The application(s) must be made before the expiry of the priority period of the OS1 search that should have been carried out prior to completion. Failure to register within the priority period will mean that the buyer and lender will lose the benefit of the priority period and would take subject to matters registered during that period.

(b) Unregistered land

An application for first registration of title must be made within two months of completion of the transaction on Form FR1. The application form and fee accompanied by the documents listed at below, should be sent to the Land Registry. Documents accompanying the application must be listed in duplicate on form DL. One copy of form DL will be returned to the applicant's solicitor, which will give an estimate of the likely time which the Land Registry expects to take to deal with the application.

The Registrar needs to investigate title on an application for first registration in order to decide which class of title can be allocated to the title. The Registrar therefore needs to have access to all the documents which formed the evidence of title supplied to the applicant by the seller's solicitor. Between 28 November 2016 and 1 October 2024, certified copies of the deeds and documents accompanying the application were acceptable, but Land Registry has now reverted to its previous practice of requiring the original deeds and documents. The documents should be numbered in chronological sequence on form DL and include such of the following documents as are relevant to the transaction:

- all the documents which formed the evidence of title supplied by the seller's solicitor
- all the buyer's pre-contract searches and enquiries relating to the title with their replies
- the contract
- requisitions on title with their replies
- all pre-completion search certificates
- the transfer deed
- the seller's mortgage, duly receipted
- SDLT/LTT certificate
- Form DI (see below)

If there is a new mortgage, the documents listed above in (a) will also be required, together with the original mortgage deed.

As part of the policy to reduce the number of overriding interests, an applicant for registration must complete form DI setting out any overriding interests that burden the title. These will then be entered on the register and therefore cease to be overriding.

Land Registry Forms AP1, DS2 and FR1 require the applicant to give details of the conveyancer acting for each party and, where a party is not represented and the value of the property is £6,000 or more in value, provide evidence of that party's identity.

The Land Registry will process the relevant application(s) for registration and insert the buyer as the new registered proprietor and the lender as the new registered proprietor of the charge. Once this has been done, the Land Registry will forward an official copy of the entries on the register, known as a Title Information Document (or 'TID') to the buyer's solicitor. Although this is not strictly a document of title, it is for the buyer to keep as evidence that it is the new owner. The buyer and lenders solicitor(s) should check it to ensure that the transfer and mortgage has been correctly registered.

Once the TID has been checked, the buyer's solicitor will need to deal with the safe custody of the TID and any other papers. Where the property has been bought with the aid of a mortgage, the lender should be asked if it wishes to retain them. Often a lender will only require the updated TID. Finally, when all the above matters have been dealt with and the bill paid, it is possible to close the file.

5.9 Remedies for delayed completion

The exchanged contract will usually contain the date for completion that the parties agreed. If it does not, SC 6.1.1 and SCPC 9.1.1 provide that the completion date is 20 working days after the date of the contract.

In both sets of conditions, the money due on completion must be paid before 2pm on the day of completion and if it is not, completion is to be treated as taking place on the next working day as a result of the buyer's default. The parties can agree to vary the completion time of 2pm in the contract: 12 noon is sometimes substituted for 2pm when there is a chain of transactions to be completed in a single day (see pre-printed special condition 5 in the SC contract in **4.5**).

The next question to consider is what happens when one of the parties is not ready to complete on time, ie before the contractual completion time on the contractual completion date. Both sets of standard conditions provide that time is not of the essence of the contract unless a notice to complete has been served (see **5.9.3** below), so there is no immediate right for the non-defaulting party to terminate or rescind the contract on the contractual completion date.

5.9.1 Contractual compensation

Both sets of standard conditions provide for compensation to be paid, with one significant distinction: in the SCs both the buyer and the seller can be asked to pay this compensation (SC 7.2), whereas under the SCPCs only the buyer can be required to pay compensation (SCPC 10.3).

The compensation is calculated at the Contract rate specified in the contract (see **4.4.3**) on the balance of the purchase price, less any deposit paid (if the defaulting party was the buyer) for the period between the contractual completion date and the date of actual completion. The compensation is calculated as a daily rate so that it can be multiplied for the number of days of default. If the non-paying party was also at fault for some of that period then those days are ignored. The compensation is payable on completion.

Example

Following an exchange of contracts incorporating the Standard Conditions, the buyer delays completion by three days. Assume that:

- *the Contract rate is 8.5%*
- *the purchase price is £300,000*
- *the buyer has paid 10% deposit.*

Calculate the compensation payable by the buyer.

Answer

The buyer will have to pay compensation on the balance of £300,000 less £30,000 deposit, which is £270,000. That sum is multiplied by the Contract rate, which is 8.5%. This produces an annual rate of compensation of £22,950, which is turned into a daily rate by dividing it by 365. Once the daily rate is established, it can be multiplied by the number of days in default.

Purchase price	£300,000
less deposit	£30,000

= £270,000 x 8.5%

= £22,950 divided by 365

= £62.88 x 3 days

= £188.64

The amount of compensation this buyer will have to pay is just under £200. That is not very much if, for example, the seller has had to check into a hotel for three nights and has significant losses such as wasted removal costs.

5.9.2 Common law damages

Failure to complete on the contractual completion date is breach of contract and the seller could make a claim for breach of contract under normal contractual principles. Damages will be assessed under *Hadley v Baxendale* with the measure being that of putting the claimant in the position it would have been in had the contract been correctly performed. Damages will be awarded for losses naturally flowing from the breach as well as for any reasonably foreseeable consequential loss. This could include wasted legal costs, putting furniture into storage, the cost of renting another property, the cost of bridging finance and any rebooking removal costs.

The fact that the seller has received contractual compensation does not prevent the seller from claiming damages for extra losses for breach of contract in the normal way. However, the contractual compensation the innocent party receives will be deducted from the contractual damages.

5.9.3 Notice to complete

Where it appears that the delay in completion is not likely to be resolved quickly, either party, if they are ready, willing and able to complete themselves may consider serving a notice to complete. A notice to complete can only be served after the contractual completion time on the contractual completion date, eg 2pm on the completion date in a contract incorporating unamended SCPCs and SCs. Once served, the notice to complete makes time of the essence and gives the other party 10 working days to complete. If the defaulting party fails to complete within 10 working days, then the party who served the notice to complete can rescind the contract (but is not obliged to do so). If the contract is rescinded and the defaulting party was the buyer, the seller is able to forfeit the deposit. If the defaulting party was the seller, then the seller must repay the deposit to the buyer. The non-defaulting party can also claim damages for any losses they suffer as a result of the other's default.

5.9.4 Rescission

Contracts incorporating the SC and the SCPC provide for rescission in specified circumstances. One such circumstance is where a party has failed to comply with a notice to complete (see **5.9.3** above). Another circumstance is where there has been a misrepresentation by the seller in a plan or statement in the contract, or in the negotiations leading up to the contract. However, rescission will only be allowed where the seller's error or omission results from fraud or recklessness, or the buyer would be obliged to accept a property differing substantially (in quantity, quality or tenure) from what the error or omission had led them to expect. Less serious misrepresentations only entitle the buyer to damages.

Summary

- Immediately after exchange of contracts, the solicitors must inform their respective clients and relevant third parties (such as the lender and the estate agent) and deal with the signed contracts and deposit as required by the contract and any undertakings given on exchange.
- The transfer is usually prepared by the buyer's solicitor. It must be a deed and where the land is registered, it must comply with Land Registry requirements.
- The transfer must always be executed by the seller and must also be executed by the buyer where it contains a covenant or declaration on the buyer's behalf.
- The purpose of pre-completion searches is to check that nothing adverse to the buyer has happened to the property or the seller since exchange, and to protect the buyer against any adverse change.
- Information about the property's title is obtained by a Land Registry search for registered land and a central land charges search for unregistered land.

- Both types of search protect the buyer by providing a priority period during which no other entries may be registered. The priority periods are different, and in each case the purchase must be completed within the relevant priority period or the priority will be lost.
- Information about the solvency of the seller is obtained by a bankruptcy search for an individual and a company search for a corporate entity. These searches do not confer the protection of a priority period and so should be done as close as possible to the date of completion.
- The buyer's solicitor issues a completion information form to the seller's solicitor to check that none of the information provided about the property before exchange has changed and to confirm the practical arrangements for completion, such as how the seller's mortgage is going to be discharged.
- The buyer's solicitor sends a certificate of title and request for funds to the lender and a completion statement to the buyer.
- The parties will agree a completion date and time and insert them into the contract before exchange. At completion, the transfer will be dated and the completion monies will be paid/released to the seller.
- Completion may take place by personal attendance or through the post using The Law Society's Code for Completing by Post.
- The buyer's solicitor will have to ensure that any SDLT/LTT payable on the purchase is paid within 14/30 days of completion.
- The buyer's solicitor must also ensure that the transfer of the property to the client is registered at Land Registry within the relevant time period. For land that is already registered, this will be the priority period conferred by the Land Registry search carried out before completion, and for land that is subject to first registration this will be within two months of completion.
- The lender's solicitor must ensure that the mortgage of the property to the lender is registered at Land Registry within the same time period. Where the borrower is a company, they must also register the charge over the property at Companies House within 21 days of its creation.
- Failure to carry out these steps within the required time periods will prejudice the client's interests and may result in the solicitor being held liable in negligence.
- If completion is delayed, the non-defaulting party will not normally be able to terminate the contract at that stage.
- Compensation may be payable under the contract by a defaulting party if there is a delay in completion beyond the completion time on the completion date specified in the contract.
- Under the SCs, either party may be liable to pay contractual compensation. Under the SCPCs, only the buyer is liable to pay contractual compensation.
- Under both sets of standard conditions, when completion is delayed, the party who is ready, willing and able to complete may serve a notice to complete on the defaulting party. This will make time of the essence, and if completion does not take place within 10 working days of the service of the notice, the aggrieved party may terminate the contract.
- If it is the buyer who has failed to comply with the notice to complete, they will forfeit the deposit.
- In addition to these procedures specified in the contract, the non-defaulting party retains their other rights and remedies in respect of a breach of contract.

Sample questions

Question 1

A solicitor is acting for the buyer on the purchase of a residential freehold property with a registered title. Title has been deduced, searches and enquiries have been carried out and contracts have been exchanged.

Is the solicitor required to carry out a search at the Land Registry prior to completion?

A Yes, because it is a part of the investigation of title.

B Yes, because the results will reveal whether there have been any changes to the register since the date of the official copies obtained prior to exchange of contracts.

C Yes, because it is needed to check that the seller is the registered proprietor.

D No, because the buyer will be protected by the priority period created when the official copies were issued.

E No, because new entries cannot be made on the registers of title without the consent of the seller.

Answer

Option B is correct. Options A and C are not the best answers because the solicitor will have already investigated title and checked that the seller is the registered proprietor before exchange of contracts. The purpose of the pre-completion search is two-fold: first, to see if there have been any changes to the register since the date of the official copies obtained prior to exchange of contracts and second, to obtain a priority period in which to register the buyer as new proprietor (and to register any lender as new chargee). Option D is wrong as this priority period is created by the issue of the Land Registry search result (OS1R), not by the issue of the official copies. Option E is wrong as third parties can apply for unilateral notices to be entered on the charges register without the consent of the registered proprietor (see **2.5.10**).

Question 2

A solicitor is acting for a lender that has advanced money for the purchase of a registered freehold property. The borrower and purchaser of the property is a limited company. The money advanced by the lender is secured by a first legal charge over the property. An official search of whole (OS1) was carried out against the property in the name of the lender prior to completion. Both the transfer of the property and the legal charge have been completed.

Which of the following best describes what steps (if any) the lender's solicitor should take after completion to protect the legal charge?

A The legal charge automatically binds any subsequent purchasers and lenders and so no further steps are required to protect it.

B The legal charge must be registered at Companies House within 14 days of its creation and at the Land Registry within the priority period conferred by the OS1 search result.

C The legal charge does not need to be registered at Companies House, but must be registered at the Land Registry within the priority period of the OS1 search.

D The legal charge must be registered at Companies House within 21 days of its creation and at the Land Registry within two months of completion of the purchase.

E The legal charge must be registered at Companies House within 21 days of its creation and at the Land Registry within the priority period conferred by the OS1 search result.

Answer

Option E is correct. As the borrower is a company, the legal charge must be registered at Companies House within 21 days of its creation to ensure constructive notice of it is given to other creditors of the company. Options A and C are wrong because further steps are necessary and the legal charge does have to be registered at Companies House. Option B is wrong as it refers to the wrong time limit of 14 days.

The legal charge must also be registered at the Land Registry to ensure the lender has a legal interest that binds those subsequently dealing with the property. Option D is not the best answer as registration at the Land Registry should be completed within the priority period conferred by the OS1 search result to ensure the lender has priority over any other applications, rather than within two months of completion.

Question 3

A solicitor acts for the buyer of a freehold property. The contract for the purchase of the property incorporates Part 1 of the Standard Commercial Property Conditions ('SCPC') without amendments. Contracts have been exchanged and the completion date is tomorrow. The seller's solicitor contacted the solicitor yesterday to confirm that they are ready for completion.

The solicitor has been contacted by the buyer today. The buyer has requested that completion be delayed for a week due to some funding issues.

Which of the following statements best describes the consequences of the delayed completion?

A Only the buyer can be liable to pay compensation under the SCPC.

B The buyer and the seller can be liable to pay compensation for late completion under the SCPC.

C The contract rate will be applied to the full purchase price to calculate the amount of compensation to be paid.

D If the seller has any actual loss resulting from the delayed completion, they will be able to claim for breach of contract and keep this in addition to any compensation paid under the SCPC.

E The seller can immediately terminate the contract.

Answer

Option A is correct. In a contract incorporating the SCPC, SCPC 10.3 only requires the buyer to pay compensation to the seller in the event of late completion and there is no corresponding requirement for the seller to pay, so option A is correct and option B is wrong.

The contract rate is applied to an amount equal to the purchase price less the deposit in order to calculate the amount of compensation, so C is incorrect.

The seller can receive damages for breach of contract, but these are reduced by the amount of any compensation paid, so option D is wrong.

Finally, the seller can terminate the contract, but only when they have served a notice to complete and the buyer has failed to complete by the expiry of the notice. Time is not of the essence until the notice to complete is served on the buyer, so option E is wrong.

6 Structure and Content of a Lease

6.1	Introduction	114
6.2	Advantages and disadvantages of owning a leasehold property	114
6.3	The structure of a typical commercial lease	115
6.4	Options for the term of a lease	116
6.5	Types of leasehold covenant	117
6.6	The full repairing and insuring lease	118
6.7	Repair	118
6.8	Insurance	119
6.9	Alterations	125
6.10	User and planning	127
6.11	Alienation	128
6.12	Rent and rent review	136
6.13	Code for Leasing Business Premises	139

SQE1 syllabus

This chapter will enable you to achieve the SQE1 Assessment Specification in relation to Functioning Legal Knowledge concerned with the following:

- Structure of a lease
- Options for the term of a lease, including break clauses
- Leasehold covenants
- Repair
- Insurance
- Alterations
- User and planning
- Alienation
- Rent and rent review
- Code for Leasing Business Premises

Note that for SQE1, candidates are not usually required to recall specific case names or cite statutory or regulatory authorities. Cases and statutory or regulatory authorities are provided for illustrative purposes only unless otherwise indicated.

Learning outcomes

By the end of this chapter you will be able to apply relevant core legal principles and rules appropriately and effectively, at the level of a competent newly qualified solicitor in practice, to realistic client-based and ethical problems and situations in the following areas:

- the purpose and structure of a lease
- the choice between a fixed term lease, a periodic tenancy and a tenancy at will
- the distinction between an absolute, qualified and fully qualified covenant
- the meaning of a tenant's covenant to repair
- the arrangements for the insurance and reinstatement of a building under a typical commercial lease
- how different types of alterations are permitted under a typical tenant's covenant for alterations
- how the user and planning covenants in a lease control the way a property can be used
- how the annual rent is made payable under a lease
- the options for reviewing the annual rent during the term of the lease
- the concept of the hypothetical lease in an open market rent review
- how a landlord controls the tenant's ability to dispose of the property through the alienation covenant in the lease
- the terms on which the tenant may be permitted to assign and/or underlet the property
- the purpose, status and content of the RICS Code for Leasing Business Premises

6.1 Introduction

It is generally thought that owning a freehold is better than owning a leasehold. People think that if they own the freehold land on which their property is built that must be better than having a lease, not least because they can never be evicted by a landlord. A freehold may last forever, whereas a lease is a depreciating asset from the date it is granted. However, leasehold property is popular - and desirable - especially in the commercial context and leasehold work will form a large part of the average commercial property lawyer's caseload. Therefore, it is important for a solicitor to understand the structure and contents of a typical commercial lease so that they can efficiently identify the relevant provisions when instructed to do so.

6.2 Advantages and disadvantages of owning a leasehold property

Looking first at the disadvantages of owning a lease from the tenant's point of view, from the date of its grant the lease will be a depreciating asset. There will be no visible return on the rent since at the end of the term the property belongs to the landlord. As the tenant does not own the property, the landlord will probably retain control and therefore specify what the tenant can and cannot do. There will probably be repairing obligations in the lease which will involve expenditure for the tenant.

From the landlord's perspective there are also disadvantages to granting a lease to a tenant instead of selling the freehold in the property. The tenant may prove unreliable and not pay the rent. The tenant may not take care of the premises, which could result in a depreciation of the landlord's investment. The income and capital are not guaranteed and are dependent on the state of the property market.

There are, however, advantages to the landlord in renting out the property rather than selling it. Positive covenants cannot be easily enforced against subsequent owners in freehold land. When buildings have multiple occupants, whether commercial, residential or a mixture of both, it is important that positive covenants, particularly in relation to repair, can be enforced and this is difficult to achieve with freehold land. Leases are therefore necessary to enforce covenants in buildings with multiple occupants.

Another advantage is that the landlord retains a capital interest in the freehold which, depending upon the market, will be an asset. The landlord can retain control of the management of the building to ensure that the capital value is preserved. If the lease is drafted properly, the landlord will be able to recover all expenditure, for example in relation to repairs and maintenance, by way of a service charge paid by the tenant. The landlord also gains a steady income by renting the property at a market rent.

Commercial tenants also have good business reasons for taking a lease. A lease is flexible: if it is a short-term lease, the tenant can move easily at the end of the term if they need smaller or larger premises. Tenants can often negotiate a break clause to enable them to terminate the lease before the end of the fixed term. Also, the tenant has no capital outlay. Although they may need to pay a capital sum (known as a premium) at the start of the lease, the capital of their business is not tied up in the premises.

Although there are disadvantages for both parties in renting out the property rather than selling the freehold, the advantages will outweigh the disadvantages for most commercial tenants and landlords.

6.3 The structure of a typical commercial lease

Most leases are now drafted with the aid of a precedent, but when the precedent clauses were first drafted, it was on the basis of practical client instructions about what was to happen in the property during the tenancy. Over the years, many of the common clauses have been the subject of statutory intervention and/or case law, so their precise meaning and practical implications might not be obvious to a client today. Solicitors need to understand the law on leases to be able to advise their clients effectively. In particular, it is important to appreciate the specific obligations on the part of the tenant and the landlord in the lease and the practical background to those obligations: these obligations continue for the length of the lease and form the basis for a continuing relationship between landlord and tenant. Leases are relatively complex documents because they attempt to deal with all the issues that might arise during the term.

Leases come in many forms and varying lengths, depending on the type of property, the length of the term and the commercial priorities of the parties. However, a typical business lease of a whole property will contain the following elements:

Prescribed clauses: leases that are dated on or after 19 June 2006 which are granted out of registered land and are compulsorily registrable (see **7.8.3**) must contain a standard set of clauses ('prescribed clauses') at the beginning of the lease, or immediately after any front cover sheet and/or front contents page. The prescribed clauses are a summary of the important details in the lease and bring together, in one place, all the information that the Land Registry needs in order complete registration. This saves time for the Land Registry which will prepare the register entries to complete registration of the lease from the information in these clauses.

Commencement: the lease starts with the words 'This lease', followed by the date of its grant and the names and addresses of the parties. Where the lease is created out of a registered title, the document will carry the usual Land Registry heading (county and district, landlord's title number, brief description of the property, and date) at the top of its first page.

Interpretation: definitions are required to avoid having to repeat detail. Definitions will appear with a first capital letter.

Grant of the lease: the operative part, whereby the landlord grants to the tenant a lease of the property for the term. The term can be fixed, periodic or at will (see **6.4** below).

Ancillary rights: these give the tenant rights over other land to enable them to use the leased property more effectively, eg a right to use roads, car parking spaces or an area for loading/unloading.

Rights excepted and reserved: these are rights in favour of the landlord over the leased property, such as a right to enter to do repairs to service media and other parts of the building.

Annual rent: this is the rent payable by the tenant, which is the landlord's income from the property. It is usually payable quarterly in advance on the historic quarter days, 25 March, 24 June, 29 September and 25 December (see **6.12** below). Other sums payable by the tenant, such as insurance premium, may also be reserved as rent because in the past, it has been easier for the landlord to exercise remedies for non-payment of rent than for breach of other obligations.

Rent review: unless the term is very short, the landlord will want to ensure that there is a mechanism to increase the annual rent in line with rises in rental value in the wider property market. There are different mechanisms available (see **6.12.1** below).

Tenant's covenants: there will be numerous obligations imposed on the tenant as to how they use and look after the property. The most important covenants are discussed at **6.7** to **6.12** below.

Landlord's covenants: there will be a few obligations imposed on the landlord, notably the obligation to insure (see **6.8** below).

Landlord's right to enter on breach of repair covenant: this gives the landlord the right to enter and inspect, give notice to the tenant to repair and if the tenant fails to do so within a certain period, then the landlord can do the work instead (see **9.4.3**).

Re-entry and forfeiture: this allows the landlord to bring the lease to an end if the tenant fails to pay the annual rent or is in breach of one of the other tenant covenants in the lease (see **9.3.4** and **9.4.4**).

A lease of part of a property will contain additional ancillary rights such as rights to use common reception areas, lifts, corridors and stairwells to access the leased property to use shared facilities such as toilets, storage and parking. A lease of part will also have a mechanism for reimbursing the landlord for a proportionate part of the common repair and maintenance expenses, usually referred to as a 'service charge'. However, leases of part are beyond the scope of this manual.

6.4 Options for the term of a lease

Most commercial properties are leased to the tenant for a *fixed term*. The fixed period can be weeks, months or years but is most likely to be years to give the tenant time to establish the business. Historically, commercial properties were let on leases for a term of 25 years, but recently leases have become much shorter and it is not uncommon to find 3–5 year leases in the retail sector. Longer leases will sometimes have a 'break clause', eg an office lease of 15 years with a tenant's right to terminate the lease on the tenth anniversary of the start of the term. At the end of the fixed term, the lease 'expires', or comes to an automatic end, without either the landlord or the tenant having to serve a notice. This option is for tenants who know exactly how long they wish to occupy property and do not object to being locked in for that period of time.

By contrast, a *periodic tenancy* is one which is not granted for a fixed period but continues indefinitely from one period to another. So while a fixed term tenancy may be for one month, a periodic tenancy would be from month to month and may last one month, two months, six months or even run into years. This option is for tenants who are not certain as to how long they wish to occupy the property. They know it will not be for less than the initial period, but after that they wish to continue on a month-to-month or periodic basis. This type of lease will run until either party decides to terminate it by giving the other party notice that they want to bring the arrangement to an end. The notice should be the length of one period of the lease, so one month's notice for a monthly tenancy and one quarter's notice for a quarterly tenancy. However, as an exception to the general rule, a yearly tenancy can be terminated on six months' notice.

The third option is a *tenancy at will*. This is where a tenant occupies the property with the permission of the landlord on the terms that the tenancy may be terminated by either party at any time. So, it is different from a fixed-term tenancy (which is for a specific fixed period) and a periodic tenancy (which is one that runs from one period to another). A tenancy at will is indefinite and might last any number of days, weeks or years. They are not often used for commercial properties as they are too uncertain, but tenancies at will can occur where the parties are not expecting them, eg where a tenant remains in occupation at the end of the formal lease, or where the parties want to create an informal agreement, such as a tenancy between family members.

Business tenants who satisfy certain criteria are able to extend the term and renew the lease under the Landlord and Tenant Act 1954 (see **10.3**).

6.5 Types of leasehold covenant

Unless there are provisions to stop them, tenants are free to do as they wish with their leasehold property, subject only to the general law. This is why landlords insist upon provisions in the lease which either prohibit certain actions by the tenant altogether, or only allow the tenant to do certain things with permission. This ensures that the landlord knows what is happening at the building, eg who is occupying and what alterations have been carried out. Landlords need this degree of control to protect their investment.

The landlord exercises this control by way of tenant covenants in the lease. These covenants fall into three categories:

1. **Absolute Covenant**

   This means the tenant absolutely cannot carry out the stated action according to the lease. The landlord may decide to allow it, either by way of a one-off consent or a permanent variation of the lease, but the landlord has total discretion on the matter.

2. **Qualified Covenant**

   This type of covenant allows the tenant to carry out the stated action, but only if it obtains landlord's consent first.

3. **Fully Qualified Covenant**

   This type of covenant allows the tenant to carry out the stated action if it obtains landlord's consent first, but goes on to say that the landlord will not be able to withhold consent unreasonably.

The landlord might be tempted to place absolute covenants on the tenant giving them no room for manoeuvre at all, but in practice, landlords appreciate that this would not be commercially acceptable to tenants. Tenants may, for example, want to be able to alter premises to suit their needs, or to sell the lease if the premises no longer meet their requirements so absolute prohibitions would not be acceptable. In addition, excessively restrictive terms could be detrimental to the landlord when the rent is reviewed.

The tenant would prefer to have no restrictions at all but, equally, will appreciate the landlord's desire to maintain control and preserve their investment. A tenant will therefore try to make covenants fully qualified so that, while landlord's consent must be obtained, the landlord cannot withhold consent unreasonably. For that reason the tenants' solicitors will try to insert the words 'reasonable' and 'reasonably' throughout the document when negotiating the lease.

6.6 The full repairing and insuring lease

For a landlord, a leasehold property is an investment product that investors buy in order to obtain a capital gain in value when the building is sold and rental income in the meantime. The tenant, and the lease under which it holds the premises, is an intrinsic part of the investment. Historically, leases of commercial property in England and Wales are 'FRI', full repairing and insuring, meaning that the landlord gets a 'clear' rental stream (all profit) and does not have to dip into it to pay for repairs, maintenance and insurance contributions. A lease which does not make the tenant pay for all this is often referred to as not being 'investment quality' or 'institutionally acceptable' to the investment institutions such as pension funds and insurance companies. These institutions see property as a long-term capital investment and as a way of securing an income in the form of rent in the short term. Institutional investors are answerable to their shareholders, pension members and policyholders and have strict views of what is an acceptable form of lease. It is important that the leases act to preserve the capital value of the property by ensuring that:

- the building is kept in good repair
- the lease reserves a market rent throughout the term (with the ability to increase the rent at regular intervals) to ensure a steady income
- the investment is readily sellable if necessary, ie the lease must be acceptable to future buyers of the freehold.

6.7 Repair

Full repairing and insuring or 'FRI' leases protect landlords from incurring any expenditure that cannot be recovered from tenants. Where one tenant has a lease of a building, it is usual to place the tenant under a full repairing obligation for the whole building. Where the tenant has a lease of part of the landlord's building, responsibility will usually be divided between landlord and tenant. The tenant will normally be responsible for the non-structural parts of the premises and the landlord will assume responsibility for the structural parts of the building and the common areas. A lease of part will usually contain provisions enabling the landlord to pass on the costs in maintaining the structure and common parts to the tenants via a service charge. Service charge provisions are beyond the scope of this manual.

Many arguments have arisen over the precise meaning of a covenant 'to repair'. Case law has established the following:

- There must be disrepair first, before the tenant can be in breach of covenant to repair. The physical condition of the property must have deteriorated from some previous physical condition (*Post Office v Aquarius Properties Ltd* [1987]).
- This is a problem if the building is brand new and will inevitably deteriorate from its original pristine condition. However, the property need not be kept in perfect repair: 'It need only be put into such a state of repair as renders it fit for the occupation of a reasonably minded tenant of the class likely to take it' (Esher LJ in *Proudfoot v Hart* [1890]).
- Works of renewal or improvement go beyond repair. Repair is restoration by renewal or replacement of parts of a whole, not renewal or replacement of the whole (*Lurcott v Wakeley* [1911]). It is a question of fact and degree and the work that the tenant has to carry out depends on the age and nature of the property at the date of the lease.
- A repairing covenant does not oblige the tenant to give back to the landlord a property that is 'wholly different' from that leased to them, but it can oblige the tenant to remedy an inherent defect in the design and/or construction of the building if that is the only way to effect the repair (*Ravenseft Properties Ltd v Davstone (Holdings) Ltd* [1980]).

The tenant should beware of repairing covenants with additional wording. A covenant to 'keep' a building in repair also means 'put' it into repair, even if that involves the tenant putting the building into a better state of repair than when they entered into the lease. A covenant to 'keep the property in good condition' is more onerous than a plain covenant to keep it in repair. It can mean that the tenant is obliged to carry out some works, even though there is no actual disrepair (*Welsh v Greenwich LBC* [2000]).

An example of a tenant's covenant is set out below:

10 Repairs

10.1 The Tenant shall repair the Property [*defined as the whole building*].

10.2 The Tenant shall not be liable to repair the Property to the extent that any disrepair has been caused by an Insured Risk, unless and to the extent that:

(a) the policy of insurance of the Property has been vitiated or any insurance proceeds withheld in consequence of any act or omission of the tenant or any person on the property with the tenant's authority; or

(b) the insurance cover in relation to that disrepair is excluded, limited or is unavailable as mentioned in [the landlord's covenant to insure - see **6.8.1** below].

Where the landlord is insuring the building, the tenant should ensure that they are not responsible for repairing damage arising as a result of insured risks as this type of damage should be covered by the insurance provisions in the lease.

6.8 Insurance

It is clearly important to ensure that adequate provisions are in place to insure the property against damage by fire, flood, etc. From a landlord's perspective, the building forms the physical basis of the investment and should be reinstated in the event of damage. Equally, the tenant will want the building to be reinstated so that they can continue to occupy the property for business purposes as intended under the lease. In the case of a letting of whole, the tenant could be made solely responsible for insurance. However, it is more common to adopt the practice used with buildings in multi-occupation where the landlord takes out the insurance, with the cost being passed on to the tenant as a separate insurance rent.

The insurance provisions in a typical lease of commercial property include the following elements:

6.8.1 A landlord's covenant to insure the property against defined risks (the 'insured risks')

There is often an inclusive list of the risks which the landlord must insure against, for example 'fire, storm, flood, etc'. The problem with this is that the landlord may continue to insure against unlikely or expensive risks and if new risks arise, these may not be covered. Accordingly, it is common for the list of risks to conclude with 'such other risks as the landlord may reasonably require'. The landlord's obligation to insure should be limited so that it does not include exclusions, limitations, excesses and conditions imposed by the insurer and any risks that are not commonly available: liability for any shortfall in the proceeds cause by these are passed on to the tenant in the repairing covenant (see clause 10.2. (b) in **6.7** above).

The property should be insured to its 'full reinstatement value', otherwise if the property is totally destroyed there will not be enough money to pay for its rebuilding. Full reinstatement value will include costs of demolition and site clearance, professional fees (eg architects, surveyors etc) and an allowance for inflation.

An example of a landlord's covenant to insure is set out below:

20 Insurance

20.1 Subject to clause 20.2 the landlord shall keep the property insured against loss or damage by the insured risks for its full reinstatement value.

20.2 The landlord's obligation to insure is subject to:

a) any exclusions, limitations, excesses and conditions that may be imposed by the insurers; and

b) insurance being available in the London insurance market on reasonable terms acceptable to the landlord.

From the interpretation section of the lease

Insured Risks: means fire, explosion, lightning, earthquake, storm, flood, bursting and overflowing of water tanks, apparatus or pipes, impact by aircraft and articles dropped from them, impact by vehicles, riot, civil commotion, malicious damage and any other risks that the landlord may reasonably require from time to time.

6.8.2 A covenant by the tenant to pay for the insurance policy

Often this covenant is to pay a sum reserved as rent (the 'insurance rent'), which includes the premium for the buildings insurance policy and an associated policy covering the landlord for loss of the annual rent (ie the income stream) during any period where the tenant is unable to use the building following the occurrence of an insured risk.

An example of a tenant's covenant to pay for the insurance of the property is set out below:

20.3 The tenant shall pay to the landlord on demand:

a) the insurance rent;

b) any amount that is deducted or disallowed by the insurers pursuant to any excess provision in the insurance policy; and

c) any costs that the landlord incurs in obtaining a valuation of the property for insurance purposes.

From the interpretation section of the lease

Insurance Rent: in each year the cost of the premium for the insurance of:

a) the Property, for its full reinstatement cost (taking inflation of building costs into account) against loss or damage by or in consequence of the Insured Risks, including costs of demolition, site clearance, site protection and shoring-up, professionals' and statutory fees and incidental expenses, the cost of any work which may be required under any law and VAT in respect of all those costs, fees and expenses;

b) loss of Annual Rent of the Property for three years; and

c) any insurance premium tax payable on the above.

6.8.3 A covenant by the landlord to reinstate the property

Often this is expressed as a covenant to use the insurance proceeds to reinstate the property (rather than an absolute obligation to reinstate even if the proceeds are insufficient). Ideally, a tenant would like this extended to include an obligation for the landlord to make good any shortfall in the insurance proceeds from its own resources as there will have been a failure to insure the property to its full reinstatement value.

There may also be a provision to deal with the situation where reinstatement is impossible. Many leases provide for the insurance monies to be retained by the landlord, whose building it is, but a tenant in a strong negotiating position (or when it is a long lease for which the tenant has paid a premium) may have agreed that the proceeds will be passed over to the tenant who has been paying the premiums, or that the proceeds will be shared between landlord and tenant proportionate to their respective interests in the building.

An example of a landlord's covenant to reinstate is set out below:

20.4 The Landlord shall, subject to obtaining all necessary planning and other consents, use all insurance money received (other than for loss of rent) to reinstate the Property. The Landlord shall not be obliged to:

a) provide accommodation identical in layout or design so long as accommodation reasonably equivalent to that previously at the Property is provided; or

b) repair or rebuild the Property after a notice has been served pursuant to [the break clause].

6.8.4 Rent suspension

In the absence of an express term to the contrary, rent will continue to be payable even if the property is rendered unusable. The tenant should therefore ensure that the lease provides for the payment of rent to be suspended during any period that the property cannot be occupied following damage by an insured risk. The landlord will normally be happy to allow such rent suspension, as they can insure against loss of rent in such circumstances. However, usually such insurance is limited in duration (often to three years) and the landlord may attempt to limit the rent suspension accordingly.

An example of a rent suspension clause is set out below:

20.5 If the property is damaged or destroyed by a risk against which the landlord is obliged to insure [see clause 20.1 and 20.2 above] so as to be unfit for occupation and use then, unless the policy of insurance of the property has been vitiated in whole or in part in consequence of any act or omission of the tenant or any other person on the property with the actual or implied authority of the tenant, payment of the annual rent, or a fair proportion of it according to the nature and extent of the damage, shall be suspended until the property has been reinstated and made fit for occupation and use, or until the end of three years from the date of damage or destruction, if sooner.

6.8.5 Termination

Unless the lease states otherwise, if the building is totally destroyed, the doctrine of frustration will only apply in exceptional circumstances. Therefore, the lease will often give the landlord the right to terminate the lease should reinstatement prove impossible. The tenant should try to ensure that they have the same right, particularly where the rent suspension is time-limited. The tenant should be able to terminate the lease if the property has not been reinstated by the end of the rent suspension period; otherwise they will be paying rent for a property they cannot use, as well as the rent on alternative premises.

Examples of termination clauses are set out below:

20.6 If, following damage to or destruction of the property, the landlord reasonably considers that it is impossible or impractical to reinstate the property, the landlord may terminate this lease by giving notice to the tenant. On giving notice this lease shall determine but this shall be without prejudice to any right or remedy of the landlord in respect of any breach of the tenant covenants of this lease. Any proceeds of the insurance shall belong to the landlord.

20.7 Provided that the tenant has complied with its obligations in this clause 20, the tenant may terminate this lease by giving notice to the landlord if, following damage or destruction by a risk against which the landlord is obliged to insure, the property has not been reinstated so as to be fit for occupation and use within three years after the date of damage or destruction. On giving this notice this lease shall determine but this shall be without prejudice to any right or remedy of the landlord in respect of any breach of the tenant covenants of this lease. Any proceeds of the insurance shall belong to the landlord.

6.8.6 Interplay between the landlord's insurance covenants and the tenant's repair covenant

If the landlord has complied with its covenants to insure the property to its full reinstatement value against the insured risks specified in the lease, then the landlord should be able to reinstate the property using the insurance proceeds from the buildings insurance policy, the premium having already been recovered from the tenant as insurance rent. The landlord will not receive the rent from the tenant while reinstatement is taking place, but will receive an equivalent sum under the loss of rent insurance policy, also paid for by the tenant. The tenant will be inconvenienced and may have to relocate on a temporary basis, but they will not be paying rent on the property and once the rent becomes payable again (ie the rent suspension provision comes to an end) they will probably be able to resume occupation of the property. If they cannot occupy the property at that point, they may be able to break the lease; if they have no break clause, they will have to start paying rent again for a property they cannot use.

Problems occur when the damage is caused by something not covered by the insurance policy. This could be because a particular risk was not insurable, or the parties agreed that the landlord should not insure against it because the premiums were too high, or where the risk was insured but the tenant has done something entitling the insurer to withhold all or part of the pay-out. In these cases, the tenant will be liable to repair the property under the repairing covenant.

Example 1

You act for the landlord of a two storey retail unit. The property director called this morning to inform you that during a recent lightning storm, a telecoms antennae collapsed causing damage to the roof structure and flooding damage to the upper floor of the property. The lease contains repair and insurance provisions identical to clause 10 (repair) and 20 (insurance) above. The landlord has obtained insurance in accordance with its covenants in the lease and the tenant has paid insurance rent due under the lease. The property director tells you that the tenant is looking to the landlord to put this damage right and is threatening to withhold the annual rent the next time it falls due until the landlord has completed the work. The tenant has previously stated that they consider the annual rent is too high and are looking for alternative premises.

The client wants to know, under the terms of the lease:

a) who is responsible for reinstating the Property;

b) whether the tenant still has to pay the rent while the works are being done; and

c) whether the tenant can use the damage as an opportunity to terminate the lease.

Answer

a) The landlord will be responsible for reinstating the Property:

- Under clause 20.1, the landlord covenants to insure the Property against loss or damage by the Insured Risks, which includes damage caused by lightning and storm, to the full reinstatement value. This is subject to Clause 20.2 but there is no information on any specific exclusions, limitations or excesses. The facts tell us that this insurance is in place.
- Clause 20.3 requires the tenant to pay the 'Insurance Rent' on demand. Insurance Rent is a defined term and covers three years loss of rent. The facts make it clear that the tenant has paid this. (Thus the actual cost of obtaining the insurance is passed on to the tenant, as is consistent with this being an FRI lease.)
- In clause 20.4, the landlord covenants to use the insurance money received to reinstate the property, subject to it obtaining all the necessary planning or other consents. There should be enough money to do this (or the landlord will have to make up the difference) as the landlord's obligation was to insure the property to the full reinstatement value.
- In clause 10.1, the tenant covenants to repair the Property, but this will not apply here as the disrepair has been caused by an Insured Risk and there is no suggestion that the 10.2 a) or b) applies.

b) The tenant will not have to pay all of the rent while the works are being done.

- Under Clause 20.5, if the Property is unfit for occupation and use as a result of the damage by a risk against which the landlord is obliged to insure, rent, or a fair proportion of it, is suspended for three years or earlier reinstatement.
- Lightning and storm are risks against which the landlord is obliged to insure.
- Rent suspension will not apply if payment under the policy has been refused due to any act or default of the tenant, but there is no suggestion of this in the facts.
- However, the damage only seems to affect the first floor, so it may be that only a fair proportion of the rent will cease to be payable.
- The landlord should be able to claim the balance under the loss of rent insurance policy, for which the tenant has paid under clause 20.3.

c) The tenant will not be able use the damage as an opportunity to terminate the lease at this stage.

- Clause 20.6 entitles the landlord, but not the tenant, to terminate the lease on notice if it considers that it is impossible or impractical to reinstate the property, but this seems unlikely on these facts.
- The tenant's right to terminate only arises if the Property has not been reinstated so as to be fit for occupation and use within three years following the date of the damage (ie when the rent suspension period expires).
- Note that if the lease is terminated, by either party, any insurance proceeds will belong to the landlord.

Example 2

You act for the landlord of a two storey retail unit. The property director called this morning to inform you that burglars got in to the shop at some point during the early hours of yesterday morning and caused some damage to the structure of the ground floor. Unfortunately, it appears that they got in as the shop manager failed to lock up the shop door properly. The lease contains repair and insurance provisions identical to clause 10 (repair) and 20 (insurance) above. The landlord has obtained insurance in accordance with its covenants in the lease and the tenant has paid insurance rent due under the lease. The property director tells you that the tenant is looking to the landlord to put this damage right and is threatening to withhold the annual rent the next time it falls due until the landlord has completed the work. The tenant has previously stated that they consider the annual rent is too high and are looking for alternative premises.

The client wants to know, under the terms of the lease:

a) who is responsible for reinstating the property;

b) whether the tenant still has to pay the rent while the works are being done; and

c) whether the tenant can use the damage as an opportunity to terminate the lease.

Answer

Failing to lock the shop door is very likely to have breached a condition in the insurance policy and so insurance is unlikely to be forthcoming. If this is the case:

a) The tenant will be responsible for reinstating the property.

- Under clause 10.1, the tenant has to keep the property in repair.
- Under clause 10.2, the tenant does not have to repair the property where the damage has been caused by an Insured Risk. Insured Risk is defined as including malicious damage and, in theory, covers the damage on the facts.
- However, clause 10.2 goes on to make it clear that the tenant will be liable to repair the property where the insurance policy has been vitiated or insurance proceeds withheld as a result of something that the tenant, or any person on the property with the tenant's authority, has done or failed to do. This would include the failure by the tenant's employee to secure the premises properly.
- The Landlord's covenant in clause 20.4 to use all insurance money received to reinstate the Property will not apply as there will be no insurance money available.

b) The tenant will have to pay all of the rent while the works are being done.

The rent suspension in clause 20.5 only applies if the property is damaged or destroyed by a risk against which the landlord is obliged to insure. The landlord's insurance covenant in clause 20.1 is subject to exclusions, limitations, excesses and conditions that may be imposed by the insurers, one of which is likely to be that the premises are properly secured when left vacant.

c) The tenant will not be able use the damage as an opportunity to terminate the lease.

- Clause 20.6 entitles the landlord, but not the tenant, to terminate the lease on notice if it considers that it is impossible or impractical to reinstate the property. In these circumstances, the landlord has no incentive to terminate as the tenant is liable to repair the property.
- The Tenant cannot terminate the lease under clause 20.7; the right to terminate only applies if the Property is damaged or destroyed by a risk against which the landlord is obliged to insure. The landlord's insurance covenant in clause 20.1 is subject to exclusions, limitations, excesses and conditions that may be imposed by the insurers, one of which is likely to be that the premises are properly secured when left vacant.

6.9 Alterations

Tenants often want to make physical alterations to the property to accommodate their business needs and landlords may have many concerns about this, eg that the works will cause mess and disruption, the alterations might not be done well, the alterations may decrease the value of the freehold reversion and/or that the tenant may not comply with planning or building control requirements. Landlords will also be concerned about alterations which are tailor-made to the current tenant's business needs but which might be off-putting to future tenants.

In the absence of an alterations covenant, the tenant would be able to make any changes it wants. So, a landlord will try and restrict the extent to which a tenant can make alterations, while not making the restrictions too onerous for the tenant. Most alterations clauses make a distinction between different types of alteration, eg:

- Alterations affecting the structure and exterior of the building
- Non-structural interior alterations
- Alterations affecting service media such as heating, lighting, communications systems
- Demountable partitioning, such as that used to separate open plan floors into different 'rooms'

Landlords can use different types of covenant to exert different levels of control over different types of alterations.

6.9.1 Absolute covenants

A landlord may impose an absolute covenant against all types of alterations, but it is more common for a lease to contain this type of covenant in relation to structural and exterior alterations. However, a tenant of business premises can use the provisions of s 3 Landlord and Tenant Act 1927 to enable it to carry out 'improvements', even where the lease contains an absolute prohibition. Under s 3, a tenant who wants to carry out improvements can serve a notice on the landlord detailing its proposals. The landlord has three months within which to object and if it does, the tenant has the right to apply to the court for authorisation to carry out the improvements. The court can authorise the improvements if they add to the letting value of the property, are reasonable and suitable to the character of the property and do not diminish the value of any other property of the landlord.

Instead of objecting or consenting to the works, a landlord can offer to carry out the works itself in return for a reasonable increase in the rent. A tenant is under no obligation to accept an offer by the landlord to carry out the works and may withdraw its notice. If it does so, the landlord then has no right to carry out the works and increase the rent. However, if the tenant rejects the landlord's offer, the court cannot give the tenant authority to do the works itself.

If the landlord does not offer to carry out the works itself, or object to the improvements within three months (or if the court authorises the work), then the tenant may lawfully carry them out, even if the lease contains an absolute covenant against the works.

6.9.2 Qualified and fully qualified covenants

Many landlords will allow tenants to make non-structural alterations and changes to service media, but with consent so that the landlord can retain control by imposing conditions about how the works are done and whether they will need to be removed and the property reinstated at the end of the term. The consent, and the conditions, will typically be imposed in a separate document called a licence to alter.

A qualified covenant against alterations prohibits alterations without the landlord's prior consent. Under s 19(2) of the Landlord and Tenant Act 1927, a term is implied into a qualified covenant against making 'improvements' that the landlord cannot unreasonably withhold its consent. Case law has established that if the works in question will increase the value or usefulness of the property to the tenant, then they will constitute an improvement, even if they will result in the reduction in the value of the landlord's reversionary interest. In relation to improvements, therefore, the landlord will not be able to withhold their consent unreasonably. However, a tenant would prefer a fully qualified covenant that makes it clear that the landlord cannot withhold their consent unreasonably to an alteration, whether or not it amounts to an improvement.

Since demountable partitioning usually has a minimal impact on the building, many landlords will allow this to be erected and removed without the need for consent at all. However, there are many variations in alterations clauses; the tenant's solicitor will need to have a practical understanding of the nature of the works and study the particular alterations clause in order to establish whether or not the tenant's proposed works are permitted by the lease and whether the works need to be removed and the property reinstated at the end of the term.

Example

Your firm is acting for the landlord of a retail property. The tenant is seeking to make some alterations to the property as it wants to make it more contemporary and more attractive to customers. The tenant wants to remove the plaster from the internal walls to reveal the bare bricks and give a more 'warehouse' look to the property. In addition, it wants to increase the height and scale of the external shop front doors. It also wants to remove the extensive recessed lighting and replace it with fewer large scale pendant lights. The alterations clause from the lease is as follows:

7 Alterations

7.1 *The tenant shall not make any external or structural alteration or addition to the property and shall not make any opening in any boundary structure of the property.*

7.2 *The tenant shall not install any service media on the exterior of the property nor alter the route of any service media at the property without the consent of the landlord, such consent not to be unreasonably withheld.*

7.3 *The tenant shall not make any internal, non-structural alteration to the property unless:*

(a) *all necessary consents from any competent authority have been obtained*
(b) *the landlord has been supplied with drawings and where appropriate a specification in duplicate prepared by an architect who must supervise the work throughout*
(c) *the reasonable fees of the landlord, any superior landlord, any mortgagee and their respective professional advisors have been paid*
(d) *the tenant has entered into such covenants as the landlord may require as to the execution and reinstatement of the alterations*
(e) *the landlord's prior written consent has been obtained (such consent not to be unreasonably withheld).*

The landlord has asked you to advise on whether it has to consent to the alterations.

Answer

Each part of the proposed works should be considered separately:

- **Remove the plaster from the internal walls, to reveal the bare bricks:** this is an internal non-structural alteration which is permitted under clause 7.3 with the consent of the landlord, which is not to be unreasonably withheld. The tenant will need to ask for consent and meet the conditions set out in the clause, but the landlord cannot unreasonably refuse consent.

- **Increase the height and scale of the shop front doors:** this is an external and structural change which is prohibited under clause 7.1 of the lease. The tenant could still seek the landlord's consent to this change, but there is no obligation on the landlord to agree to such a request. This is an alteration which affects the exterior of the property and so will require planning permission. If the landlord is minded to agree to it, you will need to check the other tenant's covenants as there is likely to be one requiring the tenant to comply with all laws relating to works carried out at the property, which will include planning laws and the need for planning permission.

  The tenant could also consider an application under s 3 Landlord and Tenant Act 1927, but this would involve delay and the works might not qualify as 'improvements' which add to the letting value of the property, are reasonable and suitable to the character of the property and do not diminish the value of any other property of the landlord.
- **Remove the recessed lighting and replace it with large-scale pendant lighting:** this will be an internal non-structural alteration and so will need consent under clause 7.3. It may also be altering the route of the service media as it will be altering the route of the electricity, so the proposal will also need the consent of the landlord under clause 7.2. Landlord's consent cannot be unreasonably withheld in either case.

6.9.3 Compensation for improvements

A tenant which has obtained prior authorisation to make the improvements by using the s 3 statutory procedure is entitled to claim compensation for improvements at the end of the term that 'add to the letting value of the holding' under s 1 of the Landlord and Tenant Act 1927, provided the claim is made within certain statutory time limits. In practice, these provisions are rarely used. Tenants usually obtain consent to carry out the alterations without using the s 3 statutory procedure, and in any event most leases contain a tenant's covenant to remove all alterations and reinstate the premises at the end of the term (so there are no improvements left in respect of which to claim compensation).

6.10 User and planning

There are many reasons why a landlord might want to restrict use of the property. So for retail premises, it could be to keep a balance of shops within a shopping centre, to keep the nature of a centre in keeping with the other shops and/or to prevent competition with its own or other shops. A landlord may therefore choose to impose a tenant's covenant which restricts the use of the property to a single purpose:

> Not to use the Premises other than as a restaurant.

However, a narrow user clause might put off a tenant who wants to retain the possibility of diversifying the business or disposing of the lease at a later stage. A narrow user clause may also depress the rent on any rent review (see **6.12.2**). The landlord may, therefore, impose a covenant which allows for the possibility of changing the user by making use of the categories set out in the Use Classes Order 1987 (see **1.7.2**):

> Not to use the Premises other than as a restaurant or such other use falling within Use Class E of the Town and Country Planning (Use Classes) Order 1987.

A landlord can impose greater control with a qualified covenant:

> Not to use the Premises other than as a restaurant or such other use falling within Use Class E of the Town and Country Planning (Use Classes) Order 1987 as the Landlord may approve in writing.

Unlike alienation covenants (see **6.11** below), there is no statutory implication that the landlord's consent cannot be unreasonably withheld for user covenants, but the landlord cannot charge a fine or an increased rent as a condition of giving consent, provided no structural alteration is involved (s 19(3) of the Landlord and Tenant Act 1927). However, a tenant would prefer a fully qualified covenant:

> Not to use the Premises other than as a restaurant or such other use falling within Use Class E of the Town and Country Planning (Use Classes) Order 1987 as the Landlord may approve in writing (such approval not to be unreasonably withheld).

Both parties need to bear in mind that in order to change the use of a property, it may be necessary to obtain planning permission (see **1.7**) and consider the terms of any covenants affecting title to the property (see **2.5.5**). It is not uncommon for the landlord to retain control of such issues by, for example, imposing a tenant's covenant not to apply for planning consents without the landlord's permission.

6.11 Alienation

Alienation is a generic term which includes different ways of creating an interest in the property for the benefit of a third party. The landlord will have chosen the original tenant of the lease carefully, based upon the tenant's 'strength of covenant', ie the tenant's ability to pay the rent and perform the covenants in the lease. In the absence of a restriction in the lease, a tenant can dispose of their interest in any way they like. The landlord will want control over whoever else might occupy the investment property and will usually insist upon restrictions in the lease against tenants dealing with the leasehold interest.

Alienation includes:

- assignment
- underletting (also known as subletting)
- charging (also known as mortgaging)
- sharing occupation (allowing a third party in while continuing to occupy, perhaps under a licence or concession arrangement)
- parting with possession (a catch-all term which covers assignment and underletting but also includes informal arrangements which may be difficult to classify).

Most leases contain an absolute covenant against all types of alienation, but then go on to permit certain types of alienation on controlled terms. An example of this type of provision is set out below:

> Except as expressly permitted by this lease, the Tenant shall not assign, underlet, charge, part with or share possession or share occupation of this lease or the Property or hold the lease on trust for any person.

Most leases will prohibit charging as the landlord will be concerned that if the borrower defaults on the mortgage, the lender may take possession of the property or exercise its power of sale. Some leases permit sharing occupation, but only with companies in the same group as the tenant and on terms such that no tenancy is created. Parting with possession is usually prohibited, other than by assignment or underletting. This chapter will consider typical tenant's covenants in the lease relating to assignment and underletting; the conveyancing procedures for these transactions are covered in **Chapter 8** (assignment) and **Chapter 7** (underletting).

6.11.1 Alienation terminology

When a lease is granted, it is possible (subject to the terms of the lease) to transfer the lease to someone else (assignment), or allow someone else to occupy the building on what is known as an underlease (or sublease, the two terms are interchangeable). After the original tenant, there may have been many different people who have owned the lease and occupied the premises. The diagram below illustrates the following transactions:

- the grant of a lease
- the assignment of lease
- the grant of an underlease

Example

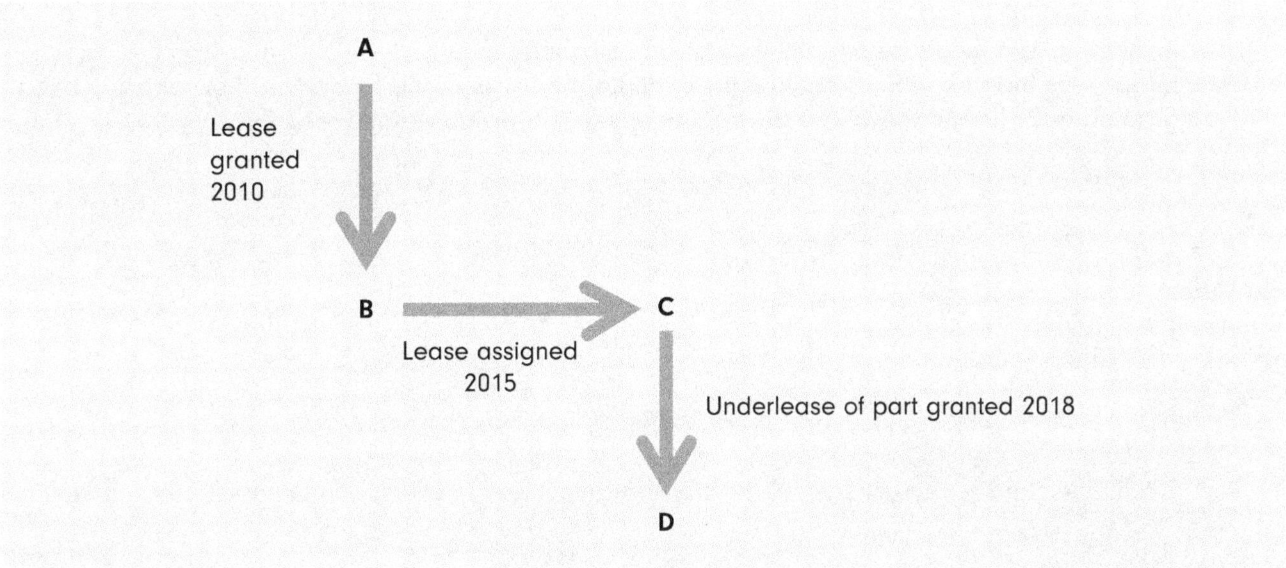

A is the freehold owner of a three-storey office property. The whole of the property was let by A to B in 2010 for a term of 20 years. B assigned the lease in 2015 to C. In 2018, C granted D an underlease of the top floor.

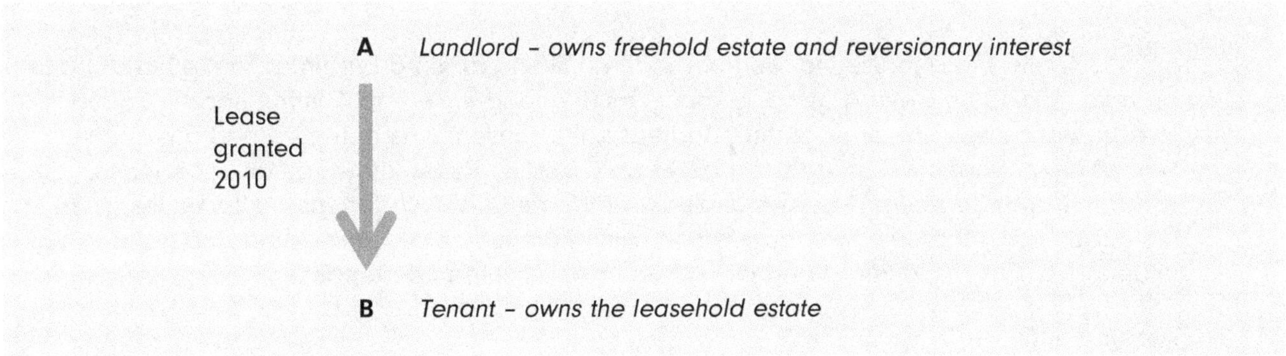

Taking each stage in turn:

When the lease was granted in 2010, A was the landlord of B. A owns the freehold estate in the building. The terms of the lease were the subject of negotiation between A and B. In 2010, upon the grant of the lease, B became A's tenant. A owns the reversionary interest and B owned the leasehold estate.

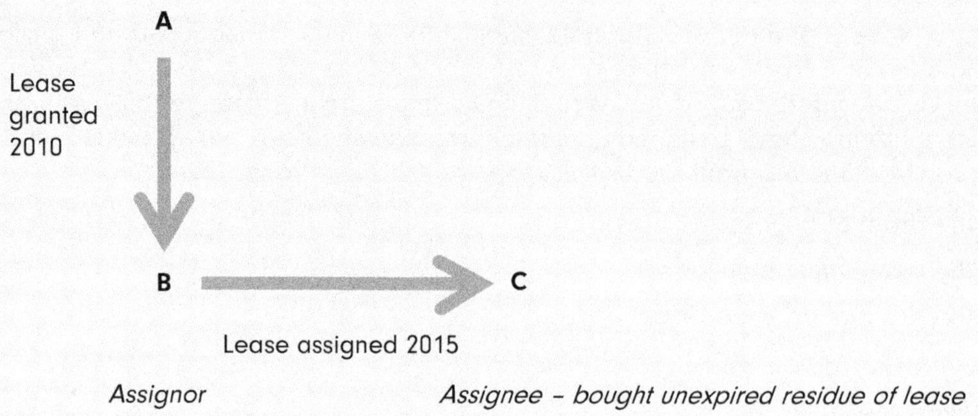

In 2015, B sold the lease to C by way of an assignment. In the transaction, B was the assignor and C was the assignee. C could not negotiate the terms of the lease as it had already been granted in 2010 and they were buying the unexpired residue of the lease.

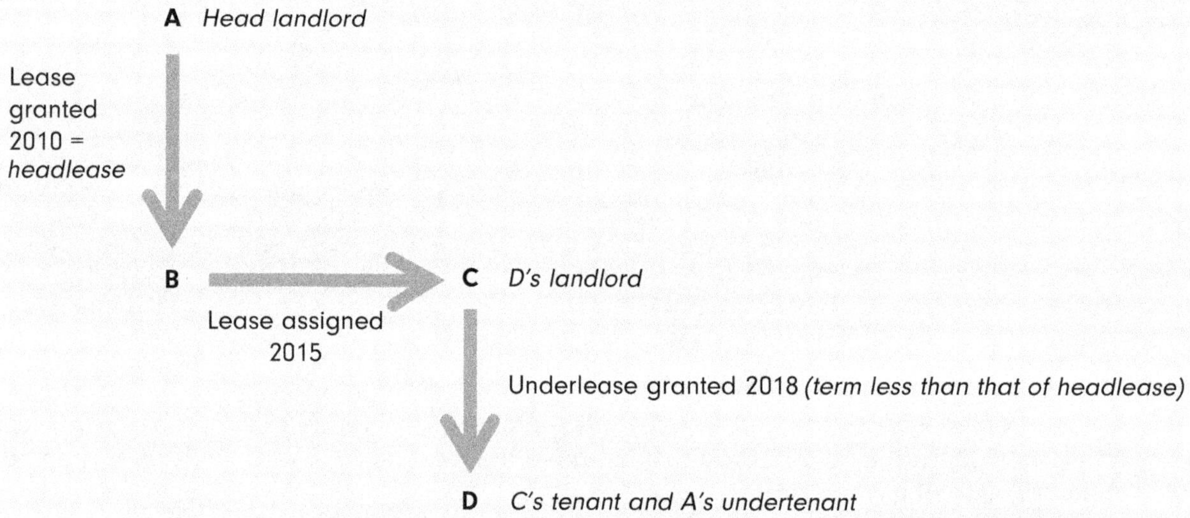

In 2018 C allowed D to use the top floor of the building to run a business. The lease granted in 2010 between A and B is known as the headlease and A is the head landlord. In accordance with the terms of the headlease, A's consent was obtained and a lease of part of the premises was negotiated between C and D. This is known as an underlease, which can also be referred to as a sublease. The term of the underlease must be less than C's headlease, otherwise the arrangement would amount to an assignment and not an underlease. C is D's landlord and in relation to A, C is the undertenant.

6.11.2 Assignment

A commercial lease will usually allow assignment of the whole property, but not of part as many properties are unsuitable for legal and physical sub-division into separate ownership. There are three statutory provisions that are relevant to assignment covenants:

1. **Section 19(1)(a) Landlord and Tenant Act 1927*:** this implies into any qualified covenant (not to assign without the landlord's consent) that it be deemed to be subject to a proviso that such consent is not to be unreasonably withheld. The effect, therefore, is to convert a qualified covenant into a fully qualified covenant.

2. **Section 19(1A) Landlord and Tenant Act 1927*:** this allows for the landlord and the tenant to agree in advance conditions and circumstances in which it would not be unreasonable for the landlord to refuse consent. Conditions are often that the assignor agrees to give an authorised guarantee agreement ('AGA' - see **8.4**) for the assignee and/or that the assignee agrees to provide guarantors. Circumstances can include that the assignor is up-to-date with the rent and/or that the assignee is of sufficient financial strength to enable it to comply with the tenant's covenants in the lease. The effect is that such pre-agreed conditions and circumstances are deemed reasonable.
3. **Section 1 Landlord and Tenant Act 1988*:** this means that where there is a qualified covenant on assignment (whether the proviso that consent is not to be unreasonably withheld is express or implied by statute) and the tenant has made a written application for consent, the landlord must within a reasonable time:
    a) give consent, except in a case where it is reasonable not to give consent
    b) serve on the tenant written notice of its decision whether or not to give consent specifying in addition:
        i) if the consent is given subject to conditions, those conditions,
        ii) if the consent is withheld, the reasons for withholding it.

* You may be required to know and be able to use these statutory authorities in the SQE1 assessments.

The Court of Appeal laid down a number of guidelines on the issue of the landlord's reasonableness under s 19(1)(a) in a 1986 case concerning an application to assign:

(a) The purpose of a fully qualified covenant against assignment is to protect the landlord from having its premises used or occupied in an undesirable way, or by an undesirable tenant or assignee.

(b) A landlord is not entitled to refuse its consent to an assignment on grounds which have nothing whatever to do with the relationship of landlord and tenant in regard to the subject matter of the lease.

(c) It is unnecessary for the landlord to prove that the conclusions which led it to refuse to consent were justified, if they were conclusions which might be reached by a reasonable person in the circumstances.

(d) It may be reasonable for the landlord to refuse its consent to an assignment on the ground of the purpose for which the proposed assignee intends to use the premises, even though that purpose is not forbidden by the lease.

(e) In general a landlord is bound to consider only its own relevant interests when deciding whether to refuse consent to an assignment of a lease. However, it would be unreasonable for a landlord not to consider the detriment which would be suffered by the tenant if consent were to be refused, if that detriment would be extreme and disproportionate in relation to the benefit gained by the landlord.

(f) Subject to the above propositions, it is, in each case, a question of fact, depending on all the circumstances, whether the landlord's consent to an assignment is being withheld unreasonably.

The following are examples of situations where consent has been held to have been *reasonably* withheld:

- where the proposed assignee's references were unsatisfactory
- where there was a long-standing and extensive breach of the repairing covenant by the assignor and the landlord could not be reasonably satisfied that the assignee would be in a position to remedy the breach
- where the assignee would be in a position to compete with the landlord's business

- where the assignment would reduce the value of the landlord's reversion (although this will not be a reasonable ground for withholding consent if the landlord has no intention of selling the reversion)
- where the proposed assignee intends to carry on a use detrimental to the premises, or a use inconsistent with the landlord's 'tenant mix' policy
- where the assignee would, unlike the assignor, acquire protection under Part II of the Landlord and Tenant Act 1954 (see **6.11.3**).

The following are examples of situations where consent has been held to have been *unreasonably* withheld:

- where the landlord has refused consent in an attempt to obtain some advantage for itself
- where there are minor breaches of the repairing covenant
- where premises had been on the market for 18 months, the rent was significant and the slight harm to the landlord would be outweighed by prejudice to the tenant.

An issue which has been before the court on more than one occasion is whether the landlord would be acting unreasonably in refusing consent where it anticipated a breach of the user covenant by the assignee. In *Ashworth Frazer Ltd v Gloucester City Council* [2002] 05 EG 133, the court considered that the correct approach is to examine what the reasonable landlord would do when asked to consent in the particular circumstances. It would usually be reasonable for a landlord to withhold consent where an assignee proposed to use the premises in breach of the terms of the lease. However, there could be circumstances where the refusal of consent on this ground alone would be unreasonable (although the court did not say what these circumstances might be). In other words, each case will be looked at on its own merits in light of what a reasonable landlord would do.

Under the provisions of the Equality Act 2010, any discrimination in withholding consent for the disposal of a property on grounds of race, sex or disability is generally unlawful.

Example

You act for the landlord of a retail property. The tenant, a DIY hardware retailer, has had some financial problems recently and has decided to close down the business at the property. It has found another prospective tenant, a women's clothing retailer, to which it wants to assign the property. The assignment provisions in the lease are as follows:

6. Assignments

6.11 *Except as expressly permitted by this lease, the tenant shall not assign, underlet, charge, part with or share possession or share occupation of this lease or the Property or hold the lease on trust for any person.*

6.12 *The tenant shall not assign the whole of this lease without the consent of the landlord, such consent not to be unreasonably withheld.*

6.13 *The tenant shall not assign part only of this lease.*

6.14 *The landlord and the tenant agree that for the purposes of section 19(1A) of the Landlord and Tenant Act 1927 the landlord may give its consent to an assignment subject to all or any of the following conditions:*

(a) *a condition that the assignor enters into an authorised guarantee agreement in the form set out in Schedule 1; and*

(b) *a condition that a person of standing acceptable to the landlord acting reasonably enters into a guarantee and indemnity of the tenant covenants of this lease in such form as the landlord may reasonably require.*

6.15 *The landlord and the tenant agree that for the purposes of s 19(1A) of the Landlord and Tenant Act 1927 the landlord may refuse its consent to an* *assignment if any of the following circumstances exist at the date of the tenant's application for consent to assign this lease:*

(a) *the Annual Rent or any other money due under this lease is outstanding or there is a material breach of covenant by the tenant that has not been remedied; or*

(b) *in the landlord's reasonable opinion the assignee is not of sufficient financial standing to enable it to comply with the tenant's covenants and conditions contained in this lease.*

The landlord has asked you for advice on whether it has to agree to the assignment and if so, what it can do to protect its position.

Answer

Clause 11.1 prohibits assignment except as expressly permitted by the lease.

11.2 provides for the tenant to assign the whole property, subject to the landlord's consent. This is a fully qualified covenant so the landlord will not be able to refuse consent unreasonably.

11.4 provides, in accordance with s 19(1A), conditions which need to be satisfied in order for the landlord to give its consent. If these conditions are not satisfied, it will not be unreasonable for the landlord to refuse consent. They are that the assignor gives an AGA and/or that the assignee provides a guarantor for its performance of the tenant's covenants.

11.5 provides for circumstances in which it will be reasonable for the landlord to refuse its consent. They are that there is rent outstanding and that the landlord does not think the assignee is in a financial position to comply with the covenants in the lease.

So, assuming that the assignor is not in arrears with the rent, the landlord will need to find out more about the assignee and its guarantor. The landlord should seek references, accounts and carry out solvency searches. The facts tell us that assignor is not doing well financially and so it may be better to have a new tenant. The landlord would also have the security of the AGA and a guarantor for the assignee which will be conditions of its consent, although the AGA may not be of much comfort if the assignor continues to have financial difficulties.

The parties should also consider whether the assignee proposes to change the use of the property (see **6.10** above).

6.11.3 Underletting

An underlease is a lease created by someone who is already a tenant. When a tenant grants an underlease, there are two leases in existence in relation to the same property, a headlease and an underlease. An underlease is an estate in land. It must be for a shorter term than the headlease out of which it is created, even if just by one day. Otherwise the transaction is an assignment of the headlease rather than the creation of a new underlease.

A tenant might choose to underlet because the property is temporarily surplus to requirements. Rather than having the property empty and wasting money on rent payable to the landlord, the tenant wants to cut its losses and recoup the rent by letting it out to someone else. In a buoyant property market, the rent the tenant can achieve on the underletting might be greater than the rent payable to the landlord, so the tenant may even make a profit. An underletting will be better than an assignment of the lease if the tenant would like to get the property back again at some time in the future, or if the tenant only wants to dispose of part of the property. So, if the property has three floors, the tenant can underlet one floor and keep the rest of the property for itself.

Another reason for a tenant deciding to underlet rather than assign is that the landlord has concerns about the financial strength of the proposed new occupier, so will not give consent for an assignment of the headlease. The landlord might, however, be prepared to consent to the creation of an underlease as the headlease will still be in place and the headtenant will still owe the rent to the landlord. The risk of the proposed new occupier not being able to pay the rent then rests with the headtenant rather than the landlord.

Alternatively it is the tenant who has concerns about the proposed new occupier. If the tenant's lease is assigned and the assignee defaults, the tenant will probably be liable for that default as it will have given an AGA to the landlord when the assignment took place. If the tenant retains the headlease and is therefore able to exercise a landlord's control over the undertenant, the tenant's ability to deal with the undertenant's difficulties will be greater and the tenant may even be able to prevent the undertenant from going into default.

It may be that the tenant would prefer to assign the lease, but cannot find anyone willing to take it. This situation arises when rent levels have been dropping and the rent reserved by the tenant's lease is too high. So the proposed new occupier will not take an assignment of the lease, but it might be willing to take an underlease of the property at a lower rent. This way at least some of the tenant's rent is covered and the other property-related costs, such as insurance and repair, are off-loaded onto the undertenant.

A landlord will be concerned about the prospect of an underletting for two main reasons:

1. It is possible that the landlord might end up with the undertenant as their direct tenant. This can occur if the headtenant's lease is forfeited and the undertenant, whose underlease would normally come to an end at the same time, successfully applies to court for relief from forfeiture (see **Chapter 9**). It can also occur if the headtenant's lease is surrendered, or disclaimed by the headtenant's liquidator, or if both leases expire and the undertenant exercises their statutory right to stay on in the property and apply for a new lease under the Landlord and Tenant Act 1954, but the headtenant does not (see **Chapter 10**).
2. Although legally the headtenant will remain liable to the landlord for the performance of the tenant's covenants under the lease, in reality it is the undertenant who will be in occupation and who will have physical control of the property. The landlord will have very limited day-to-day control over what is happening at the property as the rights reserved to the landlord, such as inspection and serving notices to repair, will be exercisable by the headtenant and the landlord will have to go through the headtenant to get anything done.

A landlord can protect itself by imposing strict controls on the tenant's ability to underlet in the lease. It is not uncommon for a lease to contain an absolute prohibition on underletting, or for it to only permit underlettings of whole rather than part. Many landlords prohibit underlettings of part because the building may not be physically suitable for sub-division, or they do not want the estate management burden of dealing with multiple tenants.

If underlettings of whole or part are permitted, there will be a requirement for the tenant to obtain the landlord's consent. The following statutory provisions apply:

Section 19(1)(a) Landlord and Tenant Act 1927: this implies into any qualified covenant (not to underlet without the landlord's consent) that it be deemed to be subject to a proviso that such consent is not to be unreasonably withheld.

Section 1 Landlord and Tenant Act 1988: this means that where there is a fully qualified covenant on underletting (whether the proviso that consent is not to be unreasonably withheld is express or implied by statute) and the tenant has made a written application for consent, the landlord must within a reasonable time:

(a) give consent, except in a case where it is reasonable not to give consent

(b) serve on the tenant written notice of its decision whether or not to give consent specifying in addition:

(i) if the consent is given subject to conditions, those conditions,

(ii) if the consent is withheld, the reasons for withholding it.

It is also likely that conditions for underletting have been imposed in the alienation covenant in the lease and if these conditions are not complied with, then the lease is at risk of forfeiture and any underlease created out of it will be at risk too.

Common conditions include:

- that the terms of the underlease mirror the terms of the headlease. That will be a problem to the undertenant if the terms of the headlease are particularly onerous, but it will reassure the landlord that the covenants in the headlease are not being watered down.
- that the annual rent reserved by the underlease is at least as high as the annual rent reserved by the headlease and that the underlease annual rent must be reviewed at the same time and on the same terms as the annual rent payable under the headlease. This reassures the landlord that rent levels in the property are being maintained and that if the headlease falls away leaving the underlease in place, there will be no loss of income. This type of condition can be very problematic for the headtenant and the undertenant in a falling market as the rent payable under the headlease might be much higher than the market rent. A compromise is a condition that says that the underlease rent must be at the market rent at the time of the underletting.
- that any underletting must exclude s 24–28 in Part II of the Landlord and Tenant Act 1954, which give business tenants the statutory right to stay on the property and renew their leases at the expiry of the contractual term (see **Chapter 10**). This means that the only way the landlord will get stuck with the undertenant at the end of the underlease is if it agrees to the undertenant being granted a new lease.
- that the undertenant enters into a 'direct covenant' with the landlord to perform the tenant's covenants in the underlease and the headlease. Only the obligation to pay the annual rent payable under the headlease is excluded from the direct covenant. The direct covenant is necessary because ordinarily there is no liability between the landlord and the undertenant, so the direct covenant creates a contractual relationship. This means that the landlord can sue the undertenant for breaches of either lease, other than the covenant to pay the headlease rent.
- that no further underletting of the property is permitted.

An example of the underletting provisions in a lease is set below:

12 Underlettings

12.1 The tenant shall not underlet the whole of the property except in accordance with this clause nor without the consent of the landlord, such consent not to be unreasonably withheld.

12.2 The tenant shall not underlet part only of the property.

12.3 Any underletting by the tenant shall be by deed and shall include:

(a) an agreement between the tenant and the undertenant that the provisions of ss 24 to 28 of the Landlord and Tenant Act 1954 are excluded from applying to the tenancy created by the underlease;

(b) the reservation of a rent which is not less than the full open market rental value of the property at the date the property is underlet and which is payable at the same times as the annual rent under this lease;

(c) provisions for the review of rent at the same dates and on the same basis as the review of rent in this lease;

(d) a covenant by the undertenant, enforceable by and expressed to be enforceable by the landlord (as superior landlord at the date of grant), to observe and perform the tenant covenants in the underlease and the tenant covenants in this lease, except the covenant to pay the rents reserved by this lease; and

(e) provisions requiring the consent of the landlord to be obtained in respect of any matter for which the consent of the landlord is required under this lease, and shall otherwise be consistent with and include tenant covenants no less onerous (other than as to the annual rent) than those in this lease.

6.12 Rent and rent review

The lease will reserve an annual rent and include a tenant's covenant to pay it. The lease should make the following matters clear:

- When rent is payable: although it is an annual rent, it is usual to spread the annual payment out into four equal instalments. Historically the rent payment dates are the 'usual quarter days' of 25 March, 24 June, 29 September and 25 December (linked to religious festivals) so although the instalment sums are equal, the quarters are of differing lengths.
- Whether rent is payable in advance or arrears: if the lease is silent, rent is deemed to be paid in arrears but it is more usual for it to be paid in advance. The landlord gets its rental income earlier and avoids the risk of getting to the end of the period and then discovering, too late, that the tenant is unable to pay.
- How instalments are to be apportioned: it is unlikely the lease will begin precisely on one of the rent payment dates in the lease. The tenant will need to make an interim payment to take it through from when it begins to occupy the property until the next rent payment day. This initial sum will be less than a full quarter's rent, so the quarterly rent will need to be apportioned. Apportionment is usually done on a daily basis.
- How the rent is to be paid: it is usual to specify how the payment is to be made, often by direct debit or electronic transfer.
- VAT: if and how it will arise and who will account for it. A grant of a commercial lease is an exempt supply, subject to the landlord's option to tax. If the landlord has opted to tax, the lease should provide that VAT can be added onto the agreed annual rent (see **1.6.3**).
- Review of the rent: the rent cannot change unless there are express provisions to that effect. This is often dealt with in a separate part of the lease.

An example of the tenant's covenant to pay rent is set out below:

7. The annual rent

7.11 The tenant shall pay the annual rent and any VAT in respect of it by four equal instalments in advance on or before the rent payment dates. The payments shall be made by banker's standing order or by any other method that the landlord requires at any time by giving notice to the tenant.

7.12 The first instalment of the annual rent and any VAT in respect of it shall be made on the date of this lease and shall be the proportion, calculated on a daily basis, in respect of the period beginning on the date of this lease and ending on the day before the next rent payment date.

From the interpretation section of the lease

Annual rent: rent at an initial rate of £120,000 per annum and then as revised pursuant to this lease.

Rent payment dates: 25 March, 24 June, 29 September and 25 December.

VAT: value added tax chargeable under the Value Added Tax Act 1994 and any similar replacement tax and any similar additional tax.

6.12.1 Types of rent review

A rent review clause is a mechanism by which the annual rent payable under a lease is periodically reassessed. There are several types of rent review clause:

(a) **Fixed increase**: it is possible to have a rent review clause which provides that, at various set dates throughout the term, the rent will increase to a set amount (eg £30,000 for the first five years, £35,000 for the next five etc). Although this has the benefits of certainty and simplicity, it is not often used because of difficulties in predicting with any certainty what rental levels are likely to be at a given point in the future.

(b) **Index-linked**: here, the rent is linked to an external index, such as the Retail Prices Index. The rationale is that this will allow rent to be altered in line with inflation. However, this does not track the property market specifically, and therefore there may still be discrepancies between the reviewed rent and actual rental values at the time of review. These types of rent review will often have a 'cap and a collar' which limit the percentage increase but also ensure a minimum increase.

(c) **Tenant's receipts**: rent review can also be linked to the tenant's receipts from its use of the property. Where this type of clause is used, it is often linked to the tenant's turnover, but could also be linked to other receipts, such as its profits or the sums it receives from subletting the property, for example. This has the advantage of tracking the tenant's actual financial health (and ability to pay the rent) and also gives the landlord an incentive to do all it can to increase the tenant's trade. However, there are obvious downsides for the landlord should the tenant's business falter.

(d) **Open market rent review**: here, rent is adjusted at regular intervals (usually every 3–5 years) during the term by reference to the open market rental value of the premises at the time of the review. This is the most common form of rent review clause.

6.12.2 Open market rent review: the basis of valuation

The aim of an open market rent review is to determine the rent which a tenant would be prepared to pay were the property to be let in the open market on the terms of the lease on the rent review date. In reality, no such exercise is going to be carried out; the tenant is staying in the premises, so it is a hypothetical assessment of what the property *would* be worth *were* it to be let on the open market, ie what a hypothetical tenant would pay for a hypothetical lease of the property.

There are two elements to consider: the physical property and the terms of the lease itself. Generally speaking, the hypothetical assessment of what the property would be worth on the rental market should be based as closely as possible on the reality of the situation. Thus, if the property is new and modern in a desirable location, the rent on review should be assessed accordingly. If the lease terms are onerous on the tenant (eg because the alienation and user provisions are very narrow), this too should be reflected in the rent review.

It is not always going to be easy to assess the reality of the situation. For example, if the premises are dilapidated and run-down, the tenant might expect the rental value be assessed accordingly. However, if the premises are dilapidated and run-down because the tenant is in breach of its repairing obligations under the lease, it would not be fair that the rent should be reduced because then the tenant would be profiting from its breach. Similarly, if the tenant has invested in voluntarily improving the property, it would not be fair to assess the rental value of the upgraded premises on that basis as the tenant would be effectively paying twice, once for the works and once by way of increased rent, while the landlord gets a windfall.

To deal with these valuation problems, a well-drafted rent review clause will make certain assumptions and certain disregards to try to balance out these sorts of issue.

Common assumptions are that the property is available to let in the open market:

- 'By a willing landlord to a willing tenant': there is a landlord who wants to grant the lease and a tenant in the market for taking it. Without them, the hypothetical letting would not take place at all.
- 'With vacant possession': the hypothetical tenant would not make an offer on a property unless it was empty.
- 'On the terms of this lease other than as to the amount of the annual rent but including the provisions for review of the annual rent': the lease should state that the provisions of the hypothetical lease are the same as the real lease, with the exception of the rent payable because the rent figure is likely to change. It would not be fair, for example, for a rent review clause to create a hypothetical lease with more generous terms (eg on user or alienation) than the actual lease, as this would increase the rent artificially. Similarly, it would not be fair to exclude the rent review provisions from the hypothetical lease as without a rent review clause, the rent would be much higher because a tenant would pay more for the certainty of knowing the rent would not go up for the whole of the term and a landlord would charge more at the outset if it knew there was no ability to increase the rent during the term. Often the solicitor will get the advice of the client's specialist valuer on this point.
- 'For a term of [?] years': the lease should specify the term of the hypothetical lease. This is a difficult point. One option is to specify the original term, eg 15 years, but if the review is taking place 10 years into a 15-year term, it might not be fair that the reviewed rent should be assessed as if there were still 15 years left to run on the lease, whereas in reality, there are only 5. This may have quite an effect on the level of rent depending on market conditions: in times of recession, tenants seek the flexibility of shorter terms and therefore a 15-year hypothetical term will tend to depress the rent. In better times, tenants might pay more for a longer term as they want stability for business growth, so a 15-year hypothetical term will tend to increase the rent. It is difficult to predict what economic conditions will be like at each rent review date, so an alternative approach is to provide that the hypothetical lease term is equal to the unexpired residue of the actual term, perhaps with a minimum term to cover the situation where the actual lease is very close to its expiry date.
- 'On the assumption that the tenant has fully complied with their obligations in this lease': since the obligations include the repair covenant, this deals with the point made above that the tenant should not profit from its failure to repair the property.
- 'On the assumption that if the property has been destroyed or damaged, it has been fully restored': if the property were to be badly damaged, say, the week before the review, it would not be fair for the annual rent to be determined for the whole of the next review period on that basis as the landlord would not have had a chance to reinstate the damage. The rent review goes ahead on the basis of an undamaged property, but the tenant will not be disadvantaged as liability to pay the increased annual rent will be suspended (see **6.8.4** above).

Common disregards are:

- 'Any effect on rent of the fact that the tenant has been in occupation of the property': the tenant's occupation is disregarded to prevent the landlord arguing that the tenant would pay an inflated annual rent in order to avoid the costs of relocation.
- 'Any goodwill attached to the property by reason of any business carried out there by the tenant': if there is existing goodwill at the property (eg a regular flow of customers, a good reputation), then it will have been generated by the tenant's business activities so should not result in the tenant having to pay a higher rent.

- 'Any effect on rent attributable to any physical improvement to the property carried out by the tenant with all necessary consents and not pursuant to an obligation to the landlord': this covers voluntary improvements made by the tenant (so not repair or works done to comply with statute) and ensures that the annual rent will not be increased (if the improvements add value) or reduced (if they detract from value).

6.12.3 Open market rent review: the process for determination

The hypothetical lease and its assumptions and disregards essentially form a set of instructions guiding the parties in making a determination as to the level of rent on review. The lease will also need to set out a process for how each rent review will be carried out, dealing with the following points:

- **Level of rent:** the rent review clause may be (and often is) upwards-only, meaning that rent will either stay the same on review, or increase. A tenant would prefer to see an upwards-downwards review which reflects the reality of the market and does not leave it paying an artificially high rent in a falling market. Landlords are not keen on this, especially institutional landlords who want a predictable yield from their FRI lease and will therefore insist on an upwards-only rent review. This can be achieved by providing that from and after each review date, the annual rent will be the *greater of* the annual rent being paid immediately before the relevant review date and the open market rent on the relevant review date.
- **Frequency of review:** the review is typically set every three or five years, on the anniversary of the commencement of the lease.
- **Instigating the review:** historically agreement as to the reviewed rent was reached by the formal service of notices and counter-notices between the parties, the idea being that offer and counter-offer on rental value would bring the parties to eventual agreement. However, this often caused disputes over the validity of service and led to unfairness. For example, if the landlord made a high offer as an opening bargaining position and the tenant failed to respond in time, the tenant would be forced to pay the amount of the landlord's offer. The more common approach now is less formal. The parties will negotiate through their specialist valuers and usually reach agreement in due course. This may be before the date when the new rent is due to begin, or it might not: time will not be of the essence for this process and most leases will provide for the tenant to keep paying the existing rent, together with interest on any delayed increase when the rent review is eventually settled to compensate the landlord for the delay.
- **Independent determination:** whichever method is used to instigate the review (formal or informal), should the parties fail to agree the revised rent, the lease should make provision for the matter to be referred to an independent third party, usually appointed through the Royal Institute of Chartered Surveyors.

6.13 Code for Leasing Business Premises

In terms of the overall balance between the parties, shortage of supply has meant that landlords have often had the upper hand in the initial negotiation for lettings of commercial property. Since the terms of a lease cannot be varied other than by agreement, if the market becomes more favourable and tenants can get better terms for new leases, a tenant of an existing lease can find it hard to find an assignee willing to take on the lease. In times of over-supply, the balance naturally tips in favour of the tenants and lease terms have been considerably reduced (the average lease length is now between 5 years to 10 years), but at various points in the economic cycle there have been attempts to redress the balance in favour of tenants in recognition of their increasingly fluid business requirements. While not wanting to jeopardise property investment (which is based around the concept of an FRI lease), the Government tried to address these tenant concerns over a number of years by the introduction of a voluntary code of practice.

Initially launched in 1995 and then again in 2002 and 2007, the code tried to introduce fairness and flexibility in leasehold transactions by advocating:

- giving tenants a choice of leasing terms, where this was practicable;
- the relaxation of alienation provisions;
- that restrictions, beyond the standard 'consent not to be unreasonably withheld', should be imposed only where necessary to protect the landlord's interests, and in particular that guarantees of the incoming tenant by the outgoing tenant under a new lease (AGAs) should be required only where the incoming tenant was of lower financial standing than the outgoing tenant.

There was a lacklustre response from landlords to these editions of the code. In fact, it was very much the norm for landlords to insist on an AGA by outgoing tenants in all circumstances, as they had lost the benefits of privity of contract. Compliance with the code was voluntary, although the Government said when it first came out that it would monitor its use and consider making it compulsory if the property industry did not cooperate.

In 2019 The Royal Institute of Chartered Surveyors published and consulted on a new version of the code as a professional statement for its members. A key objective is to improve the quality and fairness of lease negotiations and to ensure the heads of terms agreed at the outset are comprehensive. The RICS Code for leasing business premises came into operation on 1 September 2020 and replaced the earlier versions of the code, which were voluntary. The significance of the RICS Code being a professional statement (for the first time) is that all RICS members must observe those parts which are mandatory and need a justifiable good reason to depart from its other best practice statements. Failure to observe the RICS Code will support a negligence claim against the surveyor and may lead to disciplinary action. Landlords are not bound by the RICS Code (although any in-house RICS surveyors will be), nor are the landlord's solicitors, non-RICS surveyors and agents so they are free to agree non-compliant leases.

The mandatory requirements in the RICS Code are:

1. Lease negotiations must be approached in a constructive and collaborative manner.
2. Any party not represented by an RICS member or other property professional must be advised of the existence of the code and must be recommended to obtain professional advice.
3. Transaction terms must be recorded in writing, subject to contract and must summarise specified details as a minimum. The specified details relevant to the terms and conditions considered in this chapter are:
    - identity and extent of the premises, together with any special rights to be granted
    - length of term including details of any renewal or break rights
    - amount of rent, frequency of rent payments and frequency and basis of any rent review
    - liability for payment of insurance premiums
    - ability to assign, underlet, charge or share the premises
    - repairing, permitted use and alterations obligations.

The landlord is responsible for ensuring that heads of terms containing the specified provisions are agreed before the draft lease is sent to the tenant's solicitor for approval.

The remainder of the code is framed in terms of best practice, allowing an RICS member to depart from the recommendations in exceptional circumstances. The points that are relevant to the terms and covenants considered in this chapter are:

- The identity of the property should be clearly defined, a lease plan should be provided and the tenant should be granted all necessary rights for the intended use of the property
- The length of term and any break provisions should be stated
- Leases should allow either party to start the rent review process. Tenants should be made aware of the method or formula for review where appropriate to allow time to take professional advice
- Leases should contain standard provisions for assignment of whole, underletting of whole or part (where appropriate) charging and sharing with group companies
- Repairing obligations should be appropriate to the length of the lease and the condition of the premises
- Controls on alterations and change of use should be no more restrictive than are necessary to protect the value of the property and any adjoining or neighbouring premises of the landlord.

Summary

- Leases of commercial property are a balance between the landlord's investment objectives and the tenant's business requirements.
- Registerable leases granted on or after 19 June 2006 must contain certain clauses prescribed by Land Registry.
- Most leases have a similar structure: parties, extent of the demised property, tenant's covenants, landlord's covenants and provisions dealing with the landlord's remedies.
- A landlord imposes covenants on the tenant to control the way in which the property is maintained, used, altered or passed on to another tenant. A covenant may be absolute, qualified or fully qualified.
- The lease must set out who is responsible for repairing the building. The costs of repair are usually borne by the tenant. Some repairing obligations also include renewal and improvement.
- The lease should make it clear who is to insure the building, how the insurance premium is to be passed on to the tenant and what is going to happen to the building and the rent payable under the lease if the building is damaged by an insured risk.
- The tenant's alterations, user and alienation covenants should be drafted in a way that strikes a fair balance between the tenant's need for flexibility and the landlord's need to protect the value of the reversionary interest in the building.
- In relation to assignment and underletting, s 19(1)(a) of the Landlord and Tenant Act 1927 turns a qualified covenant into a fully qualified covenant. Where it would be unreasonable not to give consent, the landlord is also under a statutory duty to give consent within a reasonable time.
- In relation to assignment only, leases made on or after 1 January 1996 may contain specified circumstances in which the landlord may withhold consent and specific conditions subject to which consent to assignment may be given.
- Leases of commercial property will reserve an annual rent, usually payable in advance in four equal quarterly payments on the usual quarter days. The annual rent is the landlord's

income stream and should not need to be used for the costs of repairing and insuring the building. The lease should pass on these costs to the tenant.

- Unless the lease is very short, the landlord will require a mechanism for reviewing the annual rent at regular intervals throughout the term.
- Although there are different types of rent review, the most common type is the upward only open market rent review. With this type of review, the rent can go up or stay the same, but it can never go down.
- In an open market rent review, the valuer is instructed by the rent review clause in the lease to value a hypothetical interest in the property as at the rent review date. Assumptions and disregards are instructions to the valuer as how to conduct this hypothetical valuation in a way that will produce a result that is as close to the real open market value of the premises as possible.
- In most leases with an open market rent review, either party can initiate the rent review or time is not usually of the essence. Where the reviewed rent is agreed or determined after the relevant review date, the lease will provide that the tenant continues to pay rent at the old rate and pays any additional amount to the landlord together with interest (at a non-punitive rate) to compensate the landlord for the delay.
- When negotiating the terms of a lease, surveyors who are RICS members must comply with certain mandatory requirements in the RICS Code for leasing business premises and only depart from its other best practice statements with justifiable good reason.

Sample questions

Question 1

A solicitor acts for the tenant of a retail unit (the 'Property') under a lease granted in 2015. The lease contains a covenant not assign, underlet, charge, hold on trust, part with or share possession or occupation of the property in whole or in part, except that the tenant may, with the landlord's consent, assign the whole of the property. There are no other provisions relating to alienation in the lease. The tenant wishes to dispose of the lease and has found another retailer who is interested in the Property. However, the tenant is concerned that the landlord may refuse consent to an assignment of the lease because the other retailer is not as financially strong as the tenant.

Which of the following is the best advice to the tenant about whether the landlord will be able to refuse consent for the proposed assignment of the lease?

A The landlord cannot prevent the tenant from assigning the whole of the Property as it wishes.

B Provided the tenant has made a written application for consent, the landlord must give consent for the assignment unless it is reasonable not to do so.

C Statute allows the landlord to insist on the tenant giving an authorised guarantee agreement for the assignee as a condition of giving its consent to this proposed assignment.

D The landlord will be prevented from withholding its consent because statute implies into this covenant for assignment a proviso that the landlord's consent will not be unreasonably withheld.

E If the tenant is unable to obtain the consent of the landlord, the tenant should enter into a licence with the other retailer instead.

Answer

Option B is correct. The covenant against assignment of whole of the property in the lease is a qualified covenant and s19(1)(a) Landlord and Tenant Act 1927 implies into any qualified covenant that it be deemed to be subject to a proviso that such consent is not to be unreasonably withheld. Where there is a qualified covenant on assignment (whether the proviso that consent is not to be unreasonably withheld is express or implied by statute) and the tenant has made a written application for consent, the landlord must within a reasonable time give consent, except in a case where it is reasonable not to give consent (s 1 Landlord and Tenant Act 1988).

Option A is not the best advice as it would be reasonable for a landlord not to consent to an assignment to a proposed assignee who is not financially strong enough to pay the rent and perform the other covenants in the lease.

Option C is wrong; s 19(1A) Landlord and Tenant Act 1927 allows for the landlord and the tenant to agree conditions and circumstances in which it would not be unreasonable for the landlord to refuse consent and such conditions often include that the assignor agrees to give an authorised guarantee agreement for the assignee, but such conditions and circumstance must be agreed in advance. The facts indicate that the lease does not contain any such conditions and circumstances.

Option D correctly states the effect of s 19(1)(a) Landlord and Tenant Act 1927 on a qualified covenant, but the landlord is still able to withhold consent where it is reasonable to do so, eg if the proposed assignee is not financially strong enough to pay the rent and perform the other covenants in the lease.

Option E is not good advice as the lease contains an absolute covenant against sharing occupation, which would include allowing the other retailer into the property under a licence.

Question 2

A solicitor acts for a landlord of a high street retail unit (the 'Property'). The tenant wants to remove the existing shop front, enlarge the hole in the front wall and install bi-folding doors instead. The lease contains tenant covenants not make any external or structural alteration to the Property and not to make any non-structural alteration to the Property without the consent of the landlord.

Which of the following statements is the best advice to the landlord in this situation?

A The landlord will have to consent to the alterations as if it does not, the tenant will be able to use a statutory procedure to carry out the alterations and claim compensation from the landlord at the end of the term.

B The landlord can prevent the alterations being carried out as the relevant covenant in the lease is absolute.

C The landlord can insist that the alterations are carried out by the landlord in return for an increase in the annual rent.

D The landlord cannot refuse consent for the alterations as statute implies into the relevant covenant in the lease a term that the landlord cannot unreasonably withhold its consent.

E The landlord can refuse consent to the alterations, but the tenant may be able to carry them out using a statutory procedure.

Answer

Option E is correct. The proposed works are external and structural alterations and thus fall within the scope of the absolute covenant. However, they are not necessarily 'improvements' for the purposes of s 3 Landlord and Tenant Act 1927 so even though the tenant has a right to serve notice and apply for authorisation to carry out the alterations, it will be up to the court to decide if they add to the letting value of the property, are reasonable and suitable to the character of the property and do not diminish the value of any other property of the landlord. Option A therefore overstates the position. It also overstates the position on compensation; even if the alterations do add to the letting value of the holding, the lease is likely to contain a tenant's covenant to remove all tenant's alterations at the end of the term so there will be nothing left in respect of which to claim compensation.

Option B is not the best advice as the tenant may use the statutory procedure in s 3 Landlord and Tenant Act 1927 even where the relevant covenant in the lease is an absolute prohibition.

Option C also overstates the position; the landlord cannot insist on being able to do the alterations itself in return for an increase in the annual rent. This will only become possible if the tenant serves a notice under s 3 and even if it does, the tenant is under no obligation to accept an offer by the landlord to carry out the alterations and may withdraw its notice.

Option D is wrong as the relevant covenant in the lease is absolute, so there is no term implied by statute that consent will not be unreasonably withheld.

Question 3

A landlord is proposing to let some retail premises to a clothes shop which has only just begun trading. The prospective tenant is concerned that it might not be able to afford the rent, should it increase on review, as its business is not yet established and it cannot predict the performance of its business over the 15-year term with any certainty at this stage. The landlord insists that there must be some form of rent review provision in the lease.

Which of the following types of rent review provision is the most appropriate to address the tenant's concerns?

A A fixed increase rent review.

B An index linked rent review.

C A rent review based on the tenant's turnover.

D An open market rent review.

E An upwards-only open market rent review.

Answer

Option C is correct. A turnover rent review will be directly linked to the turnover of the tenant's business and should therefore only increase in line with the turnover of the business.

A fixed increase rent review (option A) would not be as suitable on the facts, as the tenant does not want to commit to any predictions as to the success of the business over the term. An index linked rent review (option B) is linked to an external index, such as the Retail Prices Index, so will increase in line with inflation regardless of the fortunes of the tenant's particular business.

Open market rent reviews (options D and E) will reflect the rental market as a whole, not the tenant's particular business, so do not address the tenant's concerns. Option E will be particularly harsh on the tenant as it locks in increases achieved in previous rent reviews even if the rental market has fallen and/or the tenant's business is in trouble.

7 Procedural Steps for the Grant of a Lease or Underlease

7.1	Introduction	146
7.2	Drafting the lease	146
7.3	Purpose of an agreement for lease	147
7.4	Deduction and investigation of title	148
7.5	Pre-contract enquiries and searches	148
7.6	Licence to underlet	149
7.7	Pre-completion formalities	150
7.8	Completion and post-completion steps	150

SQE1 syllabus

This chapter will enable you to achieve the SQE1 Assessment Specification in relation to Functioning Legal Knowledge concerned with the following:

- Drafting the lease
- Purpose of an agreement for lease
- Deduction and investigation of title
- Pre-contract enquiries and searches
- Purpose of and who prepares the draft of the licence to underlet
- Contractual liability and how the licence deals with this
- Key provisions in the licence
- Pre-completion formalities
- Completion and post-completion steps

Note that for SQE1, candidates are not usually required to recall specific case names or cite statutory or regulatory authorities. Cases and statutory or regulatory authorities are provided for illustrative purposes only unless otherwise indicated.

Learning outcomes

By the end of this chapter you will be able to apply relevant core legal principles and rules appropriately and effectively, at the level of a competent newly qualified solicitor in practice, to realistic client-based and ethical problems and situations in the following areas:

- Drafting and negotiating a lease/underlease
- Whether an agreement for lease is necessary
- Deduction of the superior title to the lease/underlease
- Searches and enquiries appropriate for the grant of a lease/underlease

- The process of obtaining landlord's consent to the underletting
- The purpose and content of a licence to underlet
- Preparation of the lease/underlease and counterpart
- Apportionment of the rent due at completion
- Calculation and payment of SDLT and LTT on the grant of a lease
- Registration of leases

7.1 Introduction

This chapter considers the procedure for the grant of a lease or underlease of commercial property. The conveyancing procedure is very similar to that used on a freehold transaction so this chapter deals only with those matters where the procedure differs. Where a commercial lease is for a comparatively short term, a prospective tenant may choose not to carry out some of the more usual steps, such as investigating title. However, this chapter will assume that the client wishes to these steps to be carried out.

One of the major considerations for the landlord will be the reliability of the potential tenant. The landlord will accept a tenant based upon what is known as the tenant's 'strength of covenant', ie the tenant's ability to pay the rent and perform the covenants. The landlord may consider obtaining any one or all of the following:

- references from a previous landlord
- guarantee obtained from the parent company, a bank involved in financing the transaction or from one or more of the directors
- a rent deposit (a sum of money deposited with the landlord on terms which enable the landlord to withdraw sums if rent due under lease is unpaid).

In the case of an underlease, the landlord (who will become the head-tenant on the grant of the underlease) must check the terms of its own lease to see what is permitted for underlettings. There will probably be a requirement to obtain the consent of the superior landlord to the identity of the undertenant and the terms of the underletting (see **6.11.3** and **7.6** below). The landlord should ensure that the term of the underlease is at least one day shorter than the unexpired residue of the headlease because an underlease of the whole residue will take effect as an assignment of the headlease rather than the grant of an underlease; this is probably not what the parties intended and may be a breach of the alienation covenant in the headlease.

Once a suitable tenant has been found, the parties will start the process of granting the lease or underlease.

* The tax rates set out in this chapter are correct as at the date of publication. Please note that these tax rates may no longer be current as at the date of any future SQE assessment.

7.2 Drafting the lease

The lease/underlease is the key document in the transaction as it governs the day-to-day relationship between the landlord and the tenant. In the case of a lease, the negotiation of the document is a balancing act between the landlord's desire to maintain control of the management of the building and the tenant's desire to use the property without restriction. The landlord's solicitor will draft the lease and submit it to the tenant's solicitor for approval. The tenant's solicitor will probably make amendments. The draft lease will go backwards and forwards between the solicitors until it is finally agreed. Inevitably there will be some compromise on both sides but eventually a lease should be agreed which allows the tenant to operate from the building without unnecessary restrictions but allows the landlord to maintain the necessary degree of control to protect the investment.

Where the lease is an underlease, the scope for negotiating the document will be much more restricted as it is likely that the headlease requires that the terms of the underlease mirrors the terms of the headlease (see **6.11.3**).

7.3 Purpose of an agreement for lease

Once the solicitors have agreed the form of lease/underlease and carried out all the pre-contract steps, they should be ready to complete the grant of the lease. In leasehold transactions it is quite common to by-pass the contract and proceed straight to completion by granting the lease itself. It takes a long time to negotiate a commercial lease and the parties are already financially committed, so to avoid further costs the parties may go straight to completion.

A contract, usually called an 'agreement for lease', will be useful where there is going to be a delay between agreeing the lease/underlease and actually granting it but one (or both) of the parties requires the other to be bound into the transaction. Examples of this situation are where:

(a) the landlord is in the process of constructing the property and wants to know that the tenant is bound to take the lease on completion of the works so that there will be rental income to help offset the building costs

(b) the landlord is carrying out works of repair or refurbishment at the request of the tenant (in which case the landlord may not be able to secure funding for the works unless there is a legally enforceable commitment from the tenant)

(c) the tenant is carrying out major works to the property prior to the grant of the lease

(d) the landlord requires the consent of a lender or a superior landlord to the grant of the lease

(e) the landlord is negotiating a surrender from a current tenant and wants to tie in the surrender with the grant of the new lease

(f) the tenant needs to obtain planning permission for the proposed use.

Where an agreement for lease is required, it is drafted by the landlord's solicitor in the same way that the seller's solicitor drafts the contract in the case of the sale of a freehold property. The particulars of sale must state that the property is leasehold and give details of the term to be vested in the tenant. The final agreed form of the lease/underlease should be attached to the agreement with an obligation in the agreement for the tenant to take a lease/underlease in that form on the date of completion. Incumbrances affecting the superior title must be disclosed (as these will affect the tenant in the same way as they would affect a buyer of the freehold) and the attached lease/underlease should contain an indemnity in respect of future breaches of any covenants affecting the title. In other respects, the contract will be similar to that prepared on a freehold transaction.

Standard Condition 8.2 (SCPC 11.2.3) provides for the lease/underlease to be in the form annexed to the draft contract, and for the landlord to engross the lease/underlease and supply the tenant with the engrossment at least five working days before the completion date.

7.4 Deduction and investigation of title

Before drafting the lease/underlease, the landlord's solicitor will need to investigate the client's title to ensure that the client is entitled to grant it, to anticipate any problems with the title and draft any agreement for lease. Where the property is subject to an existing mortgage, the mortgage will frequently contain a prohibition or restriction on the borrower/ landlord's ability to grant a lease of the property so the lender must be contacted and its permission obtained before the transaction proceeds.

In the case of a lease, a tenant will want the landlord to deduce title to the freehold interest. This is particularly important where a premium is to be paid for the grant of the lease, where the property is being offered as security for a loan or where a tenant is paying a significant rent. Unless the freehold is already registered, the absence of the freehold title will usually prevent the tenant from obtaining an absolute leasehold title on the subsequent registration of the lease. Even when the freehold title is registered with absolute title, the tenant will still want to see whether there is anything on the freehold title which will bind the new leasehold title. Although most landlords are happy to deduce their title, under the general law a tenant is not entitled to call for deduction of the freehold title unless the transaction is the grant of a lease for a term of more than seven years. Where this is the case and there is to be an agreement for lease, SC 8.2.4 (SCPC 11.2.4) requires the landlord to deduce such title as would enable the tenant to obtain registration with an absolute title at the Land Registry. If the landlord's title is registered, the tenant will be able to check the landlord's title under the Open Register rules in any event.

In the case of an underlease, if the headlease is registered with absolute leasehold title, there will be no need to see the title to the freehold, although the headlease itself and the official copies for the headlease title must be reviewed. Where the headlease is unregistered:

- the general law entitles the undertenant to call for the headlease and all subsequent assignments under which the headlease has been held for the last 15 years
- under the general law, the undertenant is only entitled to call for deduction of the freehold title where the transaction is the grant of a lease for a term of more than seven years.

The requirement to provide details of the freehold may cause problems to a headtenant if it did not call for the deduction of the freehold title when it took the headlease. If unable to comply, the headtenant will need to exclude this requirement by a special condition in the contract.

Investigation of title is done in exactly the same way as if the solicitor was acting in a freehold transaction (see **Chapter 2**).

7.5 Pre-contract enquiries and searches

The landlord's solicitor should provide the tenant's solicitor with the following documents:

(a) draft agreement for lease (if applicable);

(b) draft lease/underlease;

(c) evidence of the freehold/headlease title;

(d) copies of any relevant planning consents; and

(e) evidence of the lender's consent to the grant of the lease/underlease (where relevant).

The tenant's or undertenant's solicitor will want to undertake the same searches and enquiries as if the client were buying the freehold (see **Chapters 3** and **5**). There will normally be some additional queries relating specifically to a lease. For example, the tenant will want to see details of the landlord's insurance policy.

When reporting to the client, the solicitor should explain the tenant's obligations under the lease/underlease and the danger of losing the lease through forfeiture for breach of covenant (see **9.3.4** and **9.4.4**).

7.6 Licence to underlet

Most head-landlords will require formal consent to the underletting to be given in the form of a licence to underlet. This is a tripartite document entered in to by the head-landlord, headtenant and undertenant by which the head-landlord gives consent to the headtenant to underlet the property to the undertenant. The head-landlord's consent must be given by or on completion of the underletting, otherwise the headtenant is likely to be in breach of the alienation covenant in the lease. It is the head-landlord's solicitor who usually produces the first draft of the licence to underlet.

7.6.1 Contractual liability and how the licence deals with this

The usual condition of granting consent is that the undertenant is to enter into a direct covenant with the head-landlord to perform the covenants in both the underlease and the headlease. The direct covenant usually excludes the headlease covenants to pay rent and only applies in so far as the headlease covenants relate to the underlet property.

Ordinarily, there is no liability between a head-landlord and an undertenant and, therefore, the head-landlord is unable to sue an undertenant in respect of any breaches of the terms of the headlease. The direct covenant creates a contractual relationship which enables the head-landlord to sue the undertenant for any breaches of either the headlease (other than for non-payment of rent) or the underlease. (However, the head-landlord will need to obtain a new direct covenant on each and every assignment of the underlease from the proposed assignee.)

Figure 7.1 Contractual relationships in an underletting

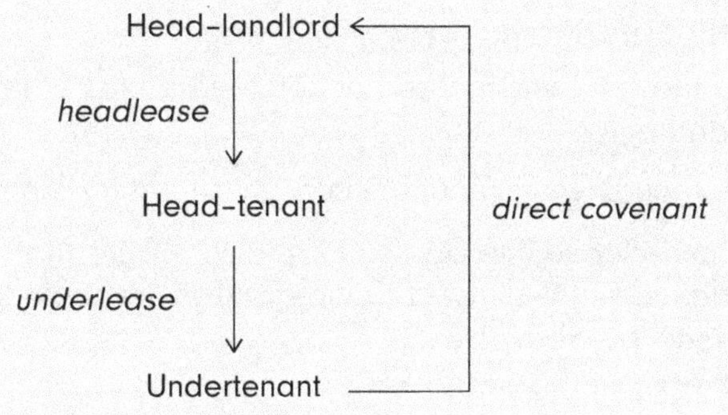

7.6.2 Key provisions in the licence

The key provisions in the licence to underlet are the consent of the head-landlord to the grant of the underlease and the direct covenant from the undertenant to the head-landlord. The licence is also likely to contain an obligation on the part of the headtenant to pay the head-landlord's costs for approving the underletting and granting the licence.

7.7 Pre-completion formalities

The lease/underlease is normally prepared in two identical parts, the lease and counterpart. The lease is executed by the landlord and the counterpart by the tenant. On completion, these are exchanged so that each party has a copy of the lease signed by the other in case of subsequent dispute.

As with the transfer deed in the case of the sale of freehold land, a top copy (or engrossment) of the lease/underlease and counterpart will need to be made and it is these that the parties will sign. The landlord will sign the lease itself in readiness for completion and the counterpart should be sent to the tenant's solicitor for execution by the tenant (at least five working days before contractual completion date if SC 8.2.5 or SCPC 11.2.5 apply).

A lease is a legal estate in land and must be created properly according to the correct legal formalities. The requirements for execution of a deed are dealt with in **5.3**.

Most leases provide that rent is payable in advance, not in arrears. Unless completion takes place on a day when rent under the lease/underlease falls due, a proportionate amount of rent calculated from the date of completion until the next rent payment day will be payable by the tenant on completion and this should be agreed in advance.

7.8 Completion and post-completion steps

7.8.1 Completion

On completion, in addition to matters relevant to a freehold transaction, the landlord will receive:

(a) the counterpart lease/underlease executed by the tenant/undertenant;

(b) any premium payable for the grant (less any deposit paid on exchange of contracts);

(c) an apportioned sum representing rent payable in advance under the lease/underlease.

The landlord should give to the tenant:

(a) the lease/underlease executed by the landlord;

(b) if not already done, properly marked or certified copies of the freehold title deeds (unregistered land only);

(c) where relevant, a certified copy of the consent of the landlord's lender to the transaction.

On the grant of an underlease, the parties must also ensure that, on or before completion, the head-landlord has given its consent to the grant of the underlease, usually in the form of a licence to underlet (see **7.6** above).

7.8.2 SDLT and LTT

(a) SDLT (England)

A land transaction return must be submitted to HMRC on the grant of a lease in the usual way. In the case of the grant of a lease, SDLT is potentially chargeable both on any capital sum being paid (referred to on the grant of a lease as a 'premium') and on the amount of the rent.

- In the case of non-residential property, the SDLT payable on any premium is calculated on the same basis as for the consideration on the sale of freehold land (see **1.6.1(b)**).
- In relation to the rental element, a complex formula is used to identify the Net Present Value ('NPV') of the rent and SDLT is then calculated using this figure. Calculating the NPV consists of working out how much rent is payable in total over the term of the lease (including any VAT) and then discounting rental payments to be made in future years by

3.5% per annum to compensate for the fact that future rent received will have a lower value than rent received today.

- SDLT is chargeable on the VAT inclusive amount of the premium and the rent so it is necessary to determine if VAT is chargeable because the landlord has opted to tax the property.
- SDLT is chargeable on the NPV as follows:

Net present value of rent	**SDLT rate**
£0 to £150,000	Zero
The portion from £150,001 to £5,000,000	1%
The portion above £5,000,000	2%

- An online calculator is provided on HMRC's website.
- the SDLT1 and payment must be submitted to HMRC within 14 days of completion of the grant of the lease.

(b) LTT (Wales)

LTT is charged on the leases of non-residential property in a similar way to SDLT, ie on the premium and on the rental element using the NPV of the rent.

- The LTT payable on any premium is calculated on the same basis as for the consideration on the sale of freehold land (see **1.6.1(d)**), except that the 0% band for premiums extending to £225,000 is not available where the 'relevant rent' exceeds £13,500. The rate of 1% will apply instead. Relevant rent is usually the highest rent payable in any year across the entire term of the lease.
- LTT is chargeable on the NPV (including any VAT) as follows:

Net present value of rent	**LTT rate**
£0 to £225,000	Zero
The portion from £1225,000 to £2,000,000	1%
The portion above £2,000,000	2%

- The Welsh Government sets the rates and bands for LTT.
- An online calculator is provided on Gov.UK website.
- The land transaction return and payment must be submitted to the Welsh Revenue Authority within 30 days of completion of the grant of the lease.

7.8.3 Registration

A legal lease for seven years or less is not capable of being registered with its own title at the Land Registry. In registered land, such a lease will take effect as an overriding interest under the Land Registration Act 2002, whether or not the tenant is in actual occupation of the land. It is possible to note leases of over three years against the landlord's title voluntarily. In unregistered land, a legal lease is binding on all subsequent owners of the land, irrespective of notice.

The grant of a lease for a term which exceeds seven years is registrable in its own right after completion, irrespective of whether the freehold title is registered. It will be registered with its own separate title and title number and, if the landlord's title is registered, it will also be noted against the landlord's title.

If the freehold is unregistered, the tenant's application to the Land Registry is for first registration and the application must be made within two months of completion of the grant of the lease. If the freehold is registered, the tenant's application is for registration of a dealing with the freehold title and the application must be made within the priority period conferred by the OSR1 search result (see **5.4.1**).

On first registration, the registered title may be classed as absolute leasehold, possessory, qualified or good leasehold title (see **2.3.2**). Good leasehold title will be awarded where the Registrar is satisfied that the title to the leasehold interest is sound but, having no access to the superior title, they are not prepared to guarantee the lease against defects in the freehold title or guarantee that the freeholder had the right to grant the lease. Good leasehold title will therefore be given where the title to the freehold reversion is unregistered and the applicant for first registration of the leasehold title does not submit title to the freehold reversion with the application, or where the freehold is registered with less than absolute title. Good leasehold title may be regarded as a title defect as it may make it difficult to sell or mortgage the lease.

Summary

- The steps involved in granting a lease of commercial property are very similar to those involved in buying a freehold property.
- The landlord's solicitor must check whether the landlord's mortgage permits the grant of a lease.
- In the case of an underlease, the landlord should check the alienation covenant in the headlease for the terms on which underletting is permitted.
- Where a lease is for more than seven years, the tenant is entitled to insist on the landlord deducing the freehold (or superior leasehold) title. If the landlord does not do so, the tenant will be unable to obtain absolute leasehold title on the registration of the lease. Where the landlord's title is registered, the tenant will always be able to investigate the landlord's title.
- The landlord's solicitor will draft the lease/underlease. Where the parties intend to enter into an agreement for lease, the terms of the lease/underlease are settled before exchange so that the agreed form may be attached to the agreement.
- The tenant's solicitor will have to report to the client on the agreed terms of the lease/underlease.
- The lease/underlease is prepared in two identical parts. The lease/underlease is executed by the landlord and given to the tenant; the counterpart is executed by the tenant and given to the landlord.
- On completion, the tenant will pay the rent due in advance for the period from the completion date to the next rent payment day under the lease/underlease.

- In all cases, a land transaction return must be submitted following completion. SDLT/LTT is payable on any premium paid for the grant of the lease and on the rent reserved by the lease.
- A lease for over seven years must be registered with its own separate title, regardless of whether the landlord's title is registered.
- A lease for seven years or less but more than three years may be noted voluntarily on the landlord's registered title.
- A lease for three years or less cannot be noted on the landlord's registered title.

Sample questions

Question 1

A solicitor is acting for a tenant who is taking a lease of a shop for a term of exactly seven years. The landlord's freehold title is unregistered. The lease has now been completed.

Does the lease have to be registered with its own title at the Land Registry?

A Yes, because the landlord's freehold title is unregistered.

B Yes, because the lease is for a term of over three years.

C Yes, because the lease is for a term of seven years.

D No, because it is not possible to register a lease unless the freehold is already registered.

E No, because it is not possible to register a lease unless the term exceeds seven years.

Answer

Option E is correct. This is a lease for a term of exactly seven years. A legal lease for seven years or less is not capable of being registered with its own title at the Land Registry, so options A, B and C are wrong. Option D is not the best answer as leases of over seven years must be registered with their own title at the Land Registry irrespective of whether the freehold title is registered.

Question 2

Yesterday a landlord granted a lease of office premises in England to a tenant for a term of 10 years. The consideration for the lease is the payment of a commercial, open-market rent with a premium of £100,000. The landlord opted to tax the property for VAT purposes before the lease was granted.

Which of the following statements best describes the position on taxation for this transaction?

A The tenant may need to pay stamp duty land tax ('SDLT') on the VAT-inclusive amount of the rent.

B The tenant may need to pay SDLT on the VAT-inclusive amount of the premium.

C The tenant may need to pay SDLT on the rent, exclusive of VAT.

D The tenant may only have to pay SDLT on the VAT-inclusive amount of the premium.

E The tenant may need to pay SDLT on the VAT-inclusive amounts of the rent and the premium.

Answer

Option A is correct. On the grant of a lease, SDLT is *potentially* payable both on any premium charged by the landlord and the rent reserved by the lease. Where VAT is chargeable (because the landlord has opted to tax the property before the grant of the lease), SDLT is charged on the VAT-inclusive amounts. This means that option C is incorrect on VAT. However, SDLT will not be charged on the premium in this instance as the applicable rate for consideration not exceeding £150,000 is 0%. Here the VAT-inclusive amount of the premium is £120,000. So options B, D and E are wrong as they all refer to the payment of SDLT on the premium.

Question 3

A solicitor is acting for a proposed undertenant who is taking an underlease of a commercial property for a term of five years. The proposed landlord is the tenant under a lease of the property granted last year for a term of 10 years. The lease was registered with absolute leasehold title. The superior landlord is the freehold owner of the property and the superior landlord's title to the property is unregistered. The undertenant wants the solicitor to investigate the superior landlord's freehold title.

Which of the following statements is the best advice as to what the proposed landlord should be expected to deduce by way of title to the freehold?

A The proposed landlord will not have to deduce title to the freehold because it is unregistered.

B The proposed landlord will have to deduce title to the freehold as the proposed undertenant is legally entitled to call for it.

C As the proposed landlord's title is registered with absolute leasehold title, there will be no need for it to deduce the freehold title.

D The proposed landlord may not be able to deduce title to the freehold as it was not entitled to call for it when its lease was granted.

E The proposed landlord should not have to deduce title to the freehold as the undertenant will be able to obtain this information under the open register rules.

Answer

Option C is correct. The proposed landlord will have registered its lease within two months of grant because leases of over seven years must be registered with their own title at the Land Registry irrespective of whether the freehold title is registered. As the proposed landlord's lease is registered with absolute leasehold title, the best class of title available, then there is no need to see the freehold title.

Option A is oversimplified as there are circumstances in which a tenant would be expected to deduce title to the freehold to a prospective undertenant. Option B is misleading on two counts; the general law allows an undertenant to call for the freehold title only when the headlease is unregistered, and then only where the underlease is for a term of more than seven years; here the headlease is registered and this underlease is for a term of five years. Option D is misleading as the proposed landlord was entitled to call for the freehold interest last year as its lease was granted for ten years, ie a term of more than seven years. Option E is wrong as the open register rules allow third parties to inspect registered titles and in this case, the freehold is unregistered.

8 Procedural Steps for the Assignment of a Lease

8.1	Introduction	156
8.2	Overview of the conveyancing procedure for the assignment of a lease	156
8.3	Landlord's consent	158
8.4	The licence to assign	159
8.5	Deduction and investigation of title	161
8.6	Pre-contract enquiries and searches	161
8.7	Deed of assignment and covenants for title	162
8.8	Pre-completion formalities	163
8.9	Completion	163
8.10	Post-completion steps	164

SQE1 syllabus

This chapter will enable you to achieve the SQE1 Assessment Specification in relation to Functioning Legal Knowledge concerned with the following:

- Landlord's consent
- Purpose of a licence to assign and who prepares the draft
- Key provisions in the licence to assign
- Contractual liability and how the licence to assign deals with this
- Authorised guarantee agreement
- Deduction and investigation of title
- Pre-contract enquiries and searches
- Deed of assignment and covenants for title
- Pre-completion formalities
- Completion and post-completion steps

Note that for SQE1, candidates are not usually required to recall specific case names or cite statutory or regulatory authorities. Cases and statutory or regulatory authorities are provided for illustrative purposes only unless otherwise indicated.

Learning outcomes

By the end of this chapter you will be able to apply relevant core legal principles and rules appropriately and effectively, at the level of a competent newly qualified solicitor in practice, to realistic client-based and ethical problems and situations in the following areas:

- The key differences between the assignment of a lease and the sale and purchase of a freehold property
- The need for, and the process of obtaining, landlord's consent to the assignment
- The purpose and content of a licence to assign
- Deduction and investigation of title to a leasehold property
- Provisions specific to leasehold property in the transfer deed
- Additional documents to collect and checks to carry out at completion for a leasehold property
- Post-completion steps, including payment of SDLT/LTT, registration of the assignment at the Land Registry and notification to the landlord.

8.1 Introduction

This chapter considers the procedure for the assignment of a lease of commercial property. An assignment is the transfer of an existing lease by the tenant (the 'seller' or 'assignor') to a third party (the 'buyer' or 'assignee'). The conveyancing procedure is very similar to that used on a freehold transaction so this chapter deals only with those matters where the procedure differs. Where the residue of the term remaining on the lease is comparatively short, the prospective assignee may choose not to carry out some of the more usual steps, such as investigating title. However, this chapter will assume that the prospective assignee wants these steps carried out.

8.2 Overview of the conveyancing procedure for the assignment of a lease

The procedure for the sale and purchase of a freehold property is set out in **Chapters 1–5**. This chapter will focus on the differences in the procedure for the assignment of a lease and these are highlighted in italics in the chart below.

One major difference between the sale of a freehold property and the assignment of a lease is the existence of the lease itself. Although there is no scope to negotiate the terms of the lease (as there is on grant of a lease), the assignee's solicitor will need to check its terms to make sure they meet the assignee's requirements. There is a possibility that the landlord will agree to vary the terms of the lease, but this is at the landlord's absolute discretion.

Another major difference is the need for the landlord's consent to the assignment, which is usually required in leases of commercial property (see **8.3** and **8.4** below).

Leases of commercial property are usually capable of assignment. Where the tenant is paying the market rent for the property, the lease is unlikely to have any capital value so no purchase price (or 'premium') will be paid by the assignee to the assignor on the assignment. If a premium is payable, it will usually be a comparatively small sum.

CONVEYANCING PROCEDURE: ASSIGNMENT OF A LEASE

SELLER/ASSIGNOR	**BOTH**	**BUYER/ASSIGNEE**
PRE-CONTRACT STAGE		
Take instructions		Take instructions
Investigate title		
Prepare pre-contract package: draft contract, *evidence of leasehold title (and possibly Landlord's reversionary title), lease etc)*		Liaise with assignor to obtain details Landlord will need to consider, eg references
Apply for Landlord's consent to the assignment and provide undertaking for Landlord's costs		Raise pre-contract searches and enquiries
		Investigate title *(leasehold and possibly Landlord's reversionary title), consider lease*
		Approve draft contract
	Exchange contracts	
PRE-COMPLETION STAGE		
		Prepare purchase deed (*transfer or deed of assignment*)
Approve purchase deed		Raise pre-completion searches *(possibly including searches against Landlord's reversionary title)*
Prepare for completion		Prepare for completion
	Agree form of Licence to Assign with Landlord	
	Completion *(including the completion of a Licence to Assign)*	
POST-COMPLETION STAGE		
Post-completion matters (comply with any undertakings given on completion)		Post-completion matters (including SDLT/LTT and registration of title) *Registration of assignment with Landlord*

8.3 Landlord's consent

Leases of commercial property usually provide for the landlord's consent to be obtained before any assignment can take place. The alienation covenants in the lease governing the requirement for landlord's consent are considered in **6.11.2**. It is the assignor's responsibility to apply for the consent and to use all reasonable endeavours to obtain it, but both parties to the assignment will need to be involved. Where the landlord's consent is required, it is usually embodied in a formal licence (a 'licence to assign').

Although the licence to assign is not finalised until completion, the assignor will need to check at the pre-exchange stage that the landlord will agree to the assignment in principle. The landlord will probably want to take up references on the prospective assignee to ensure that they are solvent and financially strong enough to pay the annual rent and perform the other tenant covenants in the lease. References are commonly required from all or some of the following sources:

(a) a current landlord;

(b) the assignee's bank;

(c) the assignee's employer;

(d) a professional person such as an accountant or solicitor;

(e) a person or company with whom the assignee regularly trades; and

(f) three years' audited accounts in the case of a company or self-employed person or partnership.

It is usual for the landlord's solicitors to require an undertaking from the assignor's solicitors for the payment of the legal and other professional costs involved in considering the proposed assignment and the licence to assign. The assignor's solicitor should first seek the assignor's authority to give the undertaking, the undertaking should be limited to the reasonable costs incurred. A cap on such costs could also be sought. The assignor's solicitor will normally want to have received the relevant sum on account from the assignor before giving the costs undertaking.

The landlord may require the assignee to provide a guarantor as a condition of the consent and/or the assignor to enter into an authorised guarantee agreement to guarantee the performance of the tenant's covenants by the assignee (see **6.11.2** and **8.4.4** below). The landlord may not require a premium to be paid by the assignor as a condition of the grant of consent unless the lease specifically allows this (which would be very unusual).

The landlord's consent must be given by or on completion of the assignment, otherwise the assignor is likely to be in breach of the assignment covenant in the lease. The contract can deal with this two in different ways, depending on which set of standard conditions are used:

- Under the SCs, either party may rescind the contract by notice if the consent has not been given three working days before the completion date or if, by that time, consent has been given subject to a condition to which the buyer reasonably objects. Although this allows contracts to be exchanged before the landlord's consent is obtained, it gives rise to uncertainty as to whether the transaction will complete. Where the timing of completion is important (eg where there is a dependent transaction), it is safest not to exchange until the landlord's consent has been obtained. Otherwise the assignment may fall through when the landlord refuses consent, whereas the dependent transaction would still be binding.
- The SCPCs provide that if the landlord's consent has not been obtained by the completion date, completion is postponed until five working days after the assignor notifies the buyer that consent has been given. The contract may not be rescinded until six months have passed since the original completion date. Either party can then rescind by serving notice on the other. Again, if timing of completion is important, it is safest not to exchange until the landlord's consent has been obtained.

8.4 The licence to assign

8.4.1 Purpose of a licence to assign and who prepares the draft

The purpose of a licence to assign is for the landlord to give consent to the assignment of the lease by the assignor to the assignee. If the assignment were to take place without that consent, the assignor may be committing a breach of the tenant's alienation covenants in the lease: the assignor may not be released from liability under the tenant's covenants (see **9.2.2**) and the lease itself could be liable to forfeiture (see **9.5**).

The draft licence to assign is produced by the landlord's solicitor and sent to the assignor's solicitor who coordinates with the assignee's solicitor to amend or agree the draft. If the assignor and assignee are to enter into covenants in the licence then all three (ie landlord, assignor and assignee) will be parties to the licence, which must be in the form of a deed. Often the licence will be prepared in triplicate, so that on completion each party receives a signed and dated part. Any guarantors of the assignee or assignee will be required to join in.

8.4.2 Key provisions in the licence to assign

A typical licence to assign will contain the following components:

(a) The landlord grants consent to the assignor to assign the lease to the assignee. Often this consent will be time-limited (eg three months) because the landlord has no control over when the assignment takes place and the assignee's financial position can change in a short time. The landlord would not want to be bound to consent to an assignment if the assignee's financial position has deteriorated since the references and accounts were checked.

(b) If the lease was granted on or after 1 January 1996, the assignor will typically give an authorised guarantee agreement to the landlord (see **8.4.4** below).

(c) If the lease was granted before 1 January 1996, a direct covenant by the assignee to the landlord to observe and perform the covenants in the lease for the remainder of the term (see **8.4.3** below).

(d) the assignor agrees to pay the landlord's legal and professional costs.

8.4.3 Contractual liability and how the licence to assign deals with this

The relationship between the landlord and the assignee will depend on whether the lease is an 'old lease' granted before 1 January 1996, or a 'new lease' granted on or after that date (see **9.2**).

An assignee of an old lease is liable under the doctrine of privity of estate for all the covenants in the lease which 'touch and concern' the land, but only for as long as the lease remains vested in the assignee. The landlord will therefore seek to extend the liability of the assignee by requiring it, as a condition of the landlord's consent, to enter into a direct covenant to observe the covenants in the lease for the remainder of the term of the lease, thereby creating privity of contract between the landlord and the assignee. This direct covenant is usually contained in the licence to assign.

An assignee of a new lease is also liable for breaches of covenant committed while the lease is vested in them (although they are liable during that time for all of the tenant covenants, not just those that touch and concern the land). However, on a future assignment of the lease, the Landlord and Tenant (Covenants) Act 1995 automatically releases the assignee from all the tenant covenants of the tenancy. If the landlord requires a direct covenant from the assignee, then this covenant should be limited to the period the assignee is actually the tenant, not the remainder of the entire term. To compensate the landlord for this loss of privity of contract for the whole of the term, statute allows the landlord to require that the assignor enters into an authorised guarantee agreement instead.

8.4.4 Authorised guarantee agreement ('AGA')

If the lease is a new lease granted on or after 1 January 1996, the landlord may have inserted the need for an AGA in the lease as a pre-condition to giving consent (see **6.11.2**). In this case, the landlord can always insist on the assignor entering into the AGA whether or not it is reasonable. In the absence of the provision in the lease, the landlord can insist on the AGA only if it is reasonable to do so.

An AGA will typically contain covenants by the assignor:

(a) guaranteeing that the assignee will perform the tenant's covenants in the lease, including the covenant to pay rent

(b) promising to perform such covenants if the assignee does not

(c) indemnifying the landlord for the assignee's failure to pay rent or to observe the other covenants

(d) promising to take a new lease if the liability of the assignee is disclaimed on insolvency.

The AGA should provide that the assignor's liability does not extend beyond that of the assignee (ie it is more limited than may be the case for an old lease), so that on the assignee being released from liability on a further assignment of the lease, so is the assignor.

Figure 8.1 The assignment of a new lease

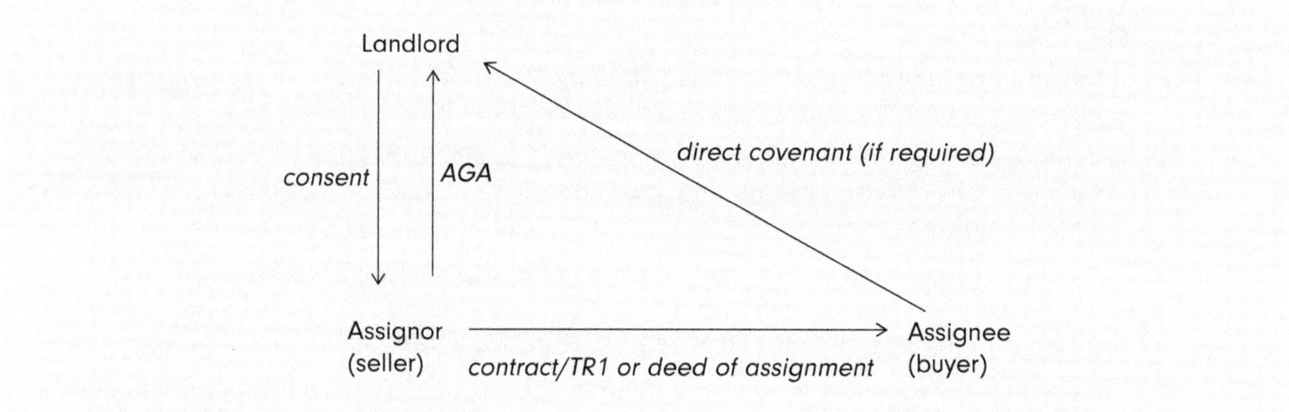

Figure 8.2 The assignment of an old lease

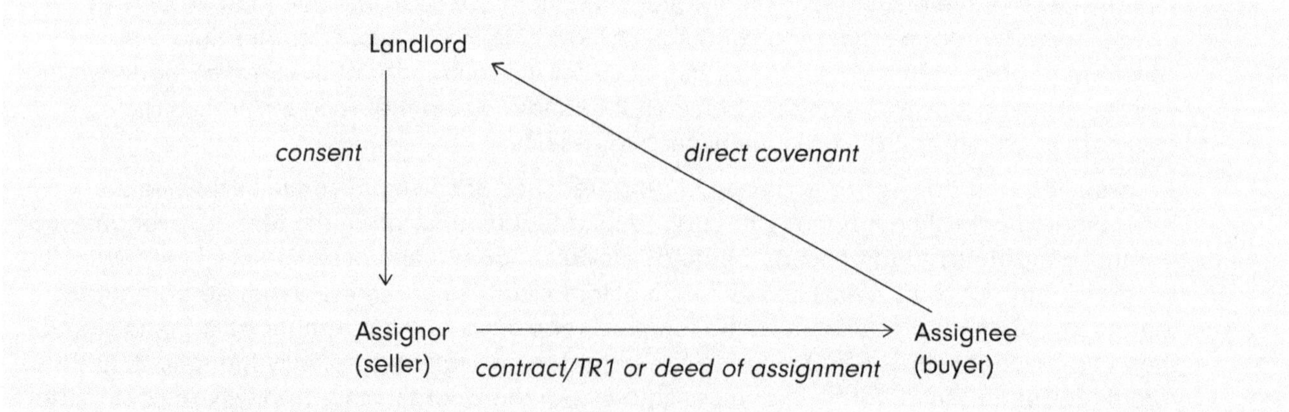

8.5 Deduction and investigation of title

The assignor's solicitor should investigate title in the same way as for the purchase of a freehold property. The superior freehold title should be checked as part of this process as well as the leasehold title, as any covenants or easements affecting the freehold will also bind the leasehold interest. Any potential problems should be identified and all relevant incumbrances disclosed in the draft contract.

The assignor's solicitor should always provide the assignee's solicitor with a copy of the lease and any licence permitting assignment to the current and previous tenants.

As to whether the superior freehold title should also be deduced:

(a) If the assignor's lease is registered with absolute title, the assignor's solicitor will be able to obtain and provide the assignee with official copies of the register and the title plan in the usual way. Since the title to the lease is guaranteed by the Land Registry, there is no need for the assignee to investigate the title to the freehold.

(b) If the lease is registered with good leasehold title, there is no guarantee of the soundness of the freehold title and so, although not entitled under the general law to do so, the assignee will try to insist on deduction of the freehold title. Without deduction of the freehold title, the lease may be unacceptable to the assignee and/or any lender. If the freehold title is registered, either party could make a search under the open register rules. Otherwise the freehold title will be deduced by the method used for unregistered land (see **2.4**). The provision for deduction of the freehold title must be dealt with by special condition in the contract because neither set of standard conditions require the assignor to deduce the freehold title.

(c) If the assignor's lease is unregistered, under the general law the assignee is entitled to call for the lease and all assignments under which that lease has been held during the last 15 years, but not for evidence of the freehold title. Without deduction of the freehold title, unless the freehold is already registered with absolute title, the assignee will only obtain a good leasehold title on registration of the lease at the Land Registry following completion, which may be unacceptable to the assignee and/or any lender. If the freehold title is registered, either party could make a search under the open register rules. Otherwise the freehold title will be deduced by the method used for unregistered land (see **2.4**). The provision for deduction of the freehold title must be dealt with by special condition in the contract because neither set of standard conditions require the assignor to deduce the freehold title.

The assignee's solicitor will need to investigate title and consider the terms of the draft contract. The terms of the lease should be checked to ensure that they will be acceptable to the assignee and any lender (see **Chapter 6**). Of particular importance is the length of the residue of the term, the permitted user, the rent and whether the landlord's consent to the assignment will be required (see **8.3** above).

8.6 Pre-contract enquiries and searches

The assignee's solicitor should make the same enquiries and searches, for the same reasons, as on a purchase of a freehold property (see **Chapter 3**). In addition, the assignee's solicitor should ask to see the insurance policy relating to the property and the receipt for the last insurance premium due. The assignee should also ask to see a copy of the receipt for the last payment of annual rent due under the lease to check that the assignor is not in breach of the lease; if there are any outstanding breaches the landlord will be able to enforce the breach against the assignee.

Where the lease has only a short period left unexpired, that the buyer may choose not to carry out some or all searches, as the risk does not justify the cost involved.

8.7 Deed of assignment and covenants for title

In order to transfer legal title to an estate in land, it is necessary to do so by deed. In the case of an assignment of a lease, the transfer deed is sometimes called a 'deed of assignment', but this document has the same effect and function as any other transfer deed. The transfer deed is usually prepared by the assignee's solicitor.

In the case of the assignment of a registered lease, irrespective of how long it has left to run, the form prescribed under the Land Registration Rules 2003 is a TR1. If the lease is unregistered, the assignment of a lease exceeding seven years in length will lead to compulsory first registration and so a TR1 will normally be used, although it is possible to use a deed of assignment similar in format to a conveyance of unregistered land. The deed of assignment format will always be used for the assignment of a lease for seven years or less as the assignment will not trigger first registration.

The drafting of the transfer deed was considered in **5.3** and the same points apply to an assignment of a lease, but the following additional points should be noted:

8.7.1 Covenants for title

If an assignor is in breach of a repairing covenant in the lease, the lack of repair could involve them in liability to the assignee after completion under the covenants for title which will be implied in the transfer deed. This is because, where the assignor sells with full or limited title guarantee, the covenants for title include a promise that the assignor has complied with the tenant's covenants in the lease, including repair. However, the principle of *caveat emptor* makes it the assignee's responsibility to check the physical state of the property and the assignor should not be expected to make any promises about it.

The conflict between the promise implied by the covenants for title and *caveat emptor* is resolved by modifying the covenants for title to exclude references to repair. This is covered in both sets of standard conditions in the contract, but there must be an express modification of the implied covenants for title in the transfer deed itself. A suggested form of wording is as follows:

> The covenants set out in section 4 of the Law of Property (Miscellaneous Provisions) Act 1994 will not extend to any breach of the tenant's covenants in the lease relating to the physical state of the property.

Panel 9 of a TR1 contains space to insert this wording, but it could also be inserted in panel 11 (additional provisions).

8.7.2 Indemnity

For the assignment of old leases granted before 1 January 1996, an indemnity covenant from the assignee to the assignor is implied except where, for unregistered leases, value is not given by the assignee for the transaction. In the latter case, an express indemnity covenant will be inserted into the transfer deed if required by the contract, and this is provided for by both sets of standard conditions.

For the assignment of leases granted on or after 1 January 1996, the assignor will usually be automatically released from future liability on the assignment and so will not require an indemnity. However, if the assignor is to remain liable (eg under the terms of an AGA), an express indemnity covenant should be included in the transfer deed. Again, both sets of standard conditions entitle the assignor to insert an indemnity in such circumstances.

8.8 Pre-completion formalities

8.8.1 Pre-completion searches

Registered lease

An official search of the registers of the leasehold title (OS1) should be carried out to check for any new entries and to gain a priority period within which to register the transfer (see **5.4.1**).

Unregistered lease

Another land charges search should be made against the name of the assignor to check that no adverse entries have been made since the pre-exchange land charges search on all the previous estate owners was made and to ensure that the priority period of 15 working days covers completion of the assignment (see **5.4.1**).

Company search

The circumstances in which company searches should be carried out are set out in **5.4.3** and apply equally to leasehold transactions.

8.8.2 The licence to assign

The landlord's solicitor will supply the engrossments (or 'top copies') of the licence, which must be by deed if it contains covenants. Where the assignee is to give a direct covenant to the landlord, the licence is usually drawn up in at least two parts, the landlord executing the original licence (which will be given to the assignor on completion for onwards transmission to the assignee) and the assignee executing the counterpart (which will be given to the landlord to take effect on completion). The assignor's AGA can be contained in the licence (in which case a third part will be needed) or created as a separate deed, in either case to take effect only on completion of the assignment.

8.8.3 Apportionments

The assignor will usually have paid rent in advance. Unless completion takes place on a day when the annual rent become due under the lease, it will be necessary for the instalment to be apportioned on completion, so that the assignee reimburses the assignor for the period from completion until the next rent day. There may also be other outgoings for which the assignor wants to claim reimbursement, such as the insurance premium. The assignor should supply a completion statement which shows the amounts due and explains how they have been calculated. Copies of the receipts or demands on which the apportionments are based should also be supplied with the completion statement, so that the assignee can check the apportioned sums.

8.9 Completion

The procedure on completion is very similar to a freehold transaction (see **Chapter 5**). The assignee will pay the assignor the balance of the purchase price (where one is to be paid) and any other sums due, including any apportionment (see **8.8.3** above).

The assignor will hand to the assignee such of the following documents as are relevant to the transaction:

(a) the lease

(b) the transfer deed (TR1 or deed of assignment, as appropriate)

(c) the licence to assign executed by the landlord

(d) evidence of the freehold title in accordance with the contract (lease not registered or not registered with absolute title)

(e) evidence of discharge of the assignee's mortgage

(f) copies of duplicate notices served by the assignor and its predecessors on the landlord in accordance with a covenant in the lease requiring the landlord to be notified of any dispositions

(g) insurance policy (or copy if insurance is effected by the landlord) and receipt (or copy) relating to the last premium due

(h) receipt for rent (and other outgoings for which the assignor wishes to claim reimbursement).

The assignee should hand to the assignor such of the following items as are relevant to the transaction:

(a) money due in accordance with the completion statement

(b) duly executed counterpart licence to assign

(c) a release of deposit (only likely where the assignee is paying a premium).

Section 45(2) of the LPA 1925 provides that, on production of the receipt for the last rent due under the lease, an assignee must assume, unless the contrary appears, that the rent has been paid and the covenants performed. The assignee's solicitor should inspect the receipt on completion (and also receipts for any other apportioned outgoings).

8.10 Post-completion steps

8.10.1 SDLT/LTT

SDLT/LTT is payable only on any purchase price charged by the assignor, and is due at the same rates using the same procedure as for the sale of freehold land (see **1.6.1**). No SLDT/LTT will be charged on the rent as it will have been paid when the lease was granted.

8.10.2 Registered lease

Where the lease is already registered at the Land Registry, an application for registration of the transfer to the assignee should be made within the priority period given by the pre-completion OS1 search. This is irrespective of the length of time left on the lease: once registered, the lease continues to be registered until it expires.

8.10.3 Unregistered lease

An unregistered lease which, at the date of the transfer to the assignee, still has over seven years of the term unexpired will need to be registered at the Land Registry within two months of the assignment or will be void in respect of the legal estate.

An application for registration with absolute title can be made where the assignee can produce satisfactory evidence relating to the superior title. In other cases, only good leasehold title can be obtained.

If the freehold title is already registered, the lease will be noted against the freehold title. In other cases, the assignee may consider lodging a caution against first registration against the freehold title, in order to protect their interests against a subsequent buyer of the freehold.

If the lease has seven years or less unexpired, it is incapable of registration with separate title.

8.10.4 Notice of assignment

Where the lease provides that notice has to be given to a landlord of an assignment (which is a standard provision), the notice should be given in duplicate accompanied by the appropriate fee set out in the lease. The landlord should be asked to sign one copy of the notice as acknowledgement of receipt and return the receipted copy to the sender to be kept with the title deeds.

Summary

- The steps involved in assigning a lease of commercial property are very similar to those involved in buying a freehold property.
- Since the lease is already in existence, the terms of the lease are not negotiable. The assignee's solicitor will have to report to the client (and any lender) on the terms of the lease.
- The assignor's solicitor must check in the lease whether the landlord's consent is required for an assignment of the lease. Consent will usually be required for leases of commercial property.
- Leases granted on or after 1 January 1996 are likely to contain detailed requirements or conditions that must be met before the landlord's consent will be given, including a requirement for the assignor to provide the landlord with an AGA guaranteeing the performance of the tenant's covenants by the assignee.
- Leases granted before 1 January 1996 are likely to contain a requirement for the assignee to give the landlord a direct covenant to perform the tenant's covenants under the lease for the remainder of the term.
- If the timing of completion is important, it is safest not to exchange until the landlord's consent has been obtained. However, both sets of standard conditions provide mechanisms for obtaining consent between exchange and completion and for rescinding the contract if consent is not obtained by a certain date.
- In the SCs, either party can rescind if consent is not obtained three working days before completion date. In the SCPCs, the parties cannot rescind until six months after the completion date.
- In the transfer deed, the assignor's solicitor should modify the implied covenants for title so that the assignor is not implying that the repair covenant in the lease has been performed.
- The transfer should contain an indemnity from the assignee where the assignor is to remain liable for breach of the tenant's covenants in the lease after the assignment has taken place.
- Apportionment of rent should take place on the completion date.
- SDLT/LTT is payable on the purchase price (if any), but not on the rent reserved by the lease.
- The assignment of a registered lease must be registered at the Land Registry.
- The assignment of an unregistered lease which has over seven years unexpired at the date of the assignment will trigger first registration.
- Notice of the assignment must be given to the landlord.

Sample questions

Question 1

A solicitor acts for the tenant of a lease of a commercial property granted in 2015. The lease contains a tenant's covenant not to assign the lease without the landlord's consent. The tenant has exchanged contracts for an assignment of the lease with a prospective assignee and the completion date is in five working days' time. The contract incorporates the Standard Conditions of Sale without amendment. The landlord has not yet said whether it consents to the assignment as it only received the references for the assignee yesterday.

Which of the following statements is the best advice for the tenant about what will happen if the landlord's consent has not been obtained by the completion date in the contract?

A The contract will automatically terminate if the consent has not been obtained within the next two working days.

B The completion date in the contract will be automatically postponed until five working days after the assignor notifies the assignee that consent has been given.

C The assignment should proceed as the landlord is being unreasonable in withholding consent.

D The assignor and the assignee can agree to defer completion to a later date when the landlord's consent has been obtained.

E The contract will automatically terminate if the consent has not been obtained by the completion date in the contract.

Answer

Option D is correct. Under the SCs, either party may rescind the contract by notice if the landlord's consent has not been given three working days before completion date, but the contract does not terminate automatically and the parties may choose not to rescind if they both still want the assignment to go ahead and believe that the landlord's consent will be forthcoming after an acceptable delay. So option D is good advice and options A and E wrongly state the contractual position.

In relation to option C, the covenant in the lease is a qualified covenant which is converted into a fully qualified covenant by s 19(1)(a) Landlord and Tenant Act 1927, so the landlord's consent cannot be unreasonably withheld. Moreover, s 1 Landlord and Tenant Act 1988 applies, which means that the landlord must give consent within a reasonable time, except in a case where it is reasonable not to give consent. However, the landlord is not acting unreasonably if it only received the references yesterday. If the assignment proceeds in breach of the alienation covenants in the lease, the assigning tenant will not be released from liability under the lease and the lease itself may be liable to forfeiture.

Option B describes the position under the SCPCs (which is different to the SCs) and is, in any event, subject to the right of either party to rescind the contract once six months have passed since the completion date.

Question 2

A solicitor acts for an assignee of a lease granted in 1998. The assignor has applied to the landlord for consent to assign the lease and the landlord's solicitor has provided a draft licence to assign. The draft licence contains a requirement for the assignor to enter into an authorised guarantee agreement with the landlord and for the assignee to give the landlord a direct covenant to observe and perform the covenants in the lease for the remainder of the term.

Is the draft licence in acceptable form?

A No, because the direct covenant should come from the assignor rather than the assignee.

B No, because the direct covenant should either be deleted or limited to the period during which the assignee is the tenant under the lease.

C No, because the assignor should not be required to enter into an authorised guarantee agreement for a lease granted in 1998.

D Yes, because the landlord needs to create privity of contract with both the assignor and the assignee.

E Yes, because the landlord is entitled to require that the assignor enters into an authorised guarantee agreement for a lease granted in 1998.

Answer

Option B is correct. The lease was granted in 1998, so it is a new lease for the purposes of the Landlord and Tenant (Covenants) Act 1995 (the 'Act'). The Act will automatically release the assignee from all the tenant covenants of the tenancy on assignment of the lease, so if the landlord requires a direct covenant from the assignee, the covenant should be limited to the period the assignee is actually the tenant, not the remainder of the entire term. It is arguable that a direct covenant is not necessary at all as it gives the landlord nothing more than they enjoy under s 3 of the Act, but landlords quite commonly require one, albeit in the restricted form.

Option A is not the best answer because the assignor will be guaranteeing performance of the tenant's covenants by the assignee in the AGA but will be automatically released from all the tenant covenants of the tenancy once the assignment takes place, so a direct covenant from the assignor serves no purpose. Option C is not the best answer because the Act, which created AGAs, does apply to leases granted on or after 1 January 1996.

Options D and E are not the best answers because they imply acceptance of an assignee's direct covenant in an inappropriate form. In addition, option D is misconceived as the Act will not allow the landlord to have continuing privity of contract with the assignor after the assignment and privity of contract with the assignee is not needed as there will be liability under s 3 of the Act. Option E overstates the position; whether the landlord is entitled to insist on an AGA from the assignor depends on the terms of the lease. The landlord may have inserted the need for an AGA in the lease as a pre-condition to its giving consent, in which case the landlord can always insist on the assignor entering into the AGA whether or not it is reasonable. In the absence of the provision in the lease, the landlord can insist on the AGA only if it is reasonable to do so.

Question 3

A solicitor acts for the assignee of a lease of commercial property granted three years ago for a term of 10 years. Contracts have been exchanged incorporating the Standard Commercial Property Conditions. The assignor obtained the landlord's consent to the assignment prior to exchange of contracts. The solicitor has drafted the transfer deed using Land Registry form TR1.

Which of the following statements best describes the way in which the transfer deed should be drafted?

A The TR1 should contain an indemnity from the assignee to the assignor to observe and perform the covenants in the lease because this is a leasehold transaction.

B The TR1 does not need to contain an indemnity from the assignee to the assignor to observe and perform the covenants in the lease as such an indemnity is implied by the general law.

C The TR1 does not need to contain an indemnity from the assignee to the assignor to observe and perform the covenants in the lease as the assignor will automatically be released from future liability on the assignment.

D The TR1 can only incorporate an indemnity from the assignee to the assignor to observe and perform the covenants in the lease if this was covered by a special condition in the contract.

E The TR1 should contain an indemnity from the assignee to the assignor to observe and perform the covenants in the lease if the assignor is giving an authorised guarantee agreement to the landlord.

Answer

Option E is correct. An indemnity from the assignee to the assignor will only serve a purpose if the assignor will continue to be liable to the landlord if there is a breach of the tenant's covenants in the lease after the assignment has taken place. Option A is overstated as an indemnity will not be appropriate for every leasehold transaction. Option B is not the best answer as the law only implies such an indemnity covenant in leases granted before 1 January 1996.

The lease was granted three years ago, so it is a new lease for the purposes of the Landlord and Tenant (Covenants) Act 1995 (the 'Act'). The Act will automatically release the assignor from all the tenant covenants of the tenancy on completion of the assignment, but the assignor may become liable under the terms of an authorised guarantee agreement instead. Option C ignores this possibility so is not the best answer.

Option D is not the best answer as both sets of standard conditions provide for an indemnity to be given in the transfer if the assignor will continue to be liable after the assignment so a special condition is not required.

9 Remedies for Breach of Leasehold Covenants

9.1	Introduction	170
9.2	Liability on covenants in leases	170
9.3	Remedies for breach of the covenant to pay rent	171
9.4	Remedies for breach of the covenant to repair	175
9.5	Remedies for breach of other covenants	178
9.6	Surrender of the lease	178

SQE1 syllabus

This chapter will enable you to achieve the SQE1 Assessment Specification in relation to Functioning Legal Knowledge concerned with the following:

- Liability on covenants in leases granted before 1 January 1996
- Liability on covenants in leases granted after 1 January 1996
- Action in debt
- Commercial Rent Arrears Recovery
- Pursue guarantors and/or rent deposit
- Forfeiture
- Specific performance
- Damages
- Self-help/*Jervis v Harris* clause

Note that for SQE1, candidates are not usually required to recall specific case names or cite statutory or regulatory authorities. Cases and statutory or regulatory authorities are provided for illustrative purposes only unless otherwise indicated.

Learning outcomes

By the end of this chapter you will be able to apply relevant core legal principles and rules appropriately and effectively, at the level of a competent newly qualified solicitor in practice, to realistic client-based and ethical problems and situations in the following areas:

- the liability of a tenant for performance of the tenant's covenants in a lease after assignment of that lease
- the remedies available to a landlord when a tenant is in breach of the tenant's covenants in the lease.

9.1 Introduction

This chapter looks at the remedies available to a landlord of commercial property should a tenant breach the covenants in its lease. This involves not only identifying the nature of the breach committed by the tenant, but also the options available to the landlord given the type of breach, the liability of any guarantors and former tenants and which, if any, of the relevant remedies available to the landlord would be most appropriate in a given set of circumstances.

9.2 Liability on covenants in leases

When there has been a breach of the tenant's covenants, the landlord will be able to look to the current tenant (and any guarantor of the current tenant) for a remedy. The landlord may also be able to look to former tenants (and any of their guarantors). How this works will depend on whether the lease is an 'old lease' granted before 1 January 1996, or a 'new' lease granted from or after that date.

9.2.1 Leases granted before 1 January 1996

The position with old leases is that the original tenant remains liable for the covenants under the lease for the full term of the lease, regardless of the fact that they may have assigned it to another tenant. So in addition to being able to sue the current tenant in privity of estate, the landlord can also sue the original tenant in privity of contract. The landlord may also be able to sue any intervening tenants in privity of contract if, as is common, the landlord required each incoming tenant to give it a direct covenant on the assignment (see **8.4.3**). This puts the landlord of an old lease in a strong position if it needs to enforce the tenant's covenants.

Figure 9.1 Leases granted before 1 January 1996

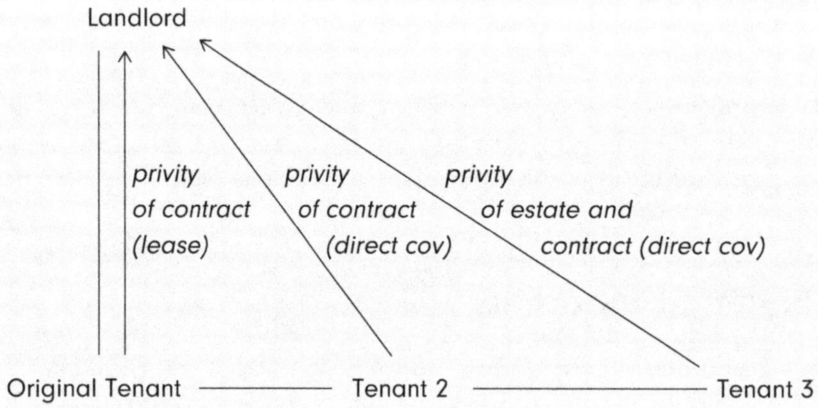

9.2.2 Leases granted on or after 1 January 1996

The Landlord and Tenant (Covenants) Act 1995 ('the Act') replaces the law of privity of contract and privity of estate with a new set of statutory rules.

With new leases, the original tenant is released from liability for the covenants in the lease as soon as it assigns the lease to another tenant. This is a worse position for the landlord than under an old lease; it means that landlords of new leases cannot always sue the original tenant. To compensate for this loss of control, the landlord is allowed to stipulate, in advance in the lease, certain circumstances and conditions which must be met before the landlord will give their consent to an assignment. For example, the landlord is allowed in certain circumstances to require an authorised guarantee agreement ('AGA') (see **8.4.4**). An AGA is a promise by the outgoing tenant that it will be liable for any breaches of the covenants in the lease by the incoming assignee.

Figure 9.2 Leases granted on or after 1 January 1996

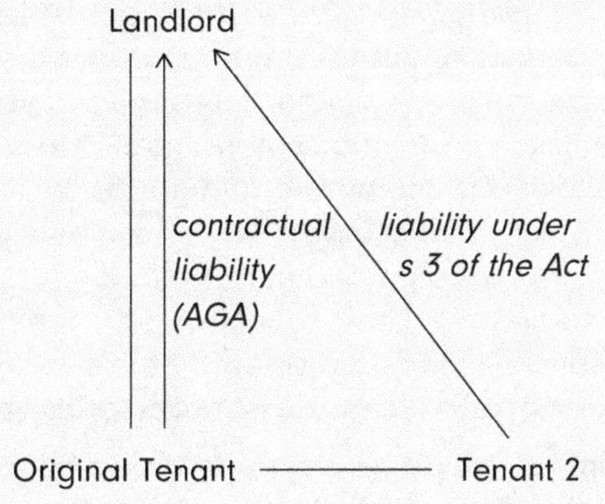

However, the AGA only lasts for the duration of that assignee's ownership of the lease and so when the assignee assigns the lease on, the tenant who gave the AGA will be released from it. The assignee (who is now the current tenant) who wants to assign will then need to give an AGA to the landlord on the assignment.

Figure 9.3 Release of tenant under a new lease

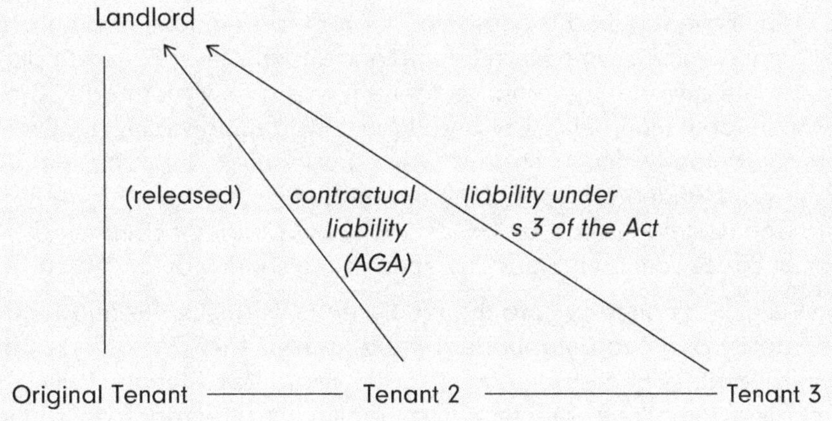

9.3 Remedies for breach of the covenant to pay rent

The remedies available depend on what type of breach has occurred. Generally there is a distinction between breaches of the covenant to pay rent and breaches of other covenants, the most important being the covenant to repair. For non-payment of rent, the first thing to check is that there is a covenant to pay rent in the lease and that the tenant has failed to pay rent by the due date (see **6.12**). If there has been a breach, there are a number of remedies available to the landlord.

9.3.1 Action in debt

Non-payment of rent is a debt and so if the current tenant, or one of the other parties mentioned above is liable for the rent, it can be recovered through the High Court or County Court. The Limitation Act 1980 puts a limitation of six years on recovery of rent.

9.3.2 Commercial Rent Arrears Recovery ('CRAR')

CRAR permits the landlord to enter the property and seize and sell goods belonging to the current tenant. This remedy applies only to commercial premises and there are strict procedural rules relating to its use. For example, the landlord must give seven days' notice of its intention to enter the premises and must use an enforcement agency to enter the premises to remove goods. The landlord is not allowed to remove certain goods, which include items or equipment up to the value of £1350 which are necessary for the tenant's business, such as computers or telephones. Also the landlord can only take items belonging to the tenant, so any items which are leased or bought on hire purchase cannot be taken. If the tenant does not pay the arrears, the landlord may sell the goods, provided that this is done at a public auction and that the tenant is given at least seven clear days' notice of the sale.

CRAR is only available in relation to rent paid for possession and use of the premises and at least seven days' rent must be outstanding. Arrears of other payments (such as insurance rent) will not be recoverable using CRAR, even if they are reserved as rent in the lease.

9.3.3 Pursue guarantors and/or rent deposit

(a) Guarantors

Whenever the tenant under a lease fails to pay rent the landlord should consider who can be sued. The current tenant who has committed the breach is always a possibility, but the current tenant may have a guarantor, or there may be former tenants and their guarantors who remain liable. These other parties may be better prospects for the landlord, especially if the current tenant is in financial difficulty.

The landlord will have required a guarantor if it had reservations about the proposed tenant's ability to maintain rental payments without financial difficulties. For example, a guarantor might have been required if the proposed tenant was a newly-formed PLC or a private company whose reputation, reliability and financial standing was unknown in the property market. The guarantee (which must be in writing) will oblige the guarantor to pay the rent and any other sums due under the lease if the tenant does not pay and to remedy, or indemnify the landlord against loss caused by, any breaches of covenant committed by the tenant. A guarantor of the current tenant may be sued in the same way as the current tenant.

The situation is more complex where the landlord wants to sue the guarantor of a former tenant. The liability of a guarantor under an old lease is likely to extend through the duration of the lease, regardless of an assignment by the guaranteed tenant. With a new lease, the guarantor is automatically released from liability on an assignment of the lease by the guaranteed tenant and any attempt by the landlord to require the guarantor *directly* to guarantee the incoming tenant is likely to be void. However, the landlord may require the guarantor of the outgoing tenant to guarantee the outgoing tenant's obligations under the AGA, thereby *indirectly* guaranteeing the incoming tenant until a further assignment takes place.

Where the landlord intends to pursue a former tenant or the guarantor of a former tenant, whether under a new or an old lease, the landlord must comply with s 17 of the Landlord and Tenant (Covenants) Act 1995*:

- The landlord must serve a 'default notice' on any former tenants or their guarantors if the landlord intends to recover a 'fixed charge' from them. A fixed charge is a monetary payment such as rent, service charge or other liquidated sum.
- The default notice must be served within six months of the current tenant's breach, otherwise the landlord will be unable to claim from the former tenant or their guarantor. The landlord does not have to start proceedings: the default notice is simply giving notice of the claim.
- Section 17 applies to all leases whenever granted, not just new leases.

Where the landlord does serve a default notice on a former tenant or its guarantor, that person may be able to regain some control over the property by paying the sum claimed under the default notice and then calling for an 'overriding lease', a headlease between the landlord and the former tenant/guarantor slotted in between the landlord and the defaulting tenant, making the former tenant/guarantor the immediate landlord of the defaulting tenant.

* s 17 notice is key term used in practice in the context of a landlord's remedies against former tenants. You may be required to know and be able to use this term in the SQE1 assessments.

(b) Rent deposits

Where a landlord has reservations about the proposed tenant's ability to maintain rental payments, it can require the tenant to deposit a cash sum as security for payment of the rent and performance of the tenant's covenants contained in the lease. The amount of the deposit (generally 6–12 months' rent due under the lease), the circumstances which entitle the landlord to withdraw money from it and the point at which it is repayable to the tenant (eg on an approved assignment) will be set out in a rent deposit deed. Provided there is no breach of the terms of the rent deposit deed by the landlord, the landlord can draw upon the money as soon as the tenant is in breach of a relevant covenant in the lease, without taking court action for debt or exercising any other remedy in respect of the breach. The deed would normally require the tenant to top the deposit up in such circumstances. The deed would also normally state that the rent deposit balance is returned to the tenant at the end of the term or on an earlier lawful assignment.

9.3.4 Forfeiture

Unlike the other remedies for non-payment of rent, forfeiture will bring the lease to end and enable the landlord to gain vacant possession of the property. To be able to use forfeiture, the lease must contain a forfeiture clause. An example of a forfeiture clause is set out below:

9. Forfeiture

9.1 Whenever:

a) any rent reserved by this lease is outstanding for twenty one days after becoming payable (whether formally demanded or not); or

b) the tenant is in breach of any of the tenant's covenants in this lease;

...

then in any of those cases the landlord may at any time (notwithstanding the waiver of any previous right of re-entry) re-enter the building or any part in the name of the whole whereupon the term will end ...

Forfeiture clauses are not always labelled as forfeiture clauses and can have other headings, such as 'provisos' or 're-entry'.

The procedure where there has been non-payment of rent is straightforward. In the example above, clause 9.1 (a) allows the landlord to proceed to forfeit if the rent has been outstanding for 21 days, whether the landlord has made a formal demand or not. Common law requires a formal demand to be made but the lease can dispense with this, as in this example. Leases also vary as to how many days the rent must have been outstanding before forfeiture can take place.

The landlord could forfeit either by taking possession through 'peaceable re-entry' (ie without force) or, if that is not possible, by obtaining a court order. The tenant can apply to the court for relief from forfeiture, whereupon the court has discretion to allow the lease to continue. This would be subject to a condition that the tenant paid all arrears and costs.

A landlord can waive its right to forfeit by carrying out any act demonstrating an intention to continue the relationship of landlord and tenant so must be careful not to demand or accept rent after the breach has arisen.

9.3.5 Choosing an appropriate remedy

Once the landlord has established that the tenant is in breach of the covenant to pay rent and has identified who may be liable for that breach, they must decide which remedy, or combination of remedies, is most likely to produce the right outcome. This will depend on a number of practical issues, such as the relative cost of the procedure, the time it will take, the effect on the continuing relationship with the tenant and the likelihood of the problem recurring in the future.

Example

You act for the landlord of a lease of one-room office premises granted in 2010 for a term of 15 years to Tenant A. Three years ago Tenant A assigned the lease to Tenant B and gave an AGA to the landlord. Tenant B is a telesales company with two employees and its only non-monetary assets are office furniture, telephones and leased computer equipment. Tenant B has been having financial difficulties and has not paid the rent for the last nine months. The landlord now wants to recover the outstanding rent.

What advice would you give to the landlord in this situation?

Although an action for debt against Tenant B is a relatively quick procedure and the landlord is likely to be successful, if Tenant B is in financial difficulties it may not be able to pay the debt or reimburse the landlord's legal costs.

CRAR would not be a suitable remedy as the landlord cannot seize certain goods up to the value of £1,350 which are necessary for the tenant's business. In any event, It is unlikely the office furniture and telephones would be worth very much. The landlord could not take the computers because they are leased. Also, this would seriously impact on Tenant B's ability to pay the rent in the future and so would not be a sensible remedy to pursue.

There does not appear to be a guarantor or rent deposit for Tenant B.

An action for debt against Tenant A is possible, but the landlord will not be able to recover the whole of the outstanding rent. Under s 17 of the Landlord and Tenant (Covenants) Act 1995, when pursuing a former tenant, the landlord can only recover sums that fall within six months of the notice being served, so it can only recover six of the nine months' rent due.

If Tenant B's problems are long term and the lease permits forfeiture, the landlord may forfeit the lease, recover possession and re-let the property to a more viable tenant. It could also pursue Tenant B for the arrears due up to forfeiture (or Tenant A for six months of those arrears). In the case of non-payment of rent, the landlord must make a formal demand for rent unless the lease relieves it of this obligation. Tenant B would have a right to apply for relief and if granted, the landlord's attempted forfeiture is frustrated, so the landlord is going to have to wait at least a short while before it can re-let the property to see if Tenant B successfully applies for relief. If the property market is depressed, the landlord could be left with an empty property for some time. However, the mere threat of forfeiture proceedings may persuade Tenant B to pay the arrears, or at least come to an agreement with the landlord about how the arrears will be paid off in future.

9.4 Remedies for breach of the covenant to repair

The first step is to establish that there has been a breach of the repair covenant. This will depend on the nature of the damage and the precise wording of the covenant (see **6.7**). If there has been a breach, there are a number of remedies available to the landlord.

9.4.1 Specific performance

The tenant's failure to repair is a breach of covenant and the equitable remedy of specific performance is available to force the tenant to comply with the positive covenant. However the courts will grant this relief only where other remedies are not appropriate. In the case of *Rainbow Estates Ltd v Tokenhold Ltd* [1999], the court granted an order for specific performance because:

- there was no forfeiture or landlord's self-help clause in the lease;
- damages were not an adequate remedy, particularly where the condition of the property was deteriorating;
- the court was sure that the order was not being sought by the landlord simply to harass or otherwise put pressure on the tenant; and
- in the circumstances, it was appropriate to grant the plaintiff an order for specific performance.

9.4.2 Damages

This remedy is always available for breach of covenant. The tenant is in breach of its contractual obligations in the lease and so an action would lie for breach of contract. However, in the case of a breach of the covenant to repair, two important statutory provisions may mean that the landlord cannot recover the full cost of the repairs:

(i) Section 18 of the Landlord and Tenant Act 1927 limits the amount of damages to the amount by which the landlord's reversion (usually the freehold building) has diminished in value as a result of the disrepair. The diminution in the capital value of the building attributable to the disrepair may be less than the cost of the repairs, so this course of action may not be attractive to the landlord.

(ii) The Leasehold Property (Repairs) Act 1938 applies to leases granted for seven or more years with more than three years left to run. If the Act applies and the landlord wants to sue for damages, a special procedure must be followed. Notice must be served on the tenant. The tenant has a right to serve a counter notice within 28 days and if the tenant does so, the landlord cannot proceed any further with the claim without leave of the court.

9.4.3 Self-help/*Jervis v Harris* clause

Most leases provide a contractual 'self-help' remedy for the landlord, allowing the landlord to recover the cost of repairs as a debt and not a damages claim. The benefit of this is that the landlord is able to avoid the statutory limitations on pursuing damages claims imposed by the 1927 and 1938 Acts. Such self-help clauses were approved in the case of *Jervis v Harris* [1996]*.

A typical self-help clause allows the landlord to enter the property to check compliance with the tenant's repair covenant. If there has been a breach, the landlord can serve a notice specifying the works required to remedy the breach. If the tenant fails to start the work within a specified period after service of the landlord's notice, or is not proceeding diligently with those works, the landlord may enter, carry out the works and recover the cost from the tenant as a debt. So a claim for damages is converted into a claim for debt, thereby avoiding the statutory restrictions on recoverability.

* *Jervis v Harris* is the term used in practice to describe this type of clause. You may be required to know and be able to use this term in the SQE1 assessments.

9.4.4 Forfeiture

The procedure used in forfeiture for non-payment of rent, which is quite straightforward, should be distinguished from forfeiture for a breach of other types of covenant where the landlord must be careful to follow the statutory procedure laid down in s 146 of the Law of Property Act 1925.

First, the landlord must serve a s 146 notice* on the tenant which will:

- specify the breach
- require the breach to be remedied within a reasonable time if it is capable of remedy
- require the tenant to pay compensation for the breach.

If the tenant does not comply with the notice, then the landlord can forfeit either by peaceable re-entry or by court order. The tenant can apply for relief from forfeiture.

There is an added complication in cases of disrepair where the lease was originally for seven years or more and has at least three years left unexpired. In this case, the Leasehold Property (Repairs) Act 1938 applies and requires the s 146 notice to include notification of the tenant's right to serve a counter notice within 28 days. If the tenant serves a counter notice, then the landlord can only proceed to forfeit with the leave of the court.

* s 146 notice is key term used in practice in the context of forfeiture. You may be required to know and be able to use this term in the SQE1 assessments.

9.4.5 Choosing an appropriate remedy

The uncertainties about the scope of repairing covenants and the statutory protection for tenants makes it more difficult for landlords to find an effective remedy for breach of the covenant to repair than non-payment of rent. The rationale for statutory protection is that tenants need protecting against landlords who would otherwise seek to use trivial or remediable disrepair to terminate leases for unrelated commercial reasons. Most landlords will try to reach a negotiated solution, but where this is not possible, practical considerations such as cost and time will need to be taken into account.

Example

Your firm acts for the landlord of a retail unit. The lease was granted to Tenant A in 2019 for a term of 10 years and assigned by Tenant A to Tenant B in 2021. Tenant A entered into an AGA with the landlord on the assignment.

The landlord visited the property last week and noticed that the shop was in a bad state of repair. The windows at the back of the property are broken and the walls beneath are damp because water is coming through. The lease contains a covenant requiring the tenant 'to keep the property clean and tidy and in good repair and condition'.

The landlord has told you that getting Tenant B out of the property is a last resort, but they would be prepared to consider it if necessary. If they decide to go down this route, then they would like Tenant B out as soon as possible so they can get on with re-letting the property. The market is not very buoyant at the moment.

What advice would you give to the landlord in this situation?

The facts make it clear that the tenant is in breach. It is unlikely that the disrepair is covered by the insurance provisions as there is no suggestion that an event classifiable as an insured risk has caused the problems identified.

Tenant B is in breach of its contractual obligations and so an action for damages should be considered. As the lease was granted for a term of seven years or more and has at least three years left to run, the landlord must comply with the requirements of Leasehold Property (Repairs) Act 1938 ('LP(R)A 1938') and must serve a s 146 notice. This is a comparatively quick procedure and if Tenant B is solvent, the landlord will get some money and the lease will continue. However, litigation costs money and the landlord may not get its award and/or legal costs if the tenant is in serious financial trouble. Also, under s 18 of the Landlord and Tenant Act 1927 ('LTA 1927'), damages for breach of repair covenants are limited to the diminution in value of the landlord's reversion. The landlord may therefore not recover the full cost of reinstating the property.

If the lease permits forfeiture, the landlord may forfeit the lease, recover possession and re-let the property. The landlord must serve a s 146 notice identifying the breach complained of, specifying remedial steps (if the breach is remediable) and requiring compensation (if required). As the lease is one to which the LP(R)A 1938 applies, the s 146 notice must also contain a statement of the tenant's rights under that Act. Essentially, if the tenant serves a counter-notice, the landlord will only be able to forfeit with leave of the court, and then only in specified circumstances. In any event, the tenant has a right to apply for relief from forfeiture. If the landlord is able to forfeit, it would get the property back and could then re-let to a more viable tenant. The difficulty comes in letting the property: if there is an over-supply of properties, the landlord could be left with an empty property bringing in no money whatsoever. Further, if Tenant B makes a successful application for relief, the landlord may have wasted valuable time.

The landlord could consider using any self-help remedy contained in the lease. The limitations in respect of the LTA 1927 and LP(R)A 1938 do not apply where the remedy being sought is a debt. Self-help provides a quick way of controlling and ensuring the remediation of any breach, returning the property to its proper state. However, the landlord does have to bear the initial cost of carrying out the repair work. Further costs (in starting court proceedings) will be incurred if the tenant refuses to reimburse the landlord. If Tenant B is in financial difficulty, it may not be able to afford to reimburse the landlord.

Specific performance is an equitable remedy so only available at the discretion of the court. There are time and cost implications of going to court (particularly if claim fails to succeed and the landlord has to bear its own costs) and all while the repair work is not being carried out. Specific performance will only be granted in unusual cases, such as where the other remedies open to the landlord (damages, forfeiture and self-help) are not available. This is unlikely to be the case here.

The landlord could pursue Tenant A under the AGA and, as this is not a claim for non-payment of rent, s 17 notice will not be required. Tenant A may be a good source from which to recover any losses suffered, but only if it is still in existence and solvent. This remedy will not, by itself, secure vacant possession of the unit and the problems with Tenant B may well recur.

9.5 Remedies for breach of other covenants

A tenants may breach the covenants in the lease in other ways. For example, they may change the use the property and/or carry out alterations without first obtaining the landlord's consent, in which case they are also likely to be in breach of covenants relating to planning and statutory consents. They may let third parties into occupation or try to assign/underlet without obtaining landlord's consent, perhaps because they know they would not get consent or they believe the landlord is unreasonably withholding consent. The following remedies are available for these types of breach:

- Forfeiture (see **9.4.4** above, although there is no need for the s 146 notice to include notification of the tenant's right to serve a counter notice).
- Injunction for breach of a negative covenant such as a user covenant, or to prevent an anticipated breach such as an assignment in breach of covenant.
- Specific performance, but only where the positive obligation is sufficiently precise, performance or supervision over a period of time is not required and damages are not an adequate remedy.
- Damages, recoverable under normal contractual rules.
- Pursuing a former tenant or their guarantor.
- Deduction from a rent deposit deed (see **9.3.3(a)** above), provided that the deed provides for deduction from the deposit for costs, losses and expenses suffered by the landlord due to a breach by the tenant of its covenants in the lease.

9.6 Surrender of the lease

This option is not a landlord's remedy in the technical sense, but it might be a practical way for the landlord and tenant to work out their problems. The tenant surrenders its lease to the landlord (see **10.2.3**). Surrender requires a mutual act by the tenant and landlord which treats the lease as no longer being in existence. Although this could be done informally by operation of law (eg by handing the keys back), with commercial leases it would probably be done formally by a deed of surrender. The deed of surrender could deal with issues such as arrears and might be attractive to the tenant as a way of terminating its obligations. It is potentially quicker and cheaper than forfeiture for both parties. It does, however, depend on both parties being willing to pursue it.

Summary

- If the lease was granted before 1 January 1996, a tenant continues to be bound by the covenants in the lease even after the lease has been assigned to another tenant.
- If the lease was granted on or after 1 January 1996, a tenant continues to be bound by the covenants in the lease while its assignee is the tenant even after the lease has been assigned to another tenant (in the case of commercial leases only) if it entered into an AGA with the landlord at the time of the assignment. Otherwise, a tenant is released from liability once the assignment has taken place.
- A landlord has a number of remedies against a tenant who is in breach of the lease, but the nature of the remedies available and the procedures that must be followed will vary according to the type of covenant that has been breached.
- The potential remedies for non-payment of rent are an action in debt, CRAR, pursuing guarantors and former tenants, deducting from the rent deposit and forfeiture.

- The potential remedies for breach of the repair covenant are an action for damages (against the current or former tenants and their respective guarantors), specific performance, using a self-help clause in the lease and forfeiture.
- The potential remedies for breaches of other covenants are an action for damages (against the current or former tenants and their respective guarantors), injunction, specific performance and forfeiture.
- Forfeiture is the only remedy which entitles the landlord to regain possession of the property.
- Forfeiture and self-help are only available if the lease contains these clauses.

Sample questions

Question 1

A solicitor acts for the landlord of a freehold property let to a tenant for a term of 15 years with eight years left to run. The tenant has not carried out repairs in accordance with its repairing obligations in the lease. Following the procedure set out in the self-help clause in the lease, the landlord has entered the property and carried out the repairs.

Will the landlord be able to recoup all of its costs from the tenant?

A No, the landlord will only be able to recoup the value by which the freehold interest in the property has reduced in value, rather than the full cost of the repair.

B No, because the landlord did not serve a s 146 notice on the tenant.

C No, because the landlord did not seek the leave of the court to pursue this claim.

D Yes, the landlord should be able to recover the full costs of the repair in a debt action.

E Yes, the landlord should be able to recover the full costs of the repair as damages.

Answer

Option D is correct. Although the breach of covenant here is a failure to repair, the case of *Jervis v Harris* confirmed that a liquidated sum sought to reimburse a landlord after exercising the self-help remedy in a lease is an action for debt rather than damages (so option E is wrong). Accordingly, the landlord is not bound by the restrictions on claims for damages in LTA 1927 (as in option A) and LP(R)A 1938 (as in options B and C).

Question 2

A solicitor acts for the landlord of a freehold office building. In 2015, the landlord let the whole of the building to an insurance company for a term of 10 years. Rent is payable monthly. In 2017, the insurance company assigned the lease to an accountancy firm, with the landlord's consent as required under the terms of the lease. In 2019, with the landlord's consent, the accountancy firm assigned the lease to a recruitment agency. As a condition of obtaining consent, the accountancy firm entered into an authorised guarantee agreement ('AGA') with the landlord. It is now 2022 and the recruitment agency has failed to pay rent for the past three months.

Which of the following statements is the best advice to the landlord in this situation?

A The landlord will only be able to sue the accountancy firm and the recruitment agency.

B The landlord will only be able to sue the recruitment agency because the insurance company and the accountancy firm will have been released from liability under the tenant's covenants in the lease by statute.

C The landlord will be able to sue all three tenants but must first serve them each with a notice under s 17 Landlord and Tenant (Covenants) Act 1995 in respect of the recruitment agency's failure to pay the rent.

D The landlord will be able to sue all three tenants, but in the case of the insurance company and the accountancy firm the landlord must first serve them each with a notice under s 17 Landlord and Tenant (Covenants) Act 1995 in respect of the recruitment agency's failure to pay the rent.

E The landlord should be able to sue the accountancy firm and the recruitment agency, but only for rent arrears of not more than six months.

Answer

The best advice is contained in option A. This a new lease under LT(C)A 1995. The current tenant, the recruitment agency, is clearly in breach of the covenant to pay rent and will be liable for the breach. Former tenants are automatically released on assignment, so the insurance company has been released. However, liability can continue if the outgoing tenant has given an AGA and as the accountancy firm has done this, it will remain liable for breaches of the tenant's covenants. Option B is not the best advice as it ignores the AGA. Options C and D incorrectly refer to the possibility of suing all three tenants.

Former tenants can only be made liable for payment of fixed sums if notified of the breach within six months of the sum falling due (or the landlord commences an action against the former tenant within that time). As there are only three months of arrears, the accountancy firm can still be sued for the recruitment agency's failure to pay rent. As long as the s 17 notice is given to the accountancy firm, there is no restriction on the amount of the arrears that can be recovered. The Limitation Act 1980 puts a limitation of six years on recovery of rent, but the lease only has another three years before it is due to expire. Option E is not the best answer as it is vague and imprecise.

Question 3

It is 2022 and a tenant is having difficulty paying the rent reserved by its lease. The quarterly payment of annual rent was due 10 days ago. The lease contains a clause entitling the landlord to forfeit the lease whenever any rent reserved by the lease is outstanding for 15 days after becoming payable, whether formally demanded or not. The tenant's problems are caused by an administrative error by its bank and the tenant has not been in breach of covenant before.

Which of the following statements is the best advice to the tenant about the landlord's remedies for the failure to pay the rent on time?

A The landlord can forfeit the lease immediately.

B The landlord cannot forfeit the lease immediately because it needs to make a formal demand first.

C The landlord is unlikely to succeed in any attempt to forfeit the lease.

D The landlord cannot forfeit the lease immediately because it needs to wait longer from the rent due date.

E The landlord can forfeit the lease if the rent is not paid in the next five days.

Answer

Option C is correct. The lease dispenses with the need to make a formal demand (so option B is wrong), but the rent has only been due for 10 days and the lease stipulates the need to wait 15 days (so option A is wrong).

Options D and E recognise that the landlord will have to wait longer before the right of forfeiture arises, but are not the best advice as they suggest that this is the only obstacle facing the landlord in a forfeiture action. The tenant can apply for relief from forfeiture and this is likely to be granted because the tenant has not been in breach before and the problem is unlikely to be repeated. The facts do not suggest that the tenant is in long-term or severe financial difficulty.

10 Lease Termination and Security of Tenure under a Business Lease

10.1	Introduction	184
10.2	Termination of leases at common law	184
10.3	The 1954 Act	186

SQE1 syllabus

This chapter will enable you to achieve the SQE1 Assessment Specification in relation to Functioning Legal Knowledge concerned with the following:

- Termination of a lease
- Effluxion of time
- Surrender
- Merger
- Security of tenure under a business lease
- Landlord and Tenant Act 1954 (Part II)
- Application of the 1954 Act
- Termination by the landlord
- Renewal lease by the tenant
- Landlord's grounds of opposition
- Terms of the new lease
- Availability of compensation

Note that for SQE1, candidates are not usually required to recall specific case names or cite statutory or regulatory authorities. Cases and statutory or regulatory authorities are provided for illustrative purposes only unless otherwise indicated.

Learning outcomes

By the end of this chapter you will be able to apply relevant core legal principles and rules appropriately and effectively, at the level of a competent newly qualified solicitor in practice, to realistic client-based and ethical problems and situations in the following areas:

- how leases come to an end under the common law
- leases qualifying for security of tenure under Part II of the Landlord and Tenant Act 1954

- letting commercial property without giving the tenant security of tenure
- termination of a secure lease by a landlord
- termination of a secure lease by a tenant
- grounds for a landlord to oppose the renewal of the lease
- terms of a renewal lease
- compensation when a secure lease is not renewed.

10.1 Introduction

This chapter starts by considering the ways in which leases can be terminated at common law when the tenant is not in breach of the tenant's covenants in the lease (see **9.3.4** and **9.4.4** for forfeiture when the tenant is in breach). However, many leases enjoy statutory protection, which means they can only be terminated in prescribed ways and the tenant may be able to renew or extend them. The generic name for this type of statutory protection is called 'security of tenure'.

This chapter considers security of tenure for business leases under Part II of the Landlord and Tenant Act 1954, which will be referred to as 'the 1954 Act'. The 1954 Act permits tenants of certain tenancies to remain in the property after the contractual term of the tenancy has expired and limits the ways in which protected tenancies can be terminated.

10.2 Termination of leases at common law

Before looking at the provisions of the 1954 Act in detail, it is important to consider how leases come to an end at common law. Then it is possible to see how the 1954 Act alters the position.

10.2.1 Effluxion of time

With a fixed-term lease, when the contractual terms ends, the lease automatically determines by what is known as 'effluxion of time'. No notice is needed. Most leases of commercial property are fixed-term leases.

10.2.2 Notice to quit

Periodic tenancies are determined by the appropriate period's notice to quit given by the landlord or tenant. A yearly tenancy is determined by at least half a year's notice expiring at the end of a completed year of the tenancy. Other periodic tenancies are determined by one full period's notice (ie one quarter, month, etc) expiring at the end of a completed period of the tenancy. For example, if a tenant has a monthly tenancy which starts on the first of each month and the landlord wants to serve a notice to quit on 14 August, the earliest date the landlord can specify for expiry of the notice is 30 September (ie the notice must be at least one month long and must expire at the end of a completed month).

10.2.3 Surrender

Surrender occurs where the tenant yields up the lease to the landlord who accepts the surrender. Accordingly, surrender can only be achieved if both the landlord and the tenant agree to it. On surrender, the lease is said to merge in the landlord's reversion and is extinguished. To be legal, surrender must be by deed (LPA 1925, s 52). See also **9.6**.

Figure 10.1 Surrender

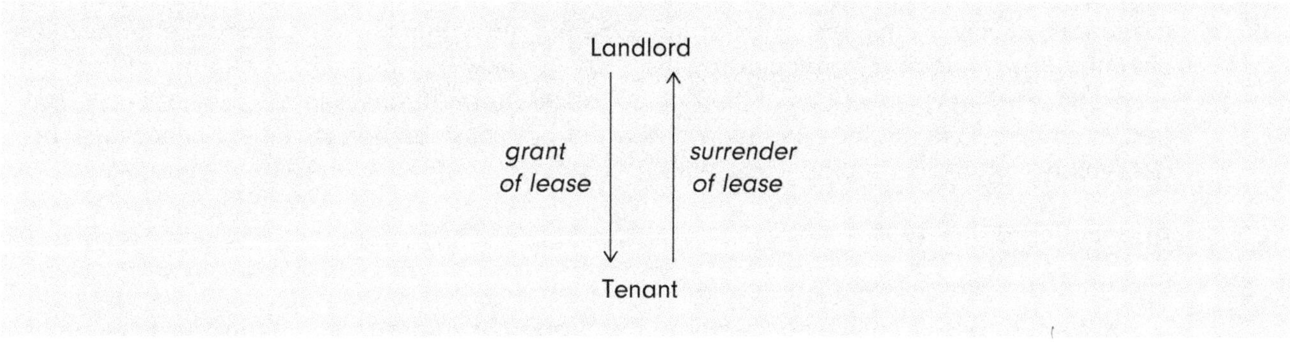

10.2.4 Merger

This occurs where the tenant acquires the immediate reversion to the lease (ie acquires the landlord's estate in land). It is the opposite of surrender.

Figure 10.2 Merger (1)

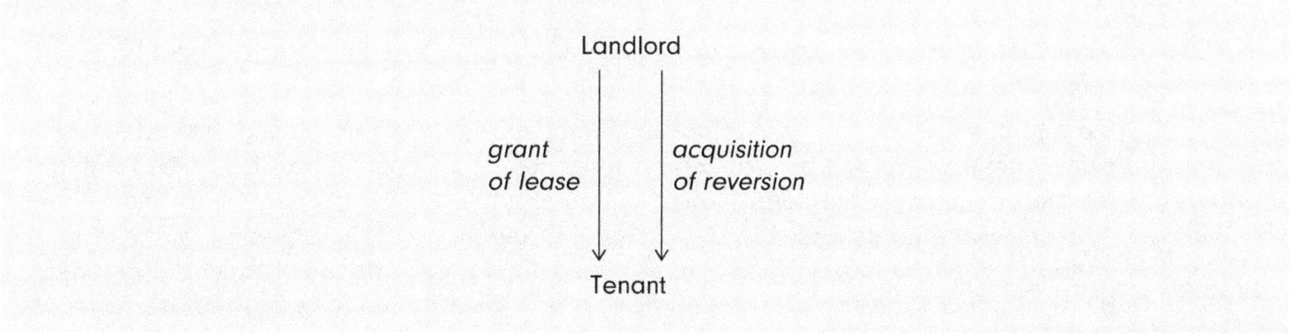

It can also occur where a third party acquires both the lease and the reversion.

Figure 10.3 Merger (2)

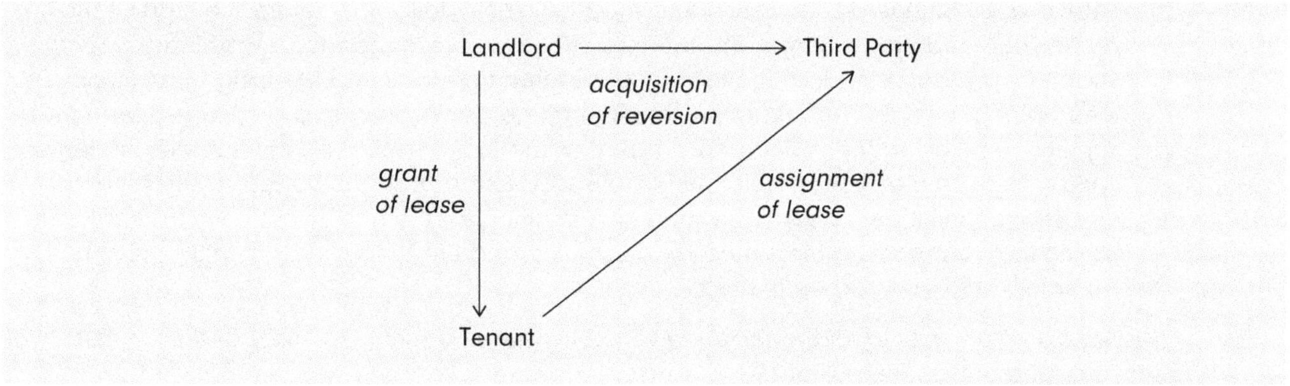

As with surrender, once the lease and the reversion are with the tenant or third party, the lease automatically merges with the reversion and is extinguished (unless the tenant/third party expressly preserves the lease in the documentation).

10.3 The 1954 Act

If a tenancy comes within the ambit of the 1954 Act, the common law methods of termination may not apply. A tenancy protected by the 1954 Act may continue until it is terminated in accordance with the provisions of the Act. So, a fixed term business lease will not necessarily end at the expiration of the fixed term and a periodic business lease will not necessarily be determined by service of a notice to quit.

10.3.1 Application of the 1954 Act

Section 23 of the 1954 Act provides that:

> this Act applies to any tenancy where the property comprised in the tenancy is or includes premises which are occupied by the tenant and are so occupied for the purposes of a business carried on by him or for those and other purposes.

So, there must be a *tenancy* (not a licence) of a property which is *occupied* by the tenant (personally, or through the medium of an agent or manager) for *business* purposes. 'Business' is widely defined and includes 'a trade, profession or employment and in the case of a body of persons any activity carried on by them'. The activity need not be a business or commercial activity; running a tennis club and a hospital have each amounted to a business use when carried on by a body of persons. However, not all types of business tenancy are protected by the Act:

- Tenancies at will, which can be terminated at any time by either party, do not have the protection of the 1954 Act.
- Fixed-term tenancies not exceeding six months are not protected. Landlords cannot circumvent the 1954 Act by granting a succession of six-month tenancies: if the tenant (or a predecessor in the same business) has already been in occupation for more than 12 months when another lease is granted, that tenant will gain protection of the Act even if the new lease is for six months or less. Also, if a tenancy does not exceed six months but contains a provision allowing renewal or extension of the term beyond the six months, then the tenancy will be protected by the Act.
- Certain types of business lease such as tenancies of agricultural holdings, farm business tenancies and mining leases are expressly excluded from the protection of the 1954 Act.
- Fixed-term tenancies that are 'contracted out' of the 1954 Act are also excluded from protection. It is possible for the landlord and tenant to agree that the tenant will not be afforded the protection of the 1954 Act but in order for this 'contracting out' to be effective, a statutory notice procedure must be strictly followed before the start of the lease. The landlord must give the tenant notice in a prescribed form warning the tenant that they are agreeing to a lease without security of tenure and advising them to obtain professional advice. The tenant must then make a declaration in a prescribed form that they have received the notice and agree that the lease should be contracted out. If the tenant is given the notice less than 14 days before the grant of the lease, the tenant's declaration must be made in the form of a statutory declaration before an independent solicitor. A reference to the service of the notice and the tenant's declaration must be contained or endorsed on the lease itself.

A landlord who wants to let the property without giving the tenant security of tenure must consider one of these exclusions.

10.3.2 Effect of the 1954 Act

A tenant who is occupying property for business purposes and who is not caught by any of these exclusions will be afforded protection by the 1954 Act. Section 24 of the 1954 Act states:

> A tenancy to which this Part of the Act applies shall not come to an end unless terminated in accordance with the provisions of this Part of the Act.

So, the tenancy will continue until terminated in accordance with the 1954 Act and even then, the tenant has a right to apply to court for a new tenancy which can only be opposed by the landlord on one of the seven statutory grounds contained in s 30 of the 1954 Act (the 's 30 grounds'). The s 30 grounds are considered in **10.3.7** below.

The 1954 Act provides for only seven methods of termination:

1) by the service of a landlord's notice under s 25
2) by the service of a tenant's request for a new tenancy under s 26
3) forfeiture (see **9.3.4** and **9.4.4**)
4) surrender (see **10.2.3** above and **9.6**)
5) in the case of a periodic tenancy, by the tenant giving the landlord a notice to quit
6) in the case of a fixed-term lease, by the tenant serving three months' written notice on the landlord under s 27, so long as the notice does not expire before the contractual expiry date
7) in the case of a fixed-term lease, by the tenant ceasing to be in occupation for business purposes at the end of the lease under s 27(1A).

Forfeiture (where the tenant is in default) and surrender (where the landlord and tenant agree) are common law methods of termination allowed by the 1954 Act. Section 27 (1A) enables the tenancy to end by effluxion of time where the tenant ceases to be in occupation for business purposes at the end of the lease. In the case of a periodic tenancy, the 1954 Act allows the tenant to serve a notice to quit on the landlord, but the landlord cannot serve notice to quit on the tenant. Similarly, s 27 of the 1954 Act allows the tenant to serve a notice on the landlord to end a fixed-term tenancy, but does not give the landlord the same right.

The purpose of the 1954 Act is to afford security of tenure to business tenants. If the tenant wishes the tenancy to come to an end it can serve a s 27 notice or just move out, but if it is the landlord wanting to terminate the tenancy, then the only common law methods available are forfeiture and surrender. If there are no grounds for forfeiture and the tenant will not agree to surrender, the only way a landlord can terminate a business tenancy protected by the 1954 Act is under s 25.

10.3.3 Termination by the landlord – s 25 notice

Section 25 can be used to terminate either a fixed term or periodic tenancy, but the landlord must follow the correct procedure. First, the landlord must serve a s 25 notice* on the tenant. The landlord serves the s 25 notice regardless of whether it wants the property back or wants to grant a new lease: there are slightly different versions of the form for both possibilities so the s 25 notice will make it clear whether the landlord opposes the grant of a new tenancy or not. Often the landlord does not oppose the renewal of the tenancy; the landlord is ending the current lease so that a new tenancy can be granted on different terms, usually a higher rent. The landlord must indicate its proposals as to the terms of the new lease in the s 25 notice. If the landlord opposes the renewal of the tenancy, the s 25 notice must state the s 30 grounds.

The s 25 notice must state the date upon which the landlord wants the tenancy to end. This date cannot be earlier than the date the tenancy could have been terminated under the common law. For example, the date cannot be earlier than the expiry of a fixed term.

There are strict time limits when calculating the date upon which the landlord wants the tenancy to end. The s 25 notice has to be served no less than six months and no more than twelve months before the termination date specified in the notice. The termination date cannot be sooner than the lease could otherwise have come to an end under the common law, but it does not have to coincide with the exact date when a fixed term lease expires. If the landlord has not served the s 25 notice in time to terminate the tenancy on the contractual expiry date and the six months would end, for example, a month after the lease expires, the tenancy continues in that extra month. Continuation tenancies are very common in practice.

Example 1

A tenant occupies an office property under a 10-year fixed term lease. The term ends on 29 September 2025 and the lease is not contracted out of the 1954 Act. If the landlord wants to terminate the tenancy on the contractual end date of 29 September, then to comply with s 25, the notice should specify 29 September 2025 as the termination date and should be served between 29 September 2024 (no more than 12 months before the termination date) and 29 March 2025 (no less than 6 months before the termination date).

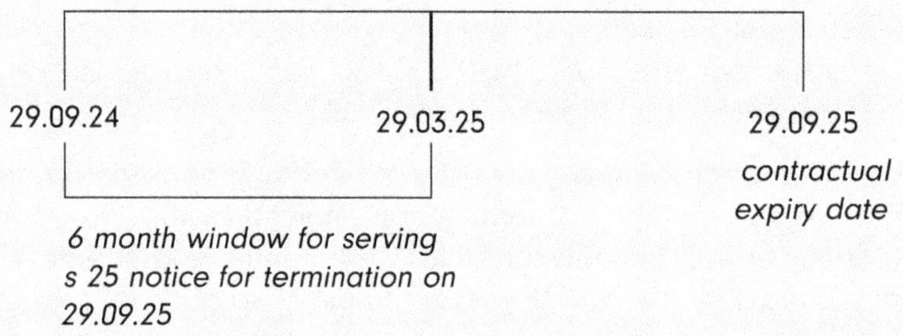

Example 2

Assume that the tenant is still in occupation of the same property under the same lease but the date is now 25 June 2025 and neither party has taken steps to terminate the tenancy. It is too late to serve a s 25 notice to end the tenancy on 29 September 2025 as the landlord will not be giving the tenant at least six months' notice. However, the landlord has not lost the opportunity to terminate the tenancy altogether; the termination date will have to be later and the tenancy will continue beyond the expiry of the contractual term. So, if the landlord served the s 25 notice on 25 June 2025, the earliest date it could specify as the termination date is 25 December 2025, as that would be giving the tenant six months' notice.

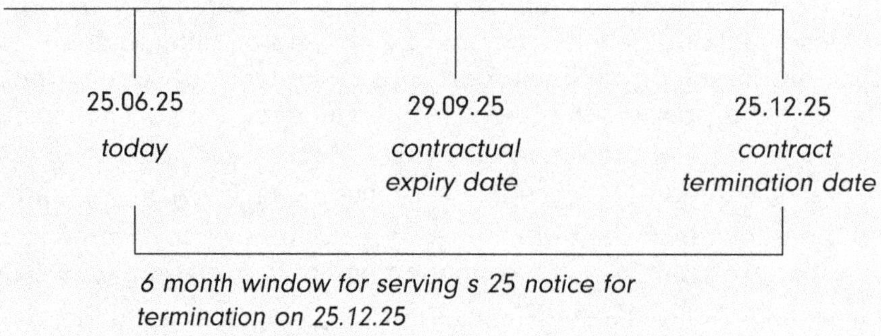

Example 3

Assuming that the notice is served on 25 June 2025, the latest termination date would be 25 June 2026 because the landlord has to give at least 6 months' but not more than 12 months' notice. The landlord can specify any date between 25 December 2025 and 25 June 2026.

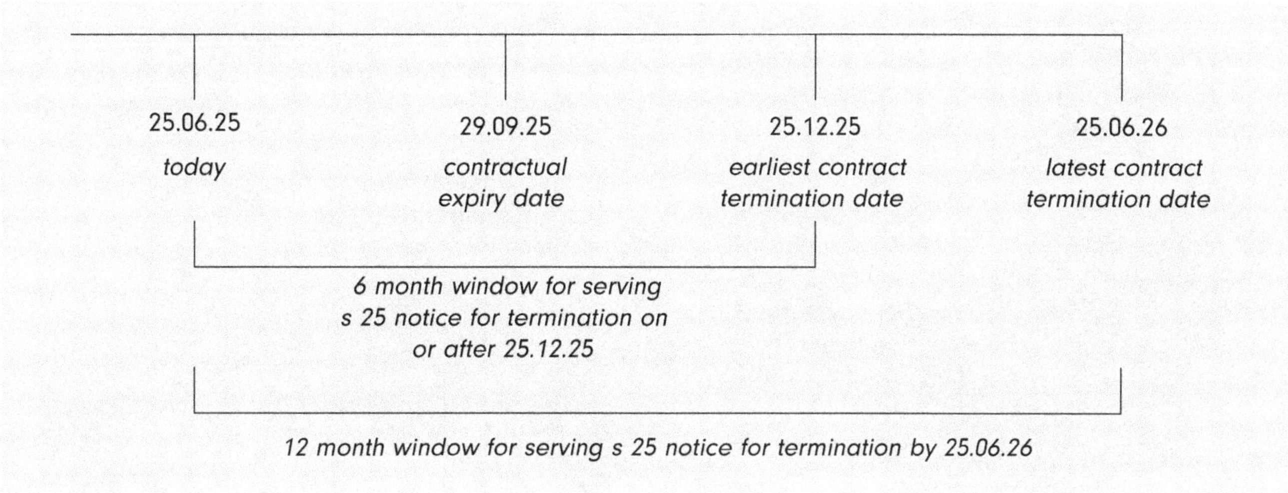

Summary

A landlord relying on the s 25 procedure to terminate a business tenancy protected by the 1954 Act must serve a s 25 notice specifying the proposed termination date (which cannot be earlier than the date the tenancy could have been terminated under the common law). The notice must be served upon the tenant no less than 6 months, but no more than 12 months, before the proposed termination date.

* s 25 notice is key term used in practice in the context of security of tenure. You may be required to know and be able to use this term in the SQE1 assessments.

10.3.4 Application to the court following service of a s 25 notice

If the landlord indicates in the s 25 notice that it will oppose the grant of a new tenancy, the tenant must apply to the court before the expiry of the s 25 notice, or they will lose their rights under the 1954 Act. The landlord can pre-empt the tenant's application to court by applying for an order to terminate the lease on the grounds stated in its s 25 notice (but not if an application has already been made by the tenant asking for the lease to be renewed).

If the landlord indicates that it will not oppose the grant of a new tenancy, the parties will enter into negotiations for the grant of a new lease, but the tenant should still apply to court within the time limit to safeguard their position. This time limit can be extended by agreement between the parties, eg where they are near to agreement on the terms of a new lease and wish to avoid the expense of court proceedings. The application is usually made to the county court.

Summary of a tenant's options on receipt of a s 25 notice

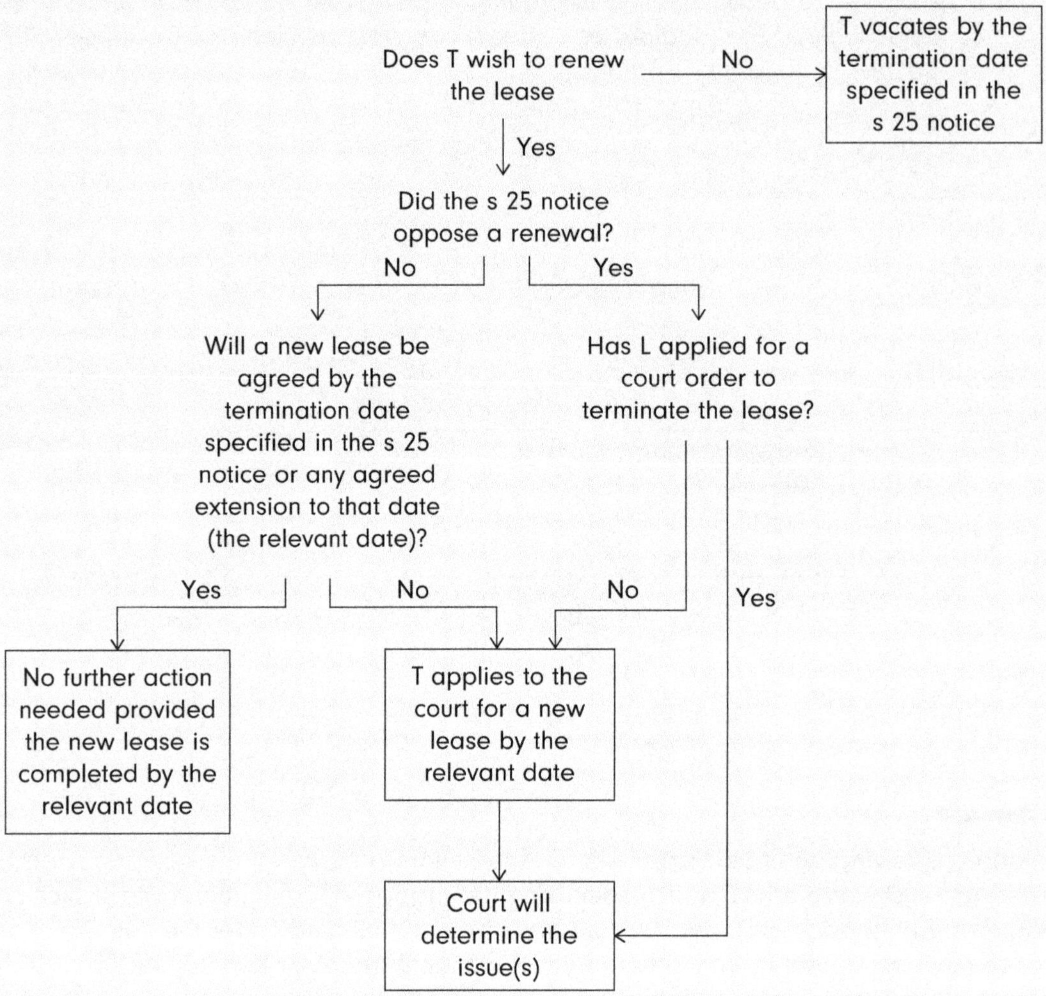

10.3.5 Renewal lease by the tenant – s 26 request

A tenant of a lease protected by the 1954 Act who wants to terminate the lease *on* the contractual expiry date may do so by ceasing to occupy for business purposes by the end of the lease (s 27(1A)) or serving a s 27 notice giving the landlord three months' prior written notice. A protected tenant who wants to terminate the lease *after* the contractual expiry date may only do so by serving a s 27 notice giving the landlord three months' notice or agreeing a voluntary surrender of the lease with the landlord.

If a protected tenant wishes to remain in the property after the contractual expiry date, they could choose to do nothing as the tenancy will continue. They could simply wait until the landlord serves a s 25 notice. Alternatively, the tenant could take the initiative and serve a s 26 request*. A s 26 request serves to bring the current tenancy to an end and constitutes a request for a new tenancy. For example, the tenant might choose to serve a s 26 request if they believe that rents have fallen and a reduced rent could be achieved for a new lease, or the tenant has plans to assign the lease and believes that the tenancy would be more attractive to a buyer if a new fixed term has been granted.

The s 26 request must state the date on which the tenant wants the new tenancy to begin and the request must contain the tenant's proposals for the new tenancy. When serving the s 26 request, the tenant must adhere to the same time limits as the landlord serving a s 25 notice, ie the tenant must give the landlord between 6 and 12 months' notice of the date they want the new tenancy to start, which cannot be earlier than the date the tenancy could have been terminated under the common law.

* s 26 request is key term used in practice in the context of security of tenure. You may be required to know and be able to use this term in the SQE1 assessments.

10.3.6 Application to the court following service of a s 26 request

If the landlord wishes to oppose the grant of a new tenancy, it must serve a counter-notice on the tenant within two months of the service of the tenant's s 26 request stating the s 30 ground(s) of opposition. The tenant must then ensure that they apply to court for a new lease or they will lose their rights under the 1954 Act. The application must be made prior to the commencement date of the new tenancy specified in the tenant's s 26 request, unless the landlord agrees an extension of this time limit. The landlord can pre-empt the tenant's application to court by applying for an order to terminate the lease on the grounds stated in its counter-notice (but not if an application has already been made by the tenant asking for the lease to be renewed).

If the landlord does not oppose the grant of a new tenancy, it need not serve a counter-notice and the parties will negotiate the terms of the new lease. However, the tenant should make an application to court before the commencement date of the new tenancy specified in the s 26 request to safeguard their position. The parties can agree to extend this time limit if negotiations are going well and it is unusual for applications to proceed to a hearing.

Summary of a landlord's options on receipt of a s 26 request

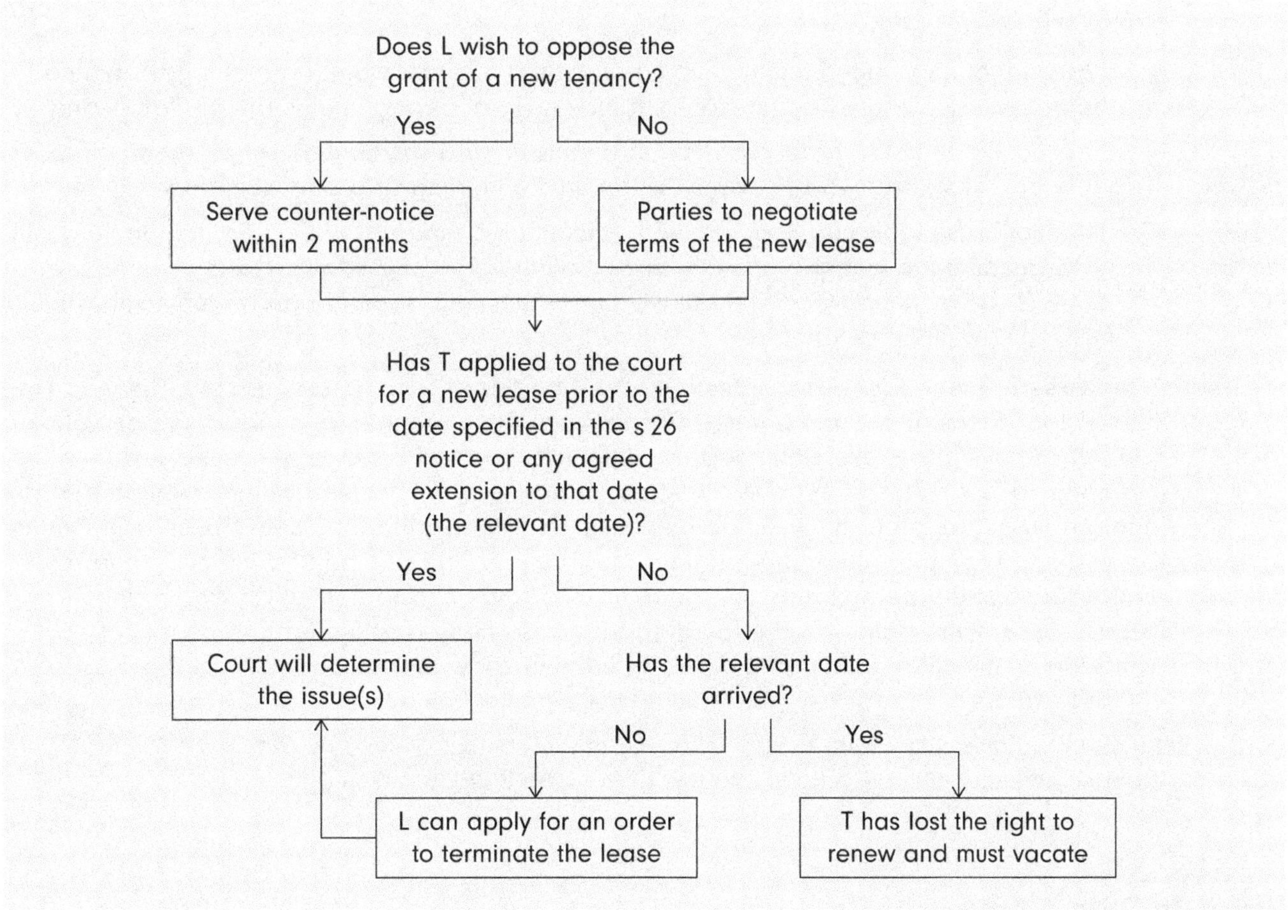

10.3.7 Landlord's grounds of opposition – s 30 grounds

If the landlord opposes the renewal of the tenancy, its s 25 notice or counter-notice to a s 26 request must state on which of the seven specified grounds* under s 30 of the 1954 Act it does so. The s 30 grounds are as follows:

(a) Tenant's failure to repair

(b) Tenant's persistent delay in paying rent

(c) Tenant's substantial breach of other obligations

(d) Landlord has offered alternative accommodation (which must be suitable to the tenant's needs and on reasonable terms)

(e) Tenancy is an underletting of part (rarely used)

(f) Landlord intends to demolish or reconstruct and could not reasonably do so without obtaining possession

(g) Landlord intends to occupy the holding for its own business or as a residence

Grounds (a), (b), (c) and (e) are all *discretionary*, ie the court will decide whether or not to allow the tenant a new lease. It is not sufficient for the landlord just to establish the ground; it also has to show that the tenant ought not to be granted a new tenancy in view of the facts giving rise to the ground. The discretion of the court means that opposed applications are expensive; there will be a court hearing on the ground(s) the landlord is relying on, with evidence and submissions is made by advocates. If the landlord wins, the court will refuse the tenant a new tenancy.

Grounds (d), (f) and (g) are *mandatory* where, for example, the landlord simply has to prove that it has offered alternative accommodation or intends to occupy itself.

Ground (f) is the most frequently used ground. The landlord must show that, on the termination of the tenancy:

i) it has a firm and settled intention to carry out the relevant work (eg that it has obtained the necessary planning permission and the financial arrangements are in place); and

ii) it intends to demolish or reconstruct the premises (or a substantial part of them), or to carry out substantial works of construction on the holding or a part of it; and

iii) it cannot reasonably carry out the work without obtaining possession (ie the landlord will not succeed if the tenant agrees to allow the landlord access to carry out the work, which can then be reasonably carried out without obtaining possession and without substantially interfering with the tenant's use).

In the case of ground (g), landlords cannot rely on this ground unless they have owned their interest for at least five years before the ending of the current tenancy. This is to prevent a landlord buying the reversion cheaply within five years of the end of the lease and then acquiring vacant possession using this ground. However, the ground will be available to a landlord who buys property with vacant possession, lets it and then seeks possession within five years of buying it. Again the landlord must have a firm and settled intention and must demonstrate at the date of the court hearing that it has considered and taken practical steps to occupy the property. The landlord must also have a reasonable prospect of achieving its intention, although it does not have to show that its business will be a success in that location.

* s 30 grounds is a key term used in practice in the context of security of tenure. You may be required to know and be able to use this term in the SQE1 assessments.

10.3.8 Terms of the new lease

The tenant is only entitled to a tenancy of the 'holding'. This means the property comprised in the current tenancy, but excluding any part not occupied by the tenant (ie those parts which the tenant has underlet). However, the landlord has the right to insist that any new tenancy will be a tenancy of the whole of the originally demised property, including those parts underlet.

This term of the new lease will be such as is reasonable in the circumstances, but cannot exceed 15 years; it will normally be much less, eg five or seven years. The term will not commence until three months after the proceedings are 'finally disposed of' (ie when the time limit for appeal has elapsed, so four weeks after the order). The new lease will thus commence three months and four weeks after the order.

The rent is the open market rent having regard to the other terms of the tenancy. In assessing this, the court must disregard:

(a) the fact that the tenant and their predecessors have been in occupation;

(b) any goodwill attached to the holding;

(c) any effect on rent of any improvements voluntarily carried out by the tenant during the tenancy; and

(d) in the case of licensed premises, any addition in value due to the tenant's licence.

The court can insert a rent review clause in the lease, even though there was not one in the previous lease.

In the absence of agreement, the other terms of the lease will again be fixed by the court, which must have regard to the terms of the current tenancy and all other relevant circumstances. It is likely that the new terms will be much the same as the old.

If the tenant finds the terms of a new lease ordered by the court unacceptable (usually the rent), they may apply for the order to be revoked. The landlord has no such right; if it is unhappy with the terms of the new lease, the only remedy is to appeal.

10.3.9 Compensation

If the landlord successfully opposes the grant of a new lease solely on one or more of the no fault grounds (ie (e), (f) or (g)), the tenant will not be granted a new lease but will be entitled to compensation. The amount of compensation will be equivalent to the rateable value of the holding, unless the tenant and their predecessors in the same business have been in occupation for at least 14 years, when it will be twice the rateable value. Any agreement restricting or excluding the payment of compensation is void if the tenant or their predecessors in the same business have been in occupation for five years or more. This means that the clause commonly found in leases contracting out of the obligation to pay compensation will only be enforceable where the tenant has been in occupation for fewer than five years.

Summary

- At common law, fixed term leases come to an end on the contractual expiry date by effluxion of time and periodic leases by service of a notice to quit.
- It is also possible for leases to be surrendered by the tenant or to merge with the reversion so that they are extinguished.

- Security of tenure under the 1954 Act means the right for the tenant to stay in the property after the expiry of the contractual term and to apply for a new tenancy, which can only be denied on certain limited statutory grounds set out in s 30 of the 1954 Act.
- To qualify for security of tenure under the 1954 Act, the tenant must have a tenancy and occupy the property for business purposes under a lease that has not been excluded from protection.
- If the parties are agreed that the tenancy should not enjoy security of tenure, it is possible do this by granting a tenancy at will, a contractual licence, a lease for six months or less or a contracted-out lease.
- A protected tenancy cannot be terminated other than by one of the seven ways laid down by the 1954 Act.
- A protected tenant who wants to terminate the lease on the contractual expiry date may do so by ceasing to occupy for business purposes by the end of the lease or serving a s 27 notice giving the landlord three months' prior written notice.
- A protected tenant who wants to terminate the lease after the expiry of the contractual expiry date may only do so by serving a s 27 notice giving the landlord three months' notice or agreeing a voluntary surrender of the lease with the landlord.
- A protected tenant who wants to stay in the property after the contractual expiry date and renew the tenancy may serve a s 26 request for a new tenancy on the landlord. The tenant may also do nothing, continue to occupy the property on the existing terms and wait for the landlord to take action.
- A landlord who is happy for the tenant to stay on may choose to do nothing and allow the tenancy to continue indefinitely. For greater certainty or a higher rent, the landlord may serve a s 25 notice terminating the tenancy on 6–12 months' notice, but without opposing a renewal.
- A landlord who wants to terminate a protected tenancy may forfeit the lease (if the tenant is in default) or agree a voluntary surrender with the tenant. Otherwise, the landlord must serve a s 25 notice on the tenant terminating the lease on or after the contractual expiry date and opposing the renewal of the tenancy on s 30 ground(s).
- The s 25 notice must be given not less than 6 or more than 12 months before the date specified in the notice for termination of the tenancy. The specified date cannot be before the tenancy would have expired under the common law.
- A protected tenant who wishes to renew their tenancy should make an application to the court before the termination date stated in the s 25 notice or the date for commencement of the new tenancy stated in the s 26 request, unless this period is extended by agreement between the parties.
- A landlord who has been served with a s 26 request and who opposes the renewal should serve a counter-notice on the tenant within two months of receiving the s 26 request and state the s 30 ground(s) on which it will be relying.
- The terms of the new lease are usually agreed between the parties, but if they are determined by the court, the renewal lease is likely to be on similar terms and conditions to the old lease. The rent is likely to be the open market rent as at the date of renewal.
- The landlord will have to pay compensation to the tenant if the new tenancy is refused, unless the reason for the refusal is that the landlord has established ground (a), (b) or (c) (where the tenant is at fault) or ground (d) (where alternative accommodation has been provided).

Sample questions

Question 1

A solicitor acts for the landlord of a retail unit. The lease was granted for a term of 10 years commencing on 5 January 2016. It is now 1 May 2025. The lease was not contracted out of the Landlord and Tenant Act 1954 (the 1954 Act) and the landlord has instructed the solicitor to serve a s 25 notice on the tenant to terminate the lease on 5 January 2026.

Can the solicitor comply with the landlord's instructions?

A No, because the tenant enjoys security of tenure so the landlord cannot terminate the lease unless the tenant is in breach of at least one of the tenant's covenants.

B No, because is too early to serve the s 25 notice.

C No, because it is too late to serve the s 25 notice.

D Yes, because the landlord will be able to comply with the requirements of the 1954 Act for service of the s 25 notice if it is served today.

E Yes, because the 1954 Act allows a landlord to terminate a tenancy in the last six months of the contractual term.

Answer

Option D is correct. The contractual expiry date of the lease is 4 January 2026 so on 1 May 2025, the landlord is within the 12–6 month window to terminate on that date. It is neither too early nor too late to serve the s 25 notice, so options B and C are wrong.

Option A is misconceived as the 1954 Act allows the landlord to terminate the lease whether or not the tenant is in breach of the lease; breaches of the lease may be relevant to whether the landlord can successfully oppose a renewal of the lease using s 30 grounds (a), (b) and (c) but this is a different point about which there is no information in the facts.

Option E is wrong as the proposed date for termination of the lease in a s 25 notice cannot be earlier than the date the tenancy could have been terminated under the common law, which for a fixed term lease is the contractual expiry date.

Question 2

A landlord owns a property which is let to a business tenant on a 10 year fixed term lease. The contractual term expires in just over six months' time and the landlord wishes to serve a s 25 notice on the tenant opposing the grant of a new tenancy today. The landlord acquired the property four and a half years ago and wishes to move into the property itself when the tenant leaves. Last year the tenant failed to pay the June instalment of the rent but has otherwise been a good tenant.

Which of the following statements is the best advice to the landlord as to which ground(s) to specify in its s 25 notice?

A The landlord cannot rely on ground (g) because it has only owned the property for four and half years.

B The landlord will be able to rely on grounds (b) and (g), but it would be better to rely on ground (b) as it is a discretionary ground.

C The landlord is unlikely to be able to rely on ground (b) but could rely on ground (g).

D The landlord will be able to rely on grounds (b) and (g), but it would be better to rely on ground (b) as the tenant will not be entitled to compensation.

E The landlord will be able to rely on grounds (b) and (g), but it would be better to rely on ground (g) as it is a mandatory ground.

Answer

Option C is correct. On the facts, the two grounds that are potentially available to the landlord are (b) and (g). Ground (b) is discretionary and ground (g) is mandatory.

Ground (b) is available where there has been a *persistent* failure by the tenant to pay rent. The tenant has only missed one rent payment and so it is unlikely that the landlord could rely upon it. Options B, D and E are, therefore, not the best advice. Option B is also misconceived as it would not be better to rely on a discretionary ground where a mandatory ground is available. Option D is correct that ground (b) is a non-compensatory ground and this might have been a reason for choosing it had it been available.

Ground (g) is available where, at the termination of the lease, the landlord intends to occupy the premises as its business or residence. This is not available if the landlord acquired its interest in the property within five years of the ending of the current tenancy. This will be the termination date specified in the s 25 notice. Although the landlord has not yet owned its interest in the property for five years on the date of service of the s 25 notice, it will have done so by the termination date specified in the s 25 notice and so will not be barred from relying on ground (g). Option A is therefore wrong.

Question 3

A solicitor acts for the freehold owner of an office building. The client needs to occupy the whole of the building in 18 months' time, but wants to raise some rental income from the building in the meantime. The client has identified a suitable short-term occupier.

Which one of the following options will best achieve the client's objective?

A Granting the occupier a lease for 18 months, contracted out of the Landlord and Tenant Act 1954.

B Granting the occupier a tenancy at will.

C Granting the occupier a contractual licence.

D Granting the occupier a lease for six months, followed by another lease of six months when the first one expires.

E Granting the occupier a lease for six months with an option to extend the term by a year once the first six months has passed.

Answer

Option A is correct. A fixed term lease of 18 months gives the client certainty of income for the whole of the period, but the occupier will not have the right to stay on in the property or renew the lease as a contracted out tenancy is excluded from security of tenure under the 1954 Act.

In relation to option B, the 1954 Act excludes tenancies at will from security of tenure, but a tenancy at will can be terminated without notice by the occupier so gives no certainty of income. In relation to option C, a contractual licence is not a tenancy within the meaning of s 23 of the 1954 Act but may be construed as a (secure) lease if, in practice, exclusive possession is enjoyed.

In relation to option D, two tenancies of exactly six months each (so not resulting in occupation for more than 12 months) will not attract security of tenure but will not guarantee income for the full 18 months. Also, the client cannot be sure that the occupier will take the second lease once the first lease expires.

In option E, the tenancy will be treated as a tenancy for more than six months so enjoy security of tenure under the 1954 Act.

Index

Locators in *italics* refer to figures.

A

absolute covenants 117, 125
absolute title 34, 148, 161
agreement for lease 147
see also grant of a lease
air and light, rights to 43
alienation 128–136
alterations
building regulations 23, 24, 25, 63
leasehold property 125–127, 143–144
planning law principles 19–24
planning permission 20–24, 63
ancillary rights 116
annual rent 116, 136
apportionments (rent) 163
assignment of lease 155–156
completion 163–164
conveyancing process - comparison to freehold 156–157
covenants for title 162
deduction of title 161
deed of assignment 162
investigation of title 161
landlord's consent 158
licence to assign 159–160, 163, 166–167
post-completion stage 164–165
pre-contract enquiries 161–162
refusal of consent 142–143
terminology 129–130
authorised guarantee agreement (AGA) 160, 171, 179–180

B

bankruptcy search 58, 103
borrowers, professional conduct issues 7–9
see also finance; mortgages
breach of condition notice 22
breach of covenant *see* leasehold covenant breaches
building regulations 23, 24, 25, 63
Building Societies Association 82
building survey 54–55
business lettings 139–141, 167–168, 186–189
buyers
deduction of title 32–33, 37
deposit from 77
professional conduct issues in a property transaction 6–7

C

Canal & River Trust search 57–58
Capital Gains Tax (CGT) 12, 15–16
caveat emptor 3, 54
certificate of title 82–83
chancel repairs search 57
Charges register 34–35, 36
Church of England chancel repairs 57
client instructions 25–26
co-ownership 43–44
Code for Leasing Business Premises 139–141
commencement 116
commercial lease, structure of 115–116
commercial lettings 139–141, 167–168, 186–189
commercial property taxation 12
Commercial Rent Arrears Recovery (CRAR) 172
common law
damages 109
termination of leases 184–186
commons search 58
Companies House 106, 111
company search 58, 102, 163
company sellers 102
compensation
completion date delay 107–108
open market rent review 193
completion dates
compensation 107–108
exchange of contracts 85
leasehold property 166
completion (freehold) 2–3, *3*
finances 103
methods and effect of 103–105
practical arrangements 102
remedies for delayed completion 107–109, 112
see also post-completion stage; pre-completion stage
completion information form 103–105

completion (leasehold) 150–152, 163–164
conflicts of interest
mortgages 83
professional conduct issues 6, 7–8
conservation areas 24, 65
contract races 9, 28
contract rate 76–77
contracts
purpose of 70–71
signature 85
special conditions 73–75, 78–79
Standard Commercial Property Conditions and Standard Conditions of Sale 71–78
see also exchange of contracts
contractual compensation 107–108
conveyancing
leasehold vs. freehold property 146, 156–157
terminology 2
Corporation Tax 12
Council of Mortgage Lenders (CML) 83
Council of Property Search Organisations (CoPSO) 62
covenants
alterations 125–127, 143–144
compensation for breach 193
investigation of title 44–47, 51
landlord's 116, 120, 121, 122–124
liability 170–171
other covenants 178
payment of rent 171–175, 179–181
positive 45–46, 76, 79, 115
remedies for breach 171–178
renewal of tenancy 192
rent suspension 121, 124
repair 122–124, 138, 162, 175–177
restrictive 19, 40, 44–45, 76, 79
surrender of the lease 178
tenant's 125–127, 143–144, 171–178
for title 162
unknown 46–47
see also leasehold covenant breaches

D

damages
breach of covenant 178
common law 109
after exchange of contracts 88–89
tenant's failure to repair 175–176
debt, rent payment 172–175
deduction of title
freehold property 32–33, 37–38
leasehold property 148, 154, 161
superior freehold title 161
deed of assignment 162, 167–168
deeds *see* title deeds; transfer deed
the deposit 77–78, 103–105
development, planning law 19–21, 24
drainage 42, 55–56

E

easements 42
effluxion of time 184
Energy Performance Certificate (EPC) 25
enforcement notice 22
enquiries *see* searches and enquiries
environmental issues
conservation areas 24, 65
Energy Performance Certificate (EPC) 25
flood search 56–57
smoke control orders 65
tree preservation orders 65
environmental searches 56
epitome of title 37–39, 41
Etridge guidelines 8–9
exchange of contracts 27–28
certificate of title 83–84
consequences of exchange 87–88
freehold property transactions 2–3, *3*
insurance and risk 79–80, 88–89
lender requirements and acting for 82–83
practice, method and authority to exchange 85–87
preparation for 84–85
reporting to the client 83–84
special conditions 78–79
Standard Commercial Property Conditions 71–78
Standard Conditions of Sale 71–78
VAT 80–81
execution
completion formalities 92–97
pre-completion formalities 150
unregistered land 39–40

F

finance
bankruptcy search 58
buyer's solvency 102
for completion 103
the deposit 77–78, 103–105
lender requirements 82
sources of 10–11
see also mortgages

fireplaces 65
fixed term leases 116–117, 184, 186
flood search 56–57
forfeiture 116, 173–174, 176, 177, 180–181
freehold property transactions 1–2
  key elements and structure 2–6
  mortgage types 11–12
  planning law principles 19–24
  professional conduct issues 6–10
  sources of finance 10–11
  taking instructions 25–26
  taxation 12–18
  see also completion; exchange of contracts; investigation of title; searches and enquiries
full repairing and insuring lease (FRI) 118
full title guarantee 76, 89–90
fully qualified covenants 118, 125–126

G

general permitted development (GPDO) 21–22, 25
grant of a lease 145–146
  completion and post-completion 150–152
  deduction of title 148, 154
  drafting 146–147
  pre-completion formalities 150
  pre-contract enquiries 148–149
  purpose of the agreement 147
  terminology 116, 129–130
grant of an underlease 145–146
  deduction of title 148, 154
  drafting 146–147
  licence to underlet 149
  pre-completion formalities 150
  pre-contract enquiries 148–149
  purpose of the agreement 147
  terminology 129–130
  underletting conditions 133–136
guarantors 172–173

H

highways access 58, 68
highways, road adoption 64–65
home rights 49
homebuyers' valuation 55

I

incumbrances 39
indemnity 162
Index Map Search (SIM) 58, 68
injunctions 22, 178
insolvency search 59
instructions checklist *26*
insurance
  exchange of contracts 79–80, 88–89
  full repairing and insuring lease 118
  lease indemnity 162
  leasehold property 119–124
investigation of title 31–32
  co-ownership 43–44
  declaration as to rights of light and air 43
  easements 42
  home rights 49
  issues revealed and further actions required 42
  leasehold property 161
  leases 48
  mines and minerals reservations 43
  mortgages 47
  notices 48–49
  positive covenants 45–46
  registered and unregistered land 32–41
  restrictive covenants 44–45
  unknown covenants 46–47

J

joint borrowers 8–9
joint buyers 7, 44
joint tenants 43–44, 50–51, 95

L

Land Charges Department search 58
land charges searches 40–41
Land Registry
  leasehold property 152, 153
  official copies 33–36
  post-completion stage 105–107
  pre-completion searches 98–100, 101, 110–111
  transfer deed 93
  see also investigation of title
land titles *see* investigation of title
Land Transaction Tax (LTT)
  leasehold property 151, 164
  payment and calculation 12–15
  post-completion stage 105–106
  VAT counting towards 18
landlord's consent 158, 166
landlord's covenants 116, 120, 121, 122–124
Law Society Code 104–105
Law Society Conveyancing Protocol 4–5
Law Society Formulae A, B, and C 85–86

lease termination *see* termination (leases)
lease to occupying tenant (freehold property) 48, 66
leasehold covenant breaches 169–170
  compensation 193
  liability 170–171
  other covenants 178
  payment of rent covenant 171–175, 179–181
  renewal of tenancy 192
  repair covenant 175–177
  surrender of the lease 178
leasehold property 113–114
  advantages and disadvantages 114–115
  alienation 128–136
  alterations 125–127
  Code for Leasing Business Premises 139–141
  conveyancing process - comparison to freehold 146, 156–157
  full repairing and insuring lease 118
  insurance 119–124
  rent and rent review 136–139
  repair 118–119
  structure of a typical commercial lease 115–116
  term of a lease 116–117
  types of leasehold covenant 117–118
  use and planning 127–128
  see also assignment of lease; grant of a lease; grant of an underlease
legal charge 111
lenders
  buyer's solvency 102
  completion 103–104
  professional conduct issues in a property transaction 7–8
  requirements of and acting for 82–83
licence to assign 159–160, 163, 166–167
licence to underlet 149
light and air, rights to 43
limited title guarantee 76, 89–90
listed buildings 24
Local Planning Authority (LPA) 19, 20, 21, 22, 23, 24, 25
local search 55

M

mergers (leases) *185*, 185
minerals reservations 43
mines 43
mining searches 57, 67–68
money *see* finance; mortgages
mortgage offers 82, 83, 85, 87–88
mortgages
  completion 103–104
  interest-only 12
  investigation of title 47
  lender requirements 82–83
  post-completion stage 105
  repayment 11–12
  types 11–12

N

National Land Information Service 61–62
notice of assignment 165
notice to complete 108–109
notice to quit 184
notices, investigation of title 48–49

O

occupiers (freehold property) 48, 66
online search providers 61–62
open market rent review 137–139, 193

P

periodic tenancy 117
permitted development 21, 24
personal inspection 55
planning law
  freehold property transactions 19–24
  leasehold property 127–128
planning permission 20–24, 29, 63–64
positive covenants 45–46, 74, 78, 115
possessory title 34
post-completion stage (freehold) *3*, 4, *6*
  leasehold property 164–165
  steps 105–107
post-completion stage (leasehold) 150–152, 157
pre-completion stage (freehold) 4, *5–6*
  key elements and structure 2–3, *3*
  searches 97–104, 110–111
  steps 92
  transfer deed and formalities for execution 92–97
pre-completion stage (leasehold) 150, 157, 163
pre-contract enquiries (freehold) 56
pre-contract enquiries (leasehold) 148–149, 161–162
pre-contract stage (freehold) *3*, 3, *5*, 27–29
  see also exchange of contracts; investigation of title; searches and enquiries
pre-contract stage (leasehold) 157

preliminary enquiries (of the seller) 56
prescribed clauses 115–116
principal private residence relief 15–16
privity of contract 170
professional conduct issues
 for borrower and lender 7–8
 contract races 9
 freehold property transactions 6–10
 for joint borrowers 8–9
 for joint buyers 7
 for seller and buyer 6–7
 undertaking 9–10
professional survey 54–55
Property register 33, 35
property transactions *see* freehold property transactions; leasehold property
Proprietorship register 33–34, 35–36, 50–51

Q

qualified covenants 117, 125–126, 127
qualified title 34

R

railways 58
ransom strips 58
re-entry 116
register of title 33–36
 see also investigation of title
registered land 32–36
 leasehold property 152
 post-completion stage 106
 pre-completion searches 98–101
 see also investigation of title
registered leases 163, 164
regulated activities 11
rent
 apportionments 163
 leasehold property 136–139
 tenant's covenants 171–175, 179–181
rent deposit 173
rent review 116, 136–139, 144, 193
rent suspension 121, 124
repair covenant 122–124, 138, 162, 175–177
repair of leasehold property 118–119, 122–124, 179
rescission 109
restrictive covenants 19, 40, 44–45, 76, 79
rights excepted and reserved 116
rights of drainage 42
rights of support 42
rights of way 42
risk
 exchange of contracts 79–80, 88–89
 leasehold property 119–125
 lender requirements and acting for 82–83
rivers 66–67
road access 58, 68
road adoption 64–65
roads 58, 68
root of title 38, 50
Royal Institute of Chartered Surveyors (RICS) 140–141

S

s 25 notice, termination of lease 189–191, 195–196
s 26 request, termination of lease 191–193
searches and enquiries 53–54
 conservation areas 65
 leasehold property 148–149, 163
 occupiers 66
 planning permissions 63–64
 pre-completion searches 97–103, 110–111
 raising enquiries 54
 range and types available 54–62
 relevance to a particular property 57–59, 62–63
 road adoption 64–65
 sample questions 66–68
 smoke control orders 65
 summary 59–61
 tree preservation orders 65
'self-help', damages 175–176
sellers
 deduction of title 32–33, 37
 preliminary enquiries 56
 professional conduct issues in a property transaction 6–7
short-term leases 196
smoke control orders 65
Solicitors Regulation Authority (SRA) 6
special conditions 73–75, 78–79
specified incumbrances 73–74
Stamp Duty Land Tax (SDLT)
 leasehold property 150–151, 153–154, 164
 payment and calculation 12–15
 post-completion stage 105–106
 unregistered land 39
 VAT counting towards 18
Standard Commercial Property Conditions 71–78, 112, 158
Standard Conditions of Sale 71–78, 158
stop notice 22

structural survey 55
superior freehold title 161
surrender of the lease 178, 184, *185*
survey 54–55

T

taxation
- freehold property transactions 12–18
- leasehold property 150–151, 153–154
- *see also* Land Transaction Tax (LTT); Stamp Duty Land Tax (SDLT); Value Added Tax (VAT)

tenancy at will 117
tenants *see* leasehold property; occupiers
tenant's covenants
- alterations 125–127, 143–144
- liability and breaches 170–171
- other covenants 178
- payment of rent 171–175, 179–181
- remedies for breach 171–178
- rent suspension 121
- repair 122–124, 138, 162, 175–177

tenants in common 43–44, 51
termination (leases)
- the 1954 Act 186–189
- common law 184–186
- forfeiture 173–174, 176, 177, 180–181
- mergers 185, *185*
- right to terminate 122
- s 25 notice 189–191, 195–196
- s 26 request 191–193
- surrender of the lease 178, 184, *185*
- types of 184–186

title deeds
- chancel repairs search 57
- highways access 68
- land charges searches 41
- leases 48
- mortgages 47
- registered and unregistered land 32
- transfer deed 92–97
- types of title 34
- unregistered land 37, 38–39
- *see also* investigation of title

title guarantee 76, 89–90
Title Information Document (TID) 107
transfer deed
- deed of assignment 162, 167–168
- pre-completion steps 92–97

tree preservation orders 65

U

underletting 133–136
- licence to underlet 149
- *see also* grant of an underlease

undertakings
- completion 103, 104
- landlord's consent 158
- professional conduct issues 9–10

unknown covenants 46–47
unregistered land 32, 36–41
- post-completion stage 105–107
- pre-completion searches 99–101
- *see also* investigation of title

unregistered land searches 58
unregistered leases 152, 162, 163, 164

V

valuation
- lender requirements 81
- open market rent review 137–139, 193
- survey 55

Value Added Tax (VAT)
- exchange of contracts 79–81
- freehold property transactions 16–18
- 'inclusive of' 79, 81, 89
- leasehold property 150–151

W

water drainage 42, 55–56
waterways 57–58, 66–67